DUBAI

DUBAI

GILDED CAGE

SYED ALI

YALE UNIVERSITY PRESS
NEW HAVEN AND LONDON

Copyright © 2010 Syed Ali

The right of Syed Ali to be identified as author of this work has been asserted by him in accordance with the Copyright, Designs and Patents Act 1988.

For information about this and other Yale University Press publications, please contact:

U.S. Office: sales.press@yale.edu   yalebooks.com
Europe Office: sales@yaleup.co.uk   www.yaleup.co.uk

Set in Janson Text by IDSUK (DataConnection) Ltd

Printed in Great Britain by Hobbs the Printers Ltd, Totton, Hampshire

Map by Martin Brown Design

Library of Congress Cataloging-in-Publication Data

Ali, Syed.
   Dubai : gilded cage / Syed Ali.
      p. cm.
ISBN 978-0-300-15217-3 (cl : alk. paper) 1. Dubayy (United Arab Emirates : Emirate)—History. 2. Dubayy (United Arab Emirates : Emirate)—Economic conditions. 3. Dubayy (United Arab Emirates : Emirate)—Politics and government. 4. Foreign workers—Legal status, laws, etc.—United Arab Emirates—Dubayy (Emirate) 5. United Arab Emirates—Emigration and immigration—Economic aspects. I. Title.
   DS247.D78A44 2010
   953.57—dc22
                                                                            2009044743
A catalogue record for this book is available from the British Library.

10 9 8 7 6 5 4 3 2 1
2014 2013 2012 2011 2010

CONTENTS

For Eli, Sami and Noura

PREFACE

IN FEBRUARY 2009, the *New York Times* published a front page article titled, 'Laid-off foreigners flee as Dubai spirals down.' One eye-opening assertion the article reported was that three thousand cars had been abandoned at Dubai International Airport, some with maxed-out credit cards inside and notes of apology taped to the windshield. The author of the piece asserted that, due to the economic crash, parts of Dubai, once hailed as the economic superpower of the Middle East, were looking more and more like a ghost town.[1]

This article, more so than similar articles being published in the local press at the time, sent government officials into a tizzy. They lambasted the critical press coverage, and denied that the economy was in a downward spiral. Or that three thousand cars had been abandoned – their official count was eleven. Officials said that more work permits were being issued than were being cancelled, implying the population was actually continuing to grow, and that talk of Dubai's demise was simply false, rumours spread by those jealous of Dubai's success.

As I am putting the final touches on the book before it goes to print, Dubai is in the midst of a recession, like much of the rest of the globe. The property market for which Dubai had built much of its fame has gone the way of Miami: down, down, down. It was a bubble six years in the making that was going to burst at some point, because that is what bubbles eventually do. The market had risen largely as a result of speculation. The timing of the bust though had more to do with global currents, specifically the major problems in the US and UK banking industries which led banks to largely stop lending, putting Dubai in a credit crunch that it could not immediately escape from. In fact, the city was in danger of defaulting on billions of dollars worth of loans that were coming due in 2009–10, and had to be rescued by Abu Dhabi, which gave Dubai and its state-owned companies USD 20 billion in bailout monies.[2]

While Dubai's phenomenal growth in the past decade led many in Dubai to believe that its meteoric rise would somehow not be subject to economic laws of gravity, the naysayers who think that Dubai is simply a house of cards are equally wrong. Dubai is not a mirage, and it is unlikely that it will revert to the sleepy regional city it was before the boom. In the pages ahead then, I will not be addressing the downturn as a central story line, though I feel it is important that I do at the least acknowledge it. What the book is about, as you will see, is the various factors that account for Dubai's rise to international prominence, and their unforeseen effects, and the ways that Dubai's system of temporary visas for foreigners shapes living and working conditions for foreigners and citizens both.

WHY I WROTE THIS BOOK

I initially came to Dubai to do research on the adult second-generation children of expatriate, foreign, workers. Expatriates account for more than 90 per cent of Dubai's population, and live there in a state of 'permanent impermanence'. That is to say, no matter how long they have lived and worked in Dubai, they cannot get permanent residency (like a US 'green card'), and it is exceedingly difficult to become a naturalized citizen. Their children, even if they are born in Dubai, are citizens of their father's (or sometimes mother's) country of passport, even if they themselves have never been there. They always remain foreigners in their homes – both in their countries of passport and the place where they actually live.

These second-generation expatriates who I encountered were all by definition at least middle class, as there is a minimum income requirement for expatriates to bring their family members, and most were living quite well. I was interested in what to me was an odd situation where a huge group of people can grow up in a place they cannot legally call their own. My intention was that the book was to revolve around their experiences. It was to be the story of a privileged class of people who were legally invisible and permanently temporary, but who for the most part had no real problem with that as generally they were leading the good life.

At this point I should note that Dubai is ruled by a benign autocrat, Sheikh Mohammed bin Rashid Al Maktoum, who fashions himself more as a CEO than a king. While he is often described glowingly as the 'CEO Sheikh' in the press, the fact remains that Dubai is a kingdom where essentially the law is what this sheikh says it is. It is not a free society. But visitors and even residents in Dubai can be forgiven for missing this fact since Dubai advertises itself as an open place, and the usual trappings of a control-obsessed dictatorship are missing here. While I was in Dubai I went about my daily routine of interviewing people and asking wide-ranging questions, writing a blog with no attempt to mask my identity, and generally going about as if no one were paying attention.

Well, that was a mistake – there are people, many people, who are paying close attention. Towards the end of my stay in Dubai, the state security police showed up at my door, took me in for a day's worth of questioning, told me politely but firmly that they disapproved of my research, and that I was being deported and was banned from returning to Dubai. (I wrote about this in more detail in a piece for the *Guardian*.[3]) In a place like Syria or Iran there is a good chance that I would have ended up in jail for an unpleasant extended stay. But Dubai is different. People want desperately to be in Dubai for the opportunities it offers, so the worst thing Dubai can really do is make them leave. Among dictatorships and democracies, this makes Dubai different.

Interestingly, many people, Emirati national citizens as well as expatriates, do not have a problem with this kind of 'Big Brother' treatment. Indeed, many welcome it. Some of the responses to my experience posted on my blog blamed me for the trouble I got into, and basically said that it was good the government kept a close eye on things.[4] This made me rethink the idea of Dubai as a free-wheeling economically and socially laissez faire oasis in the middle of the socially conservative and politically repressive Middle East. It is to a degree 'freewheeling', especially in comparison to its immediate neighbours. But there are limits to the tolerance that authorities in Dubai have, and you do not know what those limits are until you bump up against them. By then it is too late.

This book then has its beginnings in that realization, which made me reconsider the original project and expand its scope. In the pages that follow I will discuss the ways that Dubai's rulers have purposely crafted a strategy to build wealth without the benefit of oil (which makes them different from the other Arabian Gulf states), how Dubai has lured a massive population of foreign workers and how it keeps them in line, and how it keeps its citizen population happy in spite of being made numerically, socially and politically irrelevant. Again, this is not a democracy, so citizens have no say over how the show is run.

HOW I WROTE THE BOOK

I came to Dubai in the summer of 2006. My timing was quite fortunate, as I arrived right in the middle of a massive population influx, and just as Dubai was becoming a household name in the United States. (Dubai was already a recognizable brand name in the rest of the world.) Had I gone a year earlier, I might have seen a slightly more relaxed Dubai. In fact, I was scheduled to go in 2005, but delayed for a year because of the birth of my son. Had I gone a year or two later, I would have been there at the absolute height of the boom, but research would have been difficult, as taxis were nearly impossible to find, with people often waiting for more than an hour.[5] This may seem trivial, but you can't meet people in a mall unless you can get to the mall, and taxis were my way of getting to the mall.

This book was over four years in the making. Since my initial thought for the project was a study of second-generation expatriates, and since there had been nothing at all written about them, I needed to do primary research using the ethnographic method. Ethnographies generally involve a combination of participant observation and in-depth, open-ended interviews. That is academic speak for hanging out and having long chats.

The purpose of hanging out is to get a feel and a sense for how people live their lives, their patterns and rhythms, and to try to find out interesting stuff, stuff that people themselves often take for granted and do not pay much attention to. The hanging out occurred at people's houses, parties, restaurants, bars and nightclubs, and shopping malls. I was in Dubai from early June until late October 2006, the hottest time of the year, so the air conditioning in malls was a great attraction for hanging out there. I also conducted more than fifty open-ended interviews with second-generation expatriates at their homes, places of work, and more often than not in coffee shops in malls. I recorded and transcribed most of these interviews and for others I took notes. Sometimes parents or friends chimed in with their two cents, or tuppence, if you like. I also interviewed (chatted with, really) nearly every taxi driver I took a ride with (I took a lot of taxis), and one prostitute. As her time was literally money, and as I was not going to pay, that interview was particularly brief.

The chatting and hanging out gave me a good sense for a lot of the social dynamics in Dubai. I complemented this primary research with a thorough examination of the scholarly literature on Dubai and the Arabian Gulf states which have had similar experiences with expatriate labour. These states are also called the Gulf Cooperation Council (GCC), and they include the United Arab Emirates (Dubai is one of seven emirates with the capital being Abu Dhabi), Saudi Arabia, Kuwait, Bahrain, Qatar and Oman. I will refer to these countries collectively as the Gulf from here on. While I draw upon it, the scholarly literature on the Gulf, and particularly on Dubai and the United Arab Emirates (UAE), I found to be somewhat limited for my purposes.

The bulk of the information that I base my analysis on, in addition to the ethnographic material, comes from newspapers and magazines from the region and from the international press. As important as the press, perhaps even more so, are the numerous blogs written by residents of Dubai. These bloggers do a great job of picking up, analysing and critiquing news items written in the local and international press, and the various debates I read greatly shaped my own thinking. I also kept in touch with many of the people, friends, actually, with whom I hung out in Dubai to keep current with how things operate on the ground. This was particularly important, as things change rapidly in Dubai, and often things that appear in the press are not a good indicator of how things actually are.

That, in short, is the background of how this book came to be. After the following requisite section, where I thank all those who need thanking, the story of Dubai properly begins.

WHO IS RESPONSIBLE FOR THIS BOOK

Spending four years researching and writing a book means I incurred many debts. The first and most important are to the people in Dubai who gave generously of their time, who took me to dinner, driving in the desert, out to play soccer (sorry, football), and generally let me hang out with them though they hardly knew me. I am deeply grateful to them, especially Vishul, Carole, Deepak, Miriam, Sheela, Jay, Pritim, Kristin, Stanley, John, Jinu, Asifa, Mark and Abmo. I cannot thank them enough, and unfortunately I cannot thank them by their real names.

There are others that I can thank by name who helped greatly at various stages of planning and writing. James Onley reviewed the manuscript for Yale University Press and provided excellent criticisms and suggestions. My wife, Eli Pollard, also read and commented astutely on the manuscript. My best friend, critic and taskmaster, Michael Uzendoski, kept me on track throughout the research and writing process, even while he was in the Amazon jungle in Ecuador. My mentors in and out of graduate school, Murray Milner, Jr, Karen Leonard and Milton Vickerman have been instrumental in shaping my intellectual development in general and with various parts of the book. Mike Davis, Shehzad Nadeem, Sharon Hays, Xiang Biao, Christopher Lee, Peter

Gottschalk, Simon Cole and Nick from Mafiwasta have also been very helpful with advice and criticizing parts of the book. My college mate and life mentor Bill Seto came to stay with me for a few weeks while I was in Dubai, which gave me cause to play host, and see and experience things in Dubai in a new way. He's also a very smart fellow and played an important part in the ethnographic research and forced me to rethink many of my assumptions about Dubai.

Emotional support is also essential to the act of writing. My wife, Eli, and our children Sami and Noura are of course my everything. My parents, Abul Hasan and Safia, my sisters, Hafsa and Hajira, and my wife's parents, Joe and Nancy, were also of great help and support throughout. Bob Barry, Eric Jean and everyone in the pottery studio helped me keep on track in life, and critically keep up my potting skills, which oddly benefited greatly from my stay in Dubai, even though I had no time to do pottery there. Susanna Jones and Jessica Rosenberg gave me great distraction and company at the office and cheered me on every step of the way. My chairperson, Hildi Hendrickson, was very supportive, and accommodating with my teaching schedule.

I am indebted to the Fulbright Middle East, North Africa and South Asia Regional Research Program of the Bureau of Educational and Cultural Affairs of the US Department of State, which funded the research. In the very original incarnation of my research project I was going to follow migrant workers from Hyderabad, India, to Dubai to do a kind of 'before and after, here and there' study, but the Government of India rejected my proposal. (That year they either grossly delayed or rejected every Fulbright project, leading to a mini-snafu reported in the Indian press.[6]) Fortunately, Gary Garrison of the Council for International Exchange of Scholars graciously allowed me to focus my research efforts in Dubai, even though the terms of the programme required study in multiple nations in that region.

Above all I am grateful to my editor, Phoebe Clapham, who was instrumental in shaping this book. She gave me a simple directive: the book should be lively and analytical, but should not be dragged down by lengthy theoretical discussions and litera-ture reviews that too many academics find satisfying, but that the general intelligent reader (you) would likely find dull and off-putting. While these kinds of discussion have their place in academic journals, they generally do not make for good reading, and in any case would not have added much to the analytical value of this book.

To help make this a better book Ms Clapham poked and prodded and praised; when sticks needed to be swung she swung them, and when carrots needed to be dangled she did so. Where sections of the book worked, she helped to make them better; where they did not and would not, she counselled me to abandon them – something that writers too often find very difficult. To the degree the book succeeds, all praise is to her. To the degree it fails, well, that alone rests with me. Without her guidance, it is likely I would have stayed in my academic comfort zone and written a monograph interesting perhaps to specialists, but not to you.

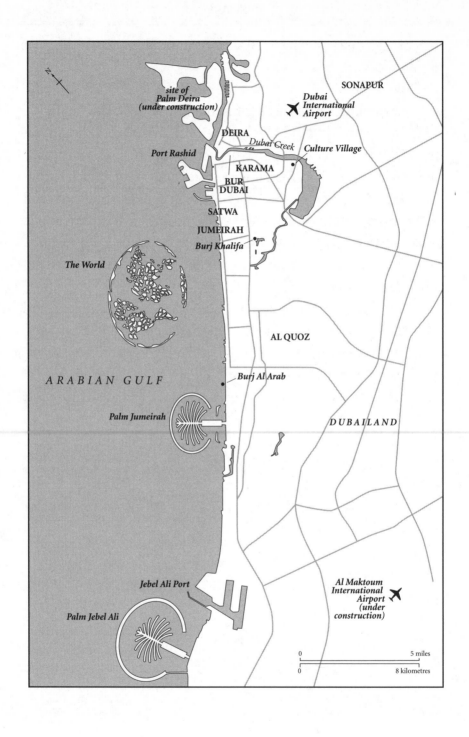

SONAPUR

Dubai International Airport

site of Palm Deira (under construction)

DEIRA

Dubai Creek

Culture Village

Port Rashid

KARAMA

BUR DUBAI

SATWA

JUMEIRAH

Burj Khalifa

The World

AL QUOZ

ARABIAN GULF

Burj Al Arab

DUBAILAND

Palm Jumeirah

Jebel Ali Port

Al Maktoum International Airport (under construction)

Palm Jebel Ali

0   5 miles

0   8 kilometres

INTRODUCTION

Dubai is:

'Manhattan-on-speed'
'A skyline on crack'
'Capitalist dream on steroids'
'Part Disney, part Scheherazade'
'A hallucinatory pastiche of the big, the bad and the ugly.'

THESE LINES ARE from recent journalistic meditations on Dubai, a city that has become central in the global imagination as the soaring cost of oil from 2001 to 2008 fuelled its latest economic boom, and the plummeting cost of oil since 2008 has just as dramatically ground its construction projects to a snail's pace. In just a few short years, Dubai has morphed from being a Middle Eastern/Indian Ocean regional city into a global megalopolis, a primary destination for companies, migrant workers and tourists on the 'New Silk Road'.

As the superlatives in the quotes above indicate, Dubai does things boldly. Dubai is purposefully branded through ever-newer, ever-grander, iconic construction projects (mostly built by government-owned or -backed companies) such as the Palm Islands, the sail-shaped Burj al Arab (formerly the world's tallest hotel), an indoor ski slope attached to the Mall of the Emirates, the Burj Khalifa (the world's tallest building) and the Rose Rayhaan, the world's tallest hotel, which was officially opened just a few days after the Burj Khalifa in early January 2010. Other projects in the works were even bigger and grander, but due to the recession these mostly have either been shelved or had their construction extremely delayed. Chief among these megaprojects is Dubailand, a complex planned to be more than twice the size of Walt Disney World with multiple theme parks, Universal Studios, a Sports City including a Manchester United soccer school, an ICC global cricket academy, a Tiger Woods golf course, luxury villas and hotels, and on and on. Very little has been built, however, and nothing has been completed.

Dubai's branding also extends to major investments in sporting events, attracting the biggest stars for some of the largest purses in tennis, golf and horse-racing. Dubai's government also brands itself abroad through purchases of landmark properties, heavy advertising and even sponsorship of sporting teams (by government-owned Emirates Airline) such as European football clubs Arsenal, AC Milan, Paris Saint Germain and Hamburger SV.

Alongside the often-fawning descriptions of its constructed wonders, Dubai has also attracted scathing media criticism. It is infamous for its exploitation of construction workers, who account for nearly one-fourth of the population and generally earn the equivalent of USD 150–200 per month for work weeks of six 10- to 12-hour days, often more. These workers live in labour camps on the edge of the desert, many in the world's largest (of course) and largely squalid labour camp, Sonapur. Until just a few short years ago, Dubai was also well known for 'employing' child camel jockeys (some as young as three), though robots have recently replaced these children. The plight of maids, who are arguably in a worse position than construction workers as their work lives are hidden behind closed doors, has been taken up by human rights organizations, most notably Human Rights Watch. And Dubai is a major centre of human trafficking, as can be seen by the incredibly large number of prostitutes from a variety of countries, visible in the clubs and bars of hotels, in brothels in apartment buildings, and working the streets.

In short, Dubai is a fascinating case study in light-speed urban development, hyper-consumerism, massive immigration and vertiginous inequality, where first-world wealth for citizens and professional expatriate workers is created through third-world wages of Asian labourers in a forest of construction cranes reclaiming the desert and the sea.

Dubai is a new city, and a unique brand of global city: a city of transients. In this book, I argue that Dubai's stories – history, economic development, culture – are dependent on the 'perma-nent impermanence' of expatriate foreign workers who comprise *more than 90 per cent* of the population and who, for the most part, live in Dubai on three-year renewable visas. Among global cities, this makes Dubai unique – nowhere else in the world do you find such a high proportion of impermanent residents.[1] This structured impermanence of Dubai's three-year visa system that regulates the lives of expatriates is the key to understanding much of the social and economic dynamics of Dubai. In other words, the story of the expatriates *is* the story of Dubai.

In spite of the glut of attention Dubai has garnered in recent years, what we know about Dubai, and the oil-rich Arabian Gulf states generally through the mass media is fairly narrow: that there is incredible wealth and consumer excess alongside equally incredible horrible living and working conditions of labourers, that there is lots of oil, and the 'fact' that the region is a breeding ground for terrorists.

Scholarly studies, oddly, have also been somewhat myopic in their discussions of Dubai. Many studies from the 1980s onwards have been focused on political developments, stemming from the transition from British colonial oversight to the formation and consolidation of the United Arab Emirates (in 1971), as well as foreign relations with other Gulf states and Western countries. Other studies have had more of an economic focus, examining especially the impact of oil on economic development, while a handful of studies have paid attention to the social aspects of the economic boom, looking at the expatriate labourers brought in to actually build up Dubai and other places in the Arabian Gulf. Recently there has been more scholarly attention paid to Dubai's economic and political development, as well as to an assessment of Dubai's architectural achievements.[2] Still, there is a paucity of scholarly studies examining one of the economic and social 'hotspots' of the early part of the twenty-first century.[3]

This book analyses how Dubai has become a global city and the living and working conditions of the people responsible for this transformation. The story I tell here has four distinct layers, but, as the book shows, these layers are all interconnected in complex ways. First, I examine how Dubai's unique – for the conservative Muslim Arabian Gulf – brand of consumerism is constructed, how it is designed to retain current residents, and how it also attracts by design new workers and, especially, tourists and new property owners. Second, I examine the foundations of 'Brand Dubai', looking at its infrastructural developments and investment strategies, and the ways Dubai manages its public relations, such as through censorship of the media. Third, I tell the story of how the government of Dubai's exclusionary legal and social policy of treating all expatriate workers as temporary shapes their living and working conditions. The ideas of exclusion and impermanence are useful to help us understand conditions of both the working class and professionals, and how lack of permanence keeps all workers under control. Fourth, I explore how two classes of long-term residents in Dubai – Dubai-born and raised professional expatriates and citizens – make their way in a place defined by a state of temporariness. I analyse how expatriates born in Dubai conceive of themselves and their relationship to Dubai when assimilation is legally and socially not possible. I end by examining how Dubai's citizens make their way in a place where they are a small permanent presence among a majority transient population, and in some ways invisible in the public sphere.

DUBAI AS A GLOBAL CITY

Globalization has become *the* buzzword of the twenty-first century. Theories of globalization come in many stripes, from often-dense academic formulations to the insistence of *New York Times* columnist and globalization cheerleader Thomas Friedman that the world is flat. Generally though, it would be fair to say, at the risk of grotesque oversimplification, that globalization theories mainly share the notion that the world is getting smaller and more tightly linked economically, politically, socially and culturally.

One major strain of theories of globalization focuses on the importance of cities as the primary sites of global interactions. The foremost theorist in this vein, Saskia Sassen, argues that global cities are essentially in a kind of dialogue with other global cities, that major flows of capital, people and ideas circulate between them. For instance, New York City has more qualitative and quantitative connections of all types with London than it does with

5

Tallahassee, Florida. Sassen posits that there are four major types of cross-border links connecting global cities to other global cities and nations: economic penetration in the form of direct investments and trade, immigrant communities, cultural links (both economic and artistic) and criminal networks.[4]

Dubai has undoubtedly become a global city of importance. In the past ten years, Dubai has – by design – emerged as a 'truly' global (rather than regional) city, standing alongside London, New York, Tokyo and Singapore. Dubai has had an outward-looking focus since the early 1900s, a locus for the Middle East, South Asia and Africa in terms of trade and as a centre of immigration. The backbone of Dubai's economy historically has been the trade in import and re-export, through licit means and by smuggling. Unlike its immediate neighbours, it does not have much in the way of oil itself – oil-related income currently accounts for less than 6 per cent of GDP. But from the 1960s Dubai has parlayed its oil wealth into building up its infrastructure and especially its construction and tourism industries, and has benefited from the rise in oil prices indirectly, as Abu Dhabi, Saudi Arabia and Kuwait invest large sums in Dubai.

This investment in infrastructure – including the dredging of Dubai's Creek, the building of two massive ports, its immense international airport and a second, larger one in the works – has been critical in making Dubai into a central hub linking Europe and East Asia (and, to a lesser extent, North America) to the Middle East, South Asia and Africa. Dubai has also attracted the attention of transnational corporations large and small from around the globe, enticed by lack of taxes and bureaucratic entanglements to come set up shop, especially in one of its many free trade zones, including Jebel Ali Port, Media City, Internet City, Healthcare City, Knowledge Village and Academic City – with other free zones in the works. Some transnational corporations, such as the American defence and energy conglomerate Halliburton, have even shifted their corporate headquarters to Dubai. One way to map Dubai's importance as a hub is simply to look at the numbers of flights and destinations of its flagship airline, Emirates. The density of connections to cities in the Middle East, South Asia, Europe, East Asia and Africa gives a sense of its importance as a commercial and social hub. Interestingly, there are currently only direct flights to four American cities, an indication of how Dubai has not (yet) effectively branded itself to Americans and American companies. But, notably, Emirates has so many direct flights to New York City that it is almost a commuter flight.

As private companies come from abroad to take advantage of Dubai's business climate, so too do international migrants. While merchants and workers from the Middle East, South Asia and Africa have been coming to Dubai since the early 1900s, today migrants come from nearly every nation to fill the demand for labour at all levels, including construction workers, maids, prostitutes, lower-level service workers in hotels, malls and restaurants, architects, bankers, real estate agents and other professionals. The private sector is staffed almost completely with foreign labour, 99 per cent, and the public sector too is staffed by more than 90 per cent expatriate labour.[5]

Of Dubai's population of nearly two million before the recession, more than 90 per cent are expatriates, with India accounting for the largest number of workers (over 40 per cent), with large numbers of Lebanese, Pakistani, Iranian, Indonesian, Filipino and British nationals, among others. For professional expatriates, working in Dubai offers the possibility of professional advancement quicker and higher than what might be possible at home. For working-class expatriates from countries such as India, Bangladesh and the Philippines, Dubai offers the promise of wages far in excess of what workers could earn at home. Even the most poorly paid construction worker is, at least until recently, able to remit a sizable portion of his income. These transnational workers exemplify just how much of a global city Dubai has become in terms of attracting workers of all skill levels from so many countries.

Dubai's globalizing strategy includes aggressively attempting to attract more well-heeled expatriates – especially from the UK – to buy property, as well as increasing the numbers of tourists. In 2002, Dubai's ruler, Sheikh Mohammed bin Rashid Al Maktoum, decreed that foreigners would be allowed to purchase property, leading to a massive real estate boom that lasted until late 2008, when the effects of the global economic meltdown finally hit Dubai. Sheikh Mohammed has also made a conscious effort to attract tourists. Seven million foreign tourists came to Dubai in 2007, and Sheikh Mohammed has stated he wants there to be fifteen million by 2010. To put this in perspective, India, a country with a population well over one billion, had five million foreign tourists in 2007.

On the cultural front, in an even shorter time span Dubai has become a major centre for art, as seen by the entrance of big market auction houses Christie's and Bonhams, who, like other transnational corporations, are drawn to Dubai by the vast amount of wealth in the area. Dubai also draws many of the biggest Western and Arab pop stars and Bollywood stars and has a thriving cosmopolitan club scene, with DJs of international renown regularly appearing. Many people I interviewed lamented Dubai's 'plastic' atmosphere, that it lacks 'culture' such as what one might find in New York or London. While until very recently there was little in the way of an 'organic' locally grown music or art scene, such as the Manchester sound of the 1980s or New York's SoHo art scene, Dubai managed to bypass this 'stage' of development and go straight to being internationally significant.

Dubai's consumer culture is largely rooted in the shopping malls, clubs and bars. The numbers and size of its malls, and the wide variety of international stores (such as H&M, Gucci, Marks and Spencer, Starbucks, etc.) match and exceed those anywhere else in the world. While shopping is of course central to the lives of people globally, it may be even more pronounced in Dubai, especially given the relative lack of non-commercial public spaces (squares, parks, museums, libraries) and the extreme heat and humidity that people must suffer for over half the year, often reaching 50 degrees Celsius in the summer months, which forces people indoors. The malls thus provide a social meeting ground and are in essence Dubai's town squares. (Except for construction workers who are often prevented from entering malls by security guards on direct orders from management. Their social meeting grounds are often, literally, patches of grass.) It is not by accident that major cultural programmes are tied in with the two summer and winter shopping festivals and enacted in malls.

Some feel that this merger of the economic and cultural is unsustainable, and ultimately will have a much-too-high human cost. For instance, George Soros, the multibillionaire and critic of unfettered globalization, insists that 'we can have a market economy, but we cannot have a market society,' meaning that 'global society' requires a moral basis beyond what the market offers to provide values and social cohesion.[6] But the Dubai model, which does away with most forms of civil society and civic participation, works precisely *because* it is a market society; in fact, it is the seductive power of Dubai's unbounded consumer culture which is in large part responsible for attracting and retaining workers. Come, make money and consume, or, in the case of lower end workers, remit. The freedoms that people so cherish in the West – free speech, democracy – are absent in Dubai. Here, 'freedom' is the freedom to do business and to engage in all manner of conspicuous consumption. Citizens and expatriates for the most part seem not to mind or miss the absence of political freedom.

The dark underbelly of processes of economic and cultural globalization and transnational flows of capital and people is the parallel transnationalisation of criminal activities, as Sassen rightly points out. The rise of smuggling rings globally in the past twenty or so years has also been felt in Dubai. The bulk of victims of human trafficking in Dubai are prostitutes, who form a veritable United Nations of sex workers, servicing expatriates, nationals, other Gulf Arab citizens and tourists. The government has recently made a show of cracking down on human smuggling and prostitution, but the extreme numbers and brazen openness of prostitution in Dubai belie this effort.

EXPATRIATE WORKERS AND THE THREE-YEAR VISA REGIME

Dubai, arguably more than any other global city, is a transitional social space. For most expatriate workers, it is a means to an end, and the meaning of Dubai varies for individuals depending on their work and nationality backgrounds. Generally, expatriates come to Dubai to earn money to send home to build villas, pay for the marriages of siblings, set up a business at home or make career advancements, or they come simply to enjoy the experience of living and working in another country, and then get out. Western migrants generally come for the short term. Of migrants from the developing world, some plan to come only for a short while, some attempt to stay as going home is something many do not desire, and some attempt to use Dubai as a springboard for migrating to the West. Dubai marks all these migrants as temporary, as there is no legal category of permanent residency, and little realistic chance of attaining citizenship for most.

As a result, expatriates are by definition there for the short term. This works well for both the government and private companies who get temporary, pliant labour who threaten neither the political nor the economic power structures.

Not unexpectedly, labourers and professionals experience their temporariness differently. Labourers (including construction workers, cab drivers, prostitutes and lower-level service workers generally), who constitute the vast majority of Dubai's population, are highly regulated in their working and social lives. Their passports are confiscated upon arrival (an illegal practice that even government departments engage in), they face deportation and temporary bans on returning to Dubai if they attempt to switch jobs or quit, their wages are often withheld for months at a time to prevent them from quitting (a practice the government tolerates), and there is a ban on unions and strikes. At any point and for practically any reason, the government or employer may cancel a worker's visa, resulting in immediate deportation and a (usually) temporary ban of six months to a year.

For professionals, these regulations are applied more subtly. They generally do not have the fear that labourers have of deportation, though it does happen, as they enter more willingly into Dubai's Faustian bargain: they give up democratic freedoms (the right to vote, free speech, the right to criticize the government) for a standard of living one might not get in Arab or South Asian countries, or even in the UK or US. It is generally not necessary for the government to enforce discipline among professionals as they so willingly give up their political freedoms. For labourers and professionals alike, political freedom is superseded by economic freedom, which for most expatriates is experienced as the most basic and important kind of freedom.

This basic legal framework of defining the bulk of the population as disposable and temporary (it is not incidental that the government insists expatriates are 'guest workers') also affects issues of identity. For expatriates, especially long-term and Dubai-born expatriates, it excludes them from making any claims on Dubai as their home. No matter how long an expatriate has been in Dubai, even if they are born in Dubai, they are not Dubaian. At some point, they must leave. This process of exclusion leaves these particular expatriates betwixt and between – they are not legally Dubaian and can be deported at any point, nor are they culturally of their countries of passport. For some, this uncertainty is liberating; it certifies them as global citizens. For others, it merely points out the dangerous condition of their liminal state.

The definition of expatriates as temporary residents also affects local citizens. Nationals (as they are known throughout Dubai and the United Arab Emirates), a small minority in their own country, feel a growing sense of estrangement from Dubai, as they see expatriates increasingly dominate numerically and culturally. Many nationals feel unease and disdain for most expatriates, who they see as insular and unwilling to accommodate nationals, whose place Dubai ostensibly is. This leads to a sense of 'reactive' identity among many nationals – the more expatriates come and come to dominate publicly, the more nationals tend to distance themselves socially and geographically from expatriates. This then leads to further tensions and misunderstandings between nationals and expatriates, among whom, according to many long-term expatriates in Dubai, there used to be much greater interaction and understanding.

Dubai, then, is a unique kind of social space, a social experiment in the construction of a new kind of global city and postmodern reality. It is in Dubai where the dreams of laissez faire economists are finding their ultimate realization. The state rarely interferes with and indeed goes to great lengths to support business interests, and the bulk of the population are treated merely as 'factors of production'; from maids and construction workers to architects and business executives, expatriate guest workers are there simply to do a job. Dubai is the 'market society' George Soros worried about, where civil society is squeezed out. While on the surface this relation seems highly exploitative of expatriates, the reality is more complex.

CHAPTER ONE

THE ROOTS OF DUBAI

DUBAI'S TRANSFORMATION INTO a brash, upstart global city has occurred in a breathtakingly short time. This was largely made possible by the aftershocks of 9/11 and the second Gulf War. But that is getting ahead of ourselves. Here I lay out the foundations of modern Dubai in its pre-9/11 incarnation and before it had acquired global cachet – its history as a trade and smuggling centre; the building of a tourist infrastructure where none reasonably should exist; and the short-term visa system that regulates how foreigners go about living their lives.

TRADE AND SMUGGLING

Dubai's modern history dates to 1833, when eight hundred members of the Al Bu Falasah section of the ruling Bani Yas family of Abu Dhabi split off to settle in Dubai. The most important family of the Al Bu Falasah section was the Al Maktoum, from which all the rulers of Dubai have come. By the early part of the twentieth century, Dubai had established itself as the main trading centre of the region, a result of a crafty move by its ruler Sheikh Maktoum bin Hasher to lure Persian-Arab and Indian traders from the Persian port cities to Dubai with promises of no taxes, protection and land. The city developed very quickly, and in 1904 a German traveller noted that the sudden influx of traders from Persia was causing high commercial and residential rents along the creek, which handsomely profited the ruler and some merchants, a situation that greatly resembled Dubai just before the bust in late 2008.[1]

In the 1950s, after twenty-odd years of relative economic depression following the collapse of the pearl trade, which had been central to Dubai's prosperity, Dubai witnessed an upsurge of commercial activity, a fair degree of it involving exports between India and Pakistan.[2] At the time, relations between these newly independent countries were icy and direct trade was not possible, so goods had to go through a third party, which was Dubai.[3] The most profitable aspect of trade with these countries was gold smuggling, indeed it was the most profitable endeavour in Dubai after the collapse of the pearl trade in the wake of the global Great Depression and before the discovery of oil. Gold would be bought in Geneva or London, imported duty free into Dubai, then smuggled to India or Pakistan. While the import and export of gold to and from Dubai was perfectly legal, importing within India and Pakistan was not – hence the use of the term 'smuggling'.

The gold smuggling trade produced a class of relatively wealthy nationals, which included a who's who of local citizen merchant families (not all the families were involved, but those that were are still prominent today) and expatriates, particularly of Indians and Iranians. Some Western expatriates were also involved as investors, but generally did not sully their hands directly and thus maintained an air of 'respectability'.[4] Most of the gold was shipped in fast, motorized dhows, some mounted with guns, and the dhow captains engaged in fantastic cat and mouse games with the Indian Coast Guard, often ending in gold being dumped into the Indian Ocean so as to avoid the authorities and sometimes in shootouts with deadly results. In the early 1970s, one smuggler supposedly had killed eighty-two Indian Coast Guard and naval personnel in his career.[5] By the early 1970s Dubai was the third largest buyer of gold in the open market, and it was believed there were 130 sterling millionaires active in the gold smuggling trade.[6]

The gold smuggling trade largely came to an end in 1973. The price of gold at this time was rising dramatically, and quickly went beyond the reach of ordinary Indian families, the end purchasers of the smuggled gold. At the same time, Prime Minister Indira Gandhi cracked down on the smugglers' agents in Bombay, imprisoning many of them. By June of that year imports of gold hit zero. While there was a minor revival in the late 1970s, the gold smuggling trade never fully recovered.[7]

While gold smuggling was a high risk/high profit venture and is the stuff that racier books are made of (such as Robin Moore's 1977 novel, *Dubai*), more basic to Dubai's economy from at least the early 1900s to today has been trade, licit and illicit, with Iran. The biggest boost to trade with Iran, and to Dubai's prominence in global trade, was the Iranian Revolution in 1979. When the American hostages were taken in the US embassy, the United States immediately imposed economic sanctions against Iran. Trade that would have gone directly to Iran was then funnelled through Dubai. While merchants were beginning to profit from this, within the year the Iran–Iraq war started and lasted until 1988, causing great economic hardship for many merchants as a result of the slowdown of trade with Iran, Dubai's main destination for exports. The war was a boon, however, for the dry docks which had just been completed in 1979, and for salvaging companies who would troll the waters for damaged boats and tow them back to the dry docks.[8]

The fortunes of Dubai's merchants improved as the war wound down in 1988 and as the United States imposed a trade embargo with Iran in 1987 – which is still continuing. In spite of the embargo – or perhaps because of it – billions of dollars of goods produced by US-based companies find their way to Iran via Dubai, smuggled by dhows. The goods are often repackaged when they arrive in Jebel Ali Port or Port Rashid to avoid US government scrutiny, though some dhow captains do not bother.[9]

During the Bush Jr years, which coincided with Dubai's second oil boom, trade with Iran increased further still, and the number of Iranians living in Dubai may have doubled. The deputy president of the Iranian Business Council of Dubai made the point that many Iranians would not be in Dubai if not for US policy. (It is difficult to assess how many Iranians live in Dubai because, aside from the lack of accurate data generally, many Iranians split their time between Dubai and Iran, so the line between Iranian residents and tourists is especially blurry.)

In large part the smuggling business today works because American companies openly flout US laws. A Middle Eastern analyst said, 'I think a majority of these companies are well plugged-in in Washington. In DC they are given mixed signals, but they have more reason to believe that the US is not going to take any action against them. So they go ahead and do it.'[10]

The legal and illegal trade with Iran, India, Pakistan and elsewhere has largely been shaped by the fast development of infrastructure, which started in the late 1950s with Sheikh Mohammed's father, Sheikh Rashid bin Saeed Al Maktoum. Rashid was keen to develop the city and its economy. The first step to this end was to dredge the creek, the city's trading lifeblood, which had become so silted that at points it was possible for camels to pass across. The dredging was completed in 1959 and allowed for a greater volume of cargo in and out of the city. One year later Rashid opened an international airport in spite of initial opposition by the British, their colonial overlords.[11]

The improved creek attracted a great deal of shipping, much of it siphoned off from the neighbouring emirate of Sharjah, which up to this time had also been an important centre of trade, and whose creek had also been silting up. Within a few short years, Dubai's creek was experiencing a 'traffic jam' and plans were made to supplement the creek, which serviced smaller vessels, with a new port that could attract bigger ships. In 1966 work was begun on Port Rashid, which initially had been planned with four berths but at the end of construction in 1971 had sixteen. This was followed five years later by construction of the massive Jebel Ali Port, one of the largest deepwater ports in the world, which on its completion in 1983 had sixty-six berths.

To complete these and other planned projects, a massive influx of workers was beginning to arrive, mainly from Pakistan and India, a necessary result of Rashid's drive to develop Dubai at breakneck speed. Out of a population of 65,000 in Dubai in 1968, there were 20–25,000 Iranians, 12,000 Pakistanis and 8–10,000 Indians. The 1968 census listed 24,500 inhabitants as 'economically active', and more than a third in trades and services, of which a high proportion were merchants and most of the rest labourers.[12] Rashid knew that many more expatriate workers were needed for the projects he envisaged, and they would require housing, which was in short stock at the time. To that end, early in the 1960s, he began building in new areas such as Karama and Satwa, with much of the construction being purposely built as low-income housing with buildings for the first time having water directly piped in and being supplied with electricity.[13] Some of this housing still exists today with rents at levels far below market rate, though most of the buildings have either been torn down or are earmarked to be torn down to make way for luxury construction. In fact, the entire Satwa area was slated to be razed, but was spared, for the time being at least, as a result of the recession that hit in late 2008.

Dubai's ascension in the 1980s and early 1990s as the region's premier port allowed legitimate trade interests to greatly expand, but at the same time made it possible for all sorts of illegitimate transactions to occur as well, as we have just seen. Dubai became the Gulf's money laundry, and home to various gangsters and terrorists in the process. These types of activity are really an extension of the smuggling trades that had been part and parcel of Dubai's development. While it has not been shown conclusively that ruling family members have an active hand in any of these illicit activities, Dubai's rulers have historically given them tacit approval by turning a blind eye in the interests of keeping commerce generally as free and uninterrupted as possible.

Before Dubai's most recent boom, the smugglers, money launderers, gangsters and terrorists were largely connected with Iran, India or Russia, using Dubai as their safe haven. For example, Bombay's number one gangster, Dawood Ibrahim, used Dubai as his home base to control his criminal enterprises in India. He came to Dubai in 1984 after being hounded out of Bombay by local police, and subsequently made a fortune as a gold smuggler, as smuggling, though on a much smaller scale than up to the early 1970s (as mentioned above), still proved profitable for some until the early 1990s, when India's economy was liberalized and many trade restrictions and customs duties were reduced. Dawood operated quite openly in Dubai, holding lavish parties and owning a number of businesses. While in Dubai, he planned and executed a series of bomb blasts in Bombay, which killed over 250 people in March 1993, in revenge for the pogrom against Muslims which had happened just months before. The Indian government put heavy pressure on Dubai to extradite him, but the Dubai government allowed him and his gang to quietly leave for Pakistan. Even so, his lieutenants continued to do business from Dubai.[14]

Again, the point here is that Dubai's positioning itself as a place of commerce, and making little in the way of judgement about commerce, has made it the preferred destination for merchants for more than a century. The type of merchandise has been of little concern to the rulers, so long as it does not adversely affect them. When it does, as with the case of Dawood Ibrahim, then the rulers act.

TOURISM

While Dubai has been an important trading centre since the early twentieth century, outside the region – that is, to the West – it was relatively unknown, even though it was indirectly ruled by the British and even though the discovery of oil had made it wealthy. Through the 1990s Dubai was an open space of beaches and desert, with a population of around 750,000 in 1999 largely concentrated on either side of the creek in Bur Dubai and Deira, with wealthier residents further south along the coast in Jumeirah, at the time a 'suburban' neighbourhood. In the 1990s, Sheikh Mohammed made a conscious decision to supplement oil revenues, which he and others knew would run out in short time. His father, Sheikh Rashid, had concentrated on improving Dubai's position as a trading hub by dredging the creek and building two massive ports, as well as building the airport. Sheikh Mohammed continued this approach, further expanding Dubai International Airport (with a second airport close to Jebel Ali Port scheduled to be open in

2010), but added to this a focus on developing tourism, specifically through the creation and expansion of Emirates Airline, and by developing Dubai as a shopping destination. Dubai basically had to create tourism from scratch as there is little to 'naturally' attract tourists in terms of culture and history, aside from a small fort dating back to the late 1700s, which today is the site of the Dubai Museum. The museum is tellingly sparse, indicating perhaps a lack of any real interest by the authorities in a non-commercial venture, a theme we will return to shortly.

'Fly Buy Dubai'

The first necessity for developing Dubai's tourism industry was simply to get people to Dubai. To this end, Sheikh Mohammed authorized the creation of Emirates Airline, which was launched in 1985 with a USD 10 million loan from the Dubai government.[15] It initially leased planes from Pakistan International Airline with just two daily flights to Karachi, but within a year it had added services to Delhi and Bombay – linking Dubai directly to its main sources of blue- and white-collar labour. By the end of the 1980s, Emirates had negotiated landing rights in Singapore, Germany, Hong Kong and the UK. By 1994, Emirates was flying to thirty-three cities, an impressive infrastructural base for the coming tourist hordes. By the end of the decade, it flew to forty-five cities on four continents. Emirates is incredibly profitable, having posted profits every year save one, supposedly without state subsidies, although they do benefit from cheap fuel and cheaper labour.[16] Emirates further benefits to a large degree from geography, lying as it does at the intersection of Europe, Africa and Asia. While the newest planes can travel roughly ten thousand miles without refuelling (for example, from New York to Singapore, a nineteen-hour flight), making the need for layovers in international travel redundant, they are not yet that common, especially for connecting emerging markets such as Cairo to Shanghai.

Still, an airline is after all just an amenity and, no matter how new and luxurious the planes are, they do not guarantee that people will actually enter the country. In the 1990s, a mere twenty years removed from independence and the first oil boom of the early 1970s, the government of Dubai made a conscious decision to make itself attractive to tourists regionally and internationally as a place to shop. This may seem trivial, but this made Dubai unique in the broader Middle East/South Asia region, where it was difficult to find quality international goods, and, if you could find them, it was at a cost even higher than in the West for items such as clothing, electronics and appliances. The CEO of Dubai's promotion board in 1996 made the reasonably accurate claim that, 'We're a little island of bargains in a sea of countries where nothing is available.'[17]

The shopping starts right at the airport. Dubai International Airport started its 'duty-free' in 1983 (the title of this section, 'Fly buy Dubai', is taken from an early advertising campaign), and it quickly grew to be one of the largest airport duty-free shopping locations in the world, going well beyond cigarettes and alcohol, the staples of duty-free shopping. Dubai's duty-free also famously offers high-end raffles for cash, gold bars and luxury cars. (While gambling is illegal, raffles are conveniently not considered to be gambling and are tremendously popular.) In 1993, Dubai's duty-free had sales of USD 132 million or 6 per cent of the worldwide duty-free market – third in the world after Amsterdam and Singapore. In 1995, this increased to USD 173 million.[18] By 2008, it was doing more than USD 1 billion in transactions.

In 1996, the government took an additional step to consolidate its standing as the shopping mall of the Middle East with the establishment of the Dubai Shopping Festival (DSF), which drew 1.6 million visitors in its first year. This was followed a few years later by the introduction of the similar Dubai Summer Surprises (DSS) to increase tourist flow, mainly from elsewhere in the Gulf and South Asia, during the unbearable (to Westerners) summer heat. To Western shoppers, DSF and DSS look simply like coordinated sales across shopping malls. And even with discounts and no taxes, most clothing and electronic items I priced (I spent a lot of time in shopping malls as I was in Dubai during the hottest time of the year) were above what I would pay online or in stores in New York City. But this misses the point. DSF (and, to a lesser degree, DSS) from its beginning was planned as spectacle, as a celebration of shopping. Fireworks, fashion shows, theatre and dance, and, for children, treasure hunts, face painting and other activities are on full display in the malls and other venues.[19] Who are these people lured by fireworks and face paint? In 1999, of the 2.4 million DSF visitors, more than a third were Saudis. And, critical for Dubai's economic engine, they are big spenders.[20] In 2008, DSF attracted 3.2 million visitors, accounting for a little less than half of all foreign tourists to Dubai.

An important part of the story of Dubai's shopping boom, largely forgotten in the economic growth of the past decade, was the breakup of the USSR. From 1992, people from the former Soviet republics would come to Dubai (or to Sharjah where it was cheaper to fly into) on dozens of daily charter flights on 'shopping tours'. Many shopkeepers in Dubai became fluent in Russian, and stores regularly had Cyrillic script on their signs and business cards, in addition to English. In the mid-1990s half a million visitors annually came from the former Soviet Union to Dubai, pumping USD 1 billion into the economy. These shoppers, *'chelnok'* professional traders, bought nearly anything and everything in bulk for resale back home.[21]

These Eastern European visitors were the social precursors to more recent British tourists – coarse and unconcerned with local cultural norms. The women often wore scandalous attire (for that time) of sundresses and miniskirts and occasionally went topless at the beaches. These tourists became a local tourist attraction themselves, bringing many men to the beaches for this particular kind of sightseeing. An Indian travel agent at the time said, 'Asian women don't want their husbands to go out anymore because they're afraid of the Russian blondes. And local men are afraid their women will start behaving like the Russians.' And the blonde Eastern Europeans, such as Marina from Kazakhstan, had their own complaints. 'It's impossible to walk on the streets here. All the local men try to touch or pinch me, probably to make sure I'm not a mirage.'[22] While it seems that everyone at the time had complaints about the social behaviour of everyone else, they all appreciated the business.

These tourists were a huge part of the Dubai story, but their numbers declined dramatically in the late 1990s – from a high of roughly 500,000 visitors per year, this dropped to around 260,000 in 1997 and 200,000 in 1998, due in large measure to the financial crisis that swept through East Asia and Russia in 1997–8.[23] This led directly to lowered sales in Dubai's stores. The former Soviets purchased nearly 40 per cent of goods in Dubai's stores in the mid-1990s, but by 1999 their purchases fell by half, leading to a painful crunch for a great number of Dubai's merchants who had become dependent on these customers.[24]

Nightlife

While today Dubai is globally famous for its nightclubs and prostitution (which we will address in the next chapter), Dubai generally drew little attention in the Western media for its social life (or anything else for that matter) before the millennium. One of the earliest sources I could find that commented on the nightlife in Dubai was a 1992 piece in the *Guardian*, ancient history by Dubai time, which reported:

> Most hotels have several bars and discos to choose from, catering for tastes from Bromley to Beirut or the Khyber Pass – it depends on which nationality you want to mix with. Besides oriental belly dancing, there are *mujras* or [South] Asian dancing clubs in many of the second-class hotels – for men only, unfortunately.[25]

An article in the *Guardian* two years later elaborated on the nightlife and its seedy nature, writing how on stage at a night-club in one hotel there are Russian dancers 'dressed in thongs and little sparkly dabs on their nipples'. The patrons were Gulf Arabs, Japanese, Lebanese, Egyptians and drunken Englishmen (a common theme in Dubai, as we will see in chapter four). In the same hotel, there were six other bars, and next door a disco for Filipinos, a bar for Africans and a nightclub for Iranians. Elsewhere in the city at the time there were British pubs for 'thirsty Englishmen' and Tex-Mex bars for visiting American oilmen and military servicemen.[26] Another travel piece, this one written in 1995, wrote of the nightlife: 'Discos are big in Dubai, although prepare yourself for chrome banisters, pile carpets and men in bad suits.'[27] Hardly a scene that could compete with Bombay or Beijing at that time, let alone with London or New York.

* * *

By the late 1990s, the tourism trade was growing rapidly, attracting Westerners in increasing numbers, including 200,000

British tourists yearly (today that number is closer to one million). Business for British travel agencies was very strong, so strong in fact that one British travel agent worried that, 'There is a danger of [Dubai] becoming another Miami Beach, with giant hotels in one big line.'[28] (This was in 2000, less than a year after the Burj al Arab, the sail-shaped, ultra-luxury hotel opened for business.)

While the British and Russians came in increasing numbers throughout the 1990s, the bulk of tourists until the mid-2000s were largely from the region, mainly Gulf Arabs and South Asians. In 2002, for instance, the largest numbers of people staying in hotels and hotel apartments were Gulf Arabs (34 per cent), not surprising given their proximity, followed by South Asians (25 per cent), non-Gulf Arabs (16 per cent), Europeans (15 per cent) and Africans (9 per cent).[29] American tourists do not even factor in these figures. It was only in the mid-2000s that they started to come in great numbers, a point we will explore in the following chapter.

THE *KAFALA* SYSTEM AND ECONOMIC DEVELOPMENT

In 1966, oil was discovered in Dubai. While Dubai's economy was already booming due to the many projects undertaken, with oil its economy exploded, especially after the spike in the price of oil in 1973, as did its population, particularly its expatriate population. By 1968, Emirati national citizens in Dubai and Abu Dhabi were already slightly in the minority. The wealth immediately accruing from oil changed in the most basic way the manner in which citizens lived, but also the conditions under which expatriates lived.

Oil wealth on its own, however, does not explain these changes, as there are many places in the world where oil has brought great wealth to the state's rulers but not to the people.

In Dubai the most basic principle underlying the relations between citizens, expatriates and the state is the *kafala* (sponsorship) system, which is common throughout the Gulf states, and is the main way – outside of direct welfare programmes – that oil wealth trickled down to the citizenry.[30] This system requires all businesses to have nationals as majority owners (outside of free zones, the first of which was Jebel Ali Free Zone Area, established in 1985), and requires all expatriate workers to be sponsored by their companies or, in the case of domestic workers, by their employers.

There are three main effects of this sponsorship system. First, it provides a very large number of Emirati nationals a way to get incomes as business partners without putting up any capital of their own. Essentially, they get money for little other than signing papers. Second, any national can sponsor workers – for their companies or as domestics. Some of these workers actually work for them, but other workers buy visas from these nationals, then go off to work elsewhere, illegally, since by law you must work for your sponsor.[31] Third, the *kafala* system makes workers beholden to their employers, a point we will return to in the next chapter.

The combination of oil wealth and the sponsorship system made it possible for citizens of the Emirates (but especially in Dubai and Abu Dhabi) to live a lifestyle far removed from that of their parents, who until the 1960s mostly lived in palm frond huts, or, in the case of the Bedouin, were nomads. (The Bedouin, even in the early part of the twentieth century accounted for only a little more than 10 per cent of the population, and their numbers have certainly declined over the years.[32]) By the time of independence in 1971 the palm frond huts had largely disappeared, and the nomadic Bedouin had become sedentary, settled in housing blocks.[33] By the early 1980s government welfare programmes had stimulated an economy and culture of mass consumption among nationals, who now had considerable disposable incomes, with little in the way of costs, as housing and many utilities were either free or heavily subsidized. What emerged early on after the first oil boom was a social order where locals were consumers and expatriates were the producers.[34] And where nationals worked in Dubai (mainly in the government), they did not perform the most menial or low paid work – this was the province of South Asians and Baluchis and other expatriate workers.[35]

While immigration controls had been put in place even before independence, half the expatriate working population at the time of independence were there illegally. Business people liked it that way, as illegal labour was cheap labour.[36] Indeed, as early as 1962, more than 900 Indians and Pakistanis a week were surreptitiously arriving by boat at Khor Fakkan on the east coast, with most making their way to Dubai.[37] This means of arrival continued into the 1980s, as a few of the adult children of expatriates I interviewed attested. In fact, illegal immigrants have always formed a large portion of the workforce – so large in fact that the UAE government has had to declare three worker amnesty programmes to get rid of them, the last one in 2007 when more than 340,000 workers (nearly all labourers or in other lower-end jobs) either got jobs that provided legitimate labour permits or left the country. In Dubai alone, almost 200,000 workers, the majority of which were Indians, took advantage of the amnesty programme.[38]

Indians have been present in Dubai as merchants since before the beginning of the twentieth century. By the mid-1970s, they constituted the third largest group in the UAE with a population of 102,000, after Pakistanis (202,000) and nationals (200,000), out of a total UAE population of 656,000. By 1979, the UAE population grew to 877,000, with Indians accounting for 152,000.[39] Today, Indians account for nearly 40 per cent of the population of Dubai and the UAE, and those from the tiny south-western coastal state of Kerala account for almost half that total. The vast majority of these workers, from the beginnings of the construction boom prior to the discovery of oil to today, were labourers, but a significant proportion have been middle-class professionals.

By the early 1980s, the presence of so many expatriates (mostly Indians and Pakistanis, but also Arabs, Iranians and a whole host of others in smaller numbers) in Dubai and the Gulf generally was already causing concern for governments and local intellectuals, who were worried that expatriates would over-whelm local populations culturally and demographically, and by extension threaten existing regimes. In actuality, for Indian and Pakistani expatriates at least, this was not the case. Expatriates, both professional and working class by and large would not, and did not, dare openly question the system as their basic livelihood depended on it. For instance, Pakistani professionals, as one observer wrote in 1984, were 'socially docile, clinging to the money they make and determined to make the most of it . . . They will not rock the boat at any cost.'[40]

Generally, expatriates found Dubai to be a quite hospitable environment for work and business, especially for those coming from unstable or corrupt regimes in the developing world, even from democratic countries. As a result, not surprisingly, by the early 1980s a great number of middle-class Indians expected to remain in the Gulf for their entire working lives, and many had brought over their wives and children.[41] A big policy shift that encouraged their numbers to increase even more came in 1986 when Dubai pushed for, and got, UAE legislation that allowed workers with monthly incomes of greater than AED 3,000 to bring in their families. (Until very recently the minimum had been AED 6,000, but in mid-2009 the UAE government proposed raising that to AED 10,000, which if enacted would greatly reduce the developing world expatriate population, especially of the Indian and Pakistani middle class, who are almost across the board the lowest paid workers in any occupation, no matter the rank.[42]) The proposal was presented as a response to a sharp drop in consumer spending, and was a break with the then current policy regarding migrants.[43] But this change was consistent with Dubai's laissez faire history, and actually hearkened back to Sheikh Maktoum bin Hasher's siren call to Persian Arab and Indian merchants to relocate to Dubai in 1902.

In the late 1970s and 1980s, British expatriates were coming to Dubai in increasing numbers, lured by opportunities in Dubai and chased by economic turmoil in the United Kingdom. By the mid-1990s, there was something of a 'gold rush' mentality for Britons. (An article in a British expatriate-focused magazine in 1995 was subtitled 'You want to work in Dubai? So does everyone else.'[44]) By 1995, there were roughly 20,000 Britons in Dubai (plus a lesser number of Canadians, Americans and other Westerners), much fewer than South Asians, but certainly a sizeable community and socially quite visible, with a greater proportion in professional positions.

The good life of luxury unattainable at home but absurdly affordable in Dubai was, and still is, a big draw for Britons. The British captain of a women's softball team was asked in the late 1980s why she stayed in Dubai, to which she replied, 'You got partying every night, water-skiing, sports. It's just a fantasy world. And you don't pay any taxes.'[45] The good life, not unlike in today's Dubai, centred around alcohol, which has always flowed freely.

Another draw for many British women was the possibility of finding a well-to-do husband. In the 1980s, the British expatriate community supposedly had a ratio of four women to every man, with 'a bumper crop of British secretaries'. An American male coach of another softball team said of his players casually that 'they're all shopping for husbands, really. Ones with money'.[46] This was not altogether dissimilar from British India, where single women would go over with the hopes of finding a proper officer gentleman husband, a catch beyond their reach in Britain itself.

* * *

Even with all the development frenzy and radical social changes through the 1990s, Dubai remained largely a sleepy, regional city, important mostly to merchants and South Asian, Iranian and Arab expatriates, and to a smaller number of Britons and other Westerners. Into the early 1990s, most of Dubai was desert. In fact, in what today is a packed skyline on Sheikh Zayed Road, until 2000, when Sheikh Mohammed's Jumeirah Group built the Emirates Towers, there was hardly anything but sand between the World Trade Center (the tallest building in the Middle East when it was built in 1979 in what was then the middle of the desert) and the Metropolitan Hotel a few miles to its south on the route to Abu Dhabi. But things changed dramatically as a result of the terrorist attacks of 11 September 2001 and the invasion of Iraq in 2003, and the incredible rise in the price of oil soon after, which concurrently fuelled Dubai's amazing economic growth and population explosion.

CHAPTER TWO

BECOMING A GLOBAL BRAND

ON MY FIRST night in Dubai in June 2006, I went to meet a friend at the Mall of the Emirates. Driving down Sheikh Zayed Road (the main highway in Dubai) at night was eerie; all the half-built skyscrapers with their white and red lights looked like 'Transformer' action figures. Once at the mall I was overwhelmed by the number and variety of high-end stores and its size: at the time it was the largest mall in the Middle East, until it was overtaken by Dubai Mall, one of the largest malls in the world, which in turn will be overtaken by the Mall of Arabia, planned to be the largest mall in the world – if it ever gets built. After a ten-minute walk inside the mall, I reached my destination, a bar/restaurant overlooking an indoor ski slope – I was not prepared for that. Like so many others around me, I was mesmerized by the audacity of people skiing indoors when it was deathly hot outside. I stood and gawked.

Where the oil boom of the 1970s allowed Dubai to become rich and regionally significant, the post-2001 oil boom had allowed Dubai to become even more extravagantly rich, to grow at a mind-boggling pace, and, importantly, to make itself internationally known. So many journalists in essays on Dubai in recent years have gawked as I did at all the things that Dubai has become known for: the seemingly never-ending construction, the extravagant consumerist excess, the prostitutes and the degraded conditions of the construction workers, maids, cleaners and others of the working class. These are all things that have helped to catapult Dubai into global fame and infamy. These are the things that, for good or bad, make up 'Brand Dubai'.

This chapter looks at how Dubai's current ruler Sheikh Mohammed has made Dubai into an internationally recognizable brand. By 'internationally recognizable' I mean that Dubai has made itself known in and relevant to the West. We will specifically examine the main factors that are the basis of Brand Dubai: its construction projects aimed at bringing in Western expatriates as well as retaining wealthier expatriates, tourism aimed at their counterparts, Westerners who spend money, and how Dubai strategically uses its sovereign wealth funds to build up its international image. We will also examine how Dubai censors its media to make certain that the good name of the brand is not besmirched.

Just below the glitzy surface of Dubai's rapid economic development and rise to international fame is how it treats its expatriate workers as temporary people. In the second part of the chapter, the conditions of their visas and the effects this has on cultural life in Dubai are outlined. Dubai's almost myopic emphasis on economic development has been at the expense of the cultural realm, specifically of art and education, which were largely ignored by the government in the rush to develop Dubai over the past few decades. Because 90 per cent of the population are treated as temporary workers, I argue this goes some way to explaining why Dubai was a culturally 'plastic' place. I then show how this changed when Dubai and other governments in the Gulf started to pay attention to art and education as opportunities of branding and profit.

BECOMING INFAMOUS

Before examining how Dubai's fame was built, it is worth briefly examining its infamy, continuing the discussion of smuggling and gangsters from the previous chapter. The UAE's flirtation with gangsters and terrorists was at its height just before 9/11 with its support of the Taliban, who harboured Osama bin Laden. The UAE was one of only three countries to officially recognize the Taliban regime in Afghanistan, and was suspected of covertly supplying arms to them.[1] 'Royal family members' (who and from which families has never been known) even went hunting with their falcons in Afghanistan. In 1999, the CIA believed that they had found bin Laden at a hunting camp where a plane with UAE markings was parked. While many in the CIA wanted to strike, seeing this as their best opportunity to kill bin Laden, they were overruled, for fear of wiping out a great number of UAE royal family members, which, pre-9/11, was thought would entail too high a political cost with an important ally.[2]

This open engagement with, or at least tolerance of, terrorist elements changed greatly as a result of American pressure in the wake of 9/11, when it came out that many of the terrorists flew to the United States from Dubai, and their funding had moved through Dubai banks. As a result, the US demanded, and the UAE agreed to, tighter banking regulations.

While the UAE has been praised recently in security circles for tightening control over banking regulations regarding 'hot money', money laundering is still widespread. Most recently, the ransom profits of Somali pirates (who gained their moment of fame in early 2009 when President Obama started to publicly take them seriously) were allegedly being laundered in Dubai, though the Dubai government vehemently contested this claim.[3] Through the 2000s, black and grey monies found a welcoming home in Dubai's booming property market, where investors would pay in full with cash for their purchases and turn around and flip their properties, in the process cleansing their cash and, as a bonus, turning a handsome profit. Drugs are also 'laundered' in Dubai. John Cassara, a former US Treasury Department agent who went in search of the routes of terrorist financing, made the assertion that in Dubai, Afghan drug lords deal in a barter system – trading opium for luxury vehicles, building materials, electronics and foodstuff, which are then shipped to Afghanistan. Cassara accused the Dubai authorities of 'wilful' blindness in turning the other way.[4] Little of this opium though finds its way to the local market – indeed the casual consumer will not find drugs anywhere near as easily as in London or New York City. Rather, it is Dubai's ease and centrality as a transit hub, with its massive ports and busy airport, that makes it so alluring for various transnational criminal elements (including human trafficking, which we will discuss in chapter three), in spite of the Dubai and UAE governments actively cracking down.

One facet of the grey/black market area that has come in for much scrutiny is Dubai's centrality in the *hawala* system. Basically, this is a way of moving money quickly and efficiently without having to go through official channels or banks. It is also cheaper, as the agents give better exchange rates and usually charge lower fees than banks or money transfer houses such as Western Union, and they deliver door to door. Basically the agent (called the *hawaladar*) at one end knows the agent at the other, and based on trust will 'transfer' funds without any funds actually moving across borders. The agents then settle their accounts with each other in various ways. This system is largely legal in most of the world, and is used legitimately by businesspeople and workers and is sometimes referred to as the 'poor man's banking system'.[5] Because of its ease of use, because it operates for the most part outside the watchful eyes of authorities, and because there is no paper trail, it is also the way that smugglers, gangsters and terrorist organizations like Al Qaeda move funds around. Even the CIA used it during the Afghan War.[6]

Dubai's association with terrorists and money laundering exploded onto the front pages in the United States in 2006 over whether Dubai's DP World would be allowed to operate US ports through its purchase of the British company P&O, which had the contract to manage these ports. Though the Bush administration approved the deal, and even though the UAE is a staunch ally of the US, the congressional uproar over 'security' issues forced DP World to sell P&O's American operations to the insurance giant AIG (who in 2008 received USD 150 billion in bailout money). The security issue was not about a foreign, private firm controlling America's ports, which was already the case, but rather whether Arabs should be allowed to control America's ports. Politicians of both US parties in Congress gleefully seized upon this issue, and in a rare show of independence from the executive branch forced the Bush administration to back down, one of the few times in eight years the Bush administration did not get its way.

Dubai took a political beating over this debacle, and officials there pointed out that they had learned a valuable lesson in American politics. However, there was a silver lining in this political defeat for Dubai: it became a household brand name in the US and piqued the interest of many Americans who had never heard of the place.[7]

BUILDING THE BIGGEST AND BEST

While Dubai has developed a degree of infamy, its international recognition rests in large part on its myriad construction projects, which serve the dual purpose of advertising Dubai and enriching the government's coffers through the sale of property. The buildings were mostly constructed after 2002, when Sheikh Mohammed decreed that non-citizens could own property outright in 'freehold' areas and would be issued a title to the property in their name, a decision that led directly to a property building and purchasing frenzy. Importantly, property owners were able to get residence visas through the master developers (Emaar, Nakheel and Dubai Properties), a big draw for expatriates from developing countries and retirees. Thus a market was born, as was a massive construction boom that expanded astronomically until it crashed at the end of 2008, more than a year after the British and American housing bubbles burst, and a few months after global credit markets froze.

Sheikh Mohammed's 2002 decree came at a fortuitous time as the US Patriot Act, enacted soon after 9/11, made investing from overseas more difficult, while at the same time the US market was in a downturn, making investing there less attractive still. Much Gulf wealth that otherwise would have been invested in the US and elsewhere in the West then found its way to a nascent property market and a welcoming stock market.[8] As a local Dubai-based European expatriate blogger, 'The Real Nick', pointed out quite astutely, 9/11 may turn out to be the best thing ever to happen to Dubai.[9]

For developers and architects, Dubai is a paradise. Almost any somewhat feasible idea can become a reality, especially if it is big and 'iconic'. World's tallest building and mall? Go for it. Replicas of the Hanging Gardens of Babylon and the French city of

Lyon? Why not. A building shaped like an iPod charging in its dock (at a 6 degree incline)? A building shaped like a man in traditional Gulf Arab robe and headdress? You get the picture.

Some of these buildings have been built or are nearing completion, some have not broken ground, and some, like the iPod and 'man in traditional garb' buildings, seem to have been quickly forgotten. Still, any idea can be brought to fruition with less difficulty than in most places as the bulk of the 'iconic' projects are run by Dubai government-owned Nakheel and Emaar, a publicly traded company but largely backed by the government. Since it is autocratic rule, all that is really required to build is Sheikh Mohammed's approval. There are no public hearings or 'not in my backyard' movements to hinder progress.

At the time of writing, the latest/greatest development to come online was the Atlantis hotel resort on Palm Jumeirah. The Atlantis is a huge, gaudy and flashy USD 1.5 billion project. Oddly, it is not unique – it is a replica of the Atlantis resort in the Bahamas. The opening ceremony for the resort in October 2008, which garnered heavy international media attention, was as outlandish as the resort itself, another branding victory for Dubai with A-list celebrities from around the world in attendance consuming thousands of bottles of champagne and lobsters. The party cost USD 20 million, with a fireworks display able to be seen from space and far in excess of those of the opening ceremonies for the Beijing Olympics, held just months before. The party was so over the top that even Atlantis's South African developer, Sol Kerzner, seemed to be a little embarrassed about the excess. Unfortunately, however, it was badly timed, as construction projects were coming to a halt all around the city and people were being laid off in their thousands as the global economic recession had hit Dubai that summer. In fact, just a few months later, the resort laid off seventy workers.

The desire to build at a nearly unprecedented speed and scale has brought Dubai more than its share of gushing admirers, but also criticism. Many people deride the form these construction projects take. For instance, one critic wrote that Dubai's architecture is 'the equivalent of a teenager experimenting with make-up'.[10] Another critic noted how, in Dubai, architecture *must* be iconic, and that the term 'iconic' itself has become a mantra that defines Dubai's architecture, indeed, Dubai itself. But this 'iconicism' suffers from inflation. He pointed out that, 'Buildings feel so much like logos that there is something strangely unsubstantial about them.'[11] Yet another critic warned that the architect Adrian Smith, who is designing six buildings over one hundred stories tall in the UAE (he led the team that designed the Burj Khalifa) without outside constraints and review, runs the risk that his buildings 'which are freed from nearly all stylistic constraints, will look ridiculous, like alien spacecraft that landed in the middle of the desert'.[12] Whatever one's reaction to the aesthetic of Dubai though, and in spite of (or possibly because of) the sometimes questionable taste of its constructions, this much is certainly undeniable: Dubai is not bland, and it is difficult to ignore.

While any appraisal of the beauty of Dubai's constructions is subjective, the negative ecological impact on the sea and desert is beginning to emerge and is difficult to deny. For instance, raw sewage was being dumped directly into the Arabian Gulf, leading to beaches that until recently were pristine being temporarily closed. With only one sewage treatment plant for the city, this was a predictable outcome.[13] An even more basic ecological threat looms – water. The demand for water has skyrocketed as the numbers of residents and tourists increase, but also to a large degree because of the insatiable thirst of golf courses (ten as of this writing), including that of golf luminary Ernie Els.

(Tiger Woods had planned a golf course that was due to open in September 2009, but it has been delayed due to the recession.) Dubai has little in the way of groundwater; over 95 per cent of its water is desalinated, and relatively expensive.[14] While the government and construction industry have adopted 'sustainability' as a supplemental ecological mantra, it is not clear what they understand this to mean. At the United Nations climate talks in Poland in 2008, the UAE Minister of Environment and Water proposed that the UAE needed to consider using nuclear power to desalinate water.[15] The renowned architect Thom Mayne summed up the threat when he decried the state of architecture in Dubai, saying it was leading to an ecological disaster, especially if architects, instead of addressing fundamental issues in construction simply added 'eco-bling'. Dubai, he pointed out, is 'a transport nightmare, it's an energy nightmare. It is absolutely bloody terrifying.'[16]

In spite of concerns of critics from various quarters, these upscale projects continue. (While the pace of construction slowed tremendously during the economic recession in 2009, many of the projects on the table continued to be developed.) The new residential constructions, luxury villas and condominiums, are aimed at drawing in new wealthy expatriates, specifically Westerners. The imagery in their promotional materials is telling. Take for example the promotional brochure for the Rotating Tower, designed by the firm Dynamic Architecture, whose individual floors will, as the name suggests, rotate.[17] One image shows Ferraris in a car lift and also parked inside the apartments themselves. (The people buying these apartments are unlikely to drive family sedans.) We also see a rendering of one elevator and three apartments within the building showing some of the people who might live there. In the elevator are a light-skinned man and woman; the man is tall and athletic looking in an elegant suit, the woman is almost as tall and model-esque in a blazer and above-the-knee skirt and high heels. In one of the apartments, you see two white women, one in the living room, and the other lying in a chaise longue on a retractable sundeck. The woman in the living room is striking a flirty pose in a very, very short red dress and impressively high heels; the other is working on her tan in a string bikini. On the floor below them is a blonde-haired woman, young and very pretty, dusting the television stand wearing what appears to be a French maid's outfit, which is odd given that maids in Dubai are generally Filipino, Indonesian, Sri Lankan or Indian. The last image in the brochure is of a beautiful young Asian woman in a bikini lounging in an 'infinity' pool with the Palm Island in the background below her.

The linking of beautiful, sexy people to property and luxury is not in itself particularly noteworthy; the beautiful computer graphic people depicted, however, are. They are Western (or Westernized), cosmopolitan and modern. The target audience for high-end properties, again, is largely Westerners, and, of those, the British are the main targets, and Britons account for a huge portion of those buying property. For example, 25 per cent of property purchases on the Palm Jumeirah were by Britons.[18] While UAE nationals, Gulf Arabs, Arab expatriates and South Asian expatriates are not prevented from buying into luxury properties like the Rotating Towers – indeed, I met many South Asian expatriates who had bought freehold villas and condominiums – they are not the ones being aggressively wooed.

While Britons probably account for the largest number of property purchasers, and speculators of all nationalities for even more (final homeowners account for only 30 per cent of the market), a substantial number of purchasers of freehold property are South Asian and Arab expatriates, and retirees, including many Britons. For many of these people, part of the lure of investing in these properties was the promise of residence visas not beholden to employers (a central issue in the living conditions of expatriates as we will see in the coming chapters). Property owners were led by developers to believe that they would be provided with residence visas. Indeed, there was a clause in their contracts attesting to this, and many owners had been provided with three-year residence visas based on the purchase of property.[19] In June 2008, however, the chief of the Real Estate Regulatory Agency clearly and bluntly announced that this was no longer the policy, that there would no longer be a link between property ownership and residence visas, and further that developers should not promise residence visas to prospective buyers.[20]

This change of policy could have an adverse affect upon the housing market, as the promise of a residence visa was an important selling point for many purchasers from developing world countries, as well as for those who purchased properties for their retirements. The de-linking of visas from property purchases could mean that those not working or owning businesses would not be able to enjoy living in their homes. A few months later, in early 2009, as the housing market was in free fall, a law at the federal level was passed allowing six-month renewable residence visas for property owners. While this provides some level of security for property owners, it has proved expensive and time consuming as individuals have to pay fees each time they renew their visas. In fact, many developers felt that six months is not enough, that a two- or three-year visa would be more likely to entice purchasers from countries such as Iran and India.[21] It remains to be seen, if and when the housing market bounces back, if that is enough of a guarantee for people to buy into the market.

TOURISM

Along with construction, tourism is the other industry upon which Dubai's international fame is built. Today, tourism is much more central to Dubai's economy than ever, with tourism and travel accounting for 30 per cent of Dubai's GDP.[22] The industry is built upon two pillars – shopping and hedonism – and is geared towards aggressively courting high-end, especially British, tourists. This is reflected in the quality of hotels. While there are a number of one- and two-star hotels in Dubai, nearly all the recently constructed hotels are four and five stars. Today there are roughly 7 million tourists a year (Sheikh Mohammed's vision was to more than double this to 15 million per year by 2010, but, with the global economic crisis, this seems highly unlikely). In 2007, Western tourists accounted for nearly 40 per cent of the almost 7 million guests staying in hotels, with nearly 750,000 Britons, 475,000 Russians and other Eastern Europeans, and almost 400,000 Americans. (In comparison, there were slightly more than 400,000 Iranian tourists, 400,000 Indian tourists and nearly 450,000 Saudi Arabian tourists.) Nearly half of all the guests in five-star hotels were Europeans.[23]

Shopping as we saw in the last chapter was central to building Dubai's position as the premier tourist destination in the region. While the Russians and others in the 1990s did much of their shopping in smaller stores as there were only a few malls at the time, today shopping is largely in the malls, where Russians again are a big tourist and shopping presence, though this time mainly as high-end leisure tourists and shoppers, not as profes- sional shoppers.[24] The forty or so malls in Dubai today are a central attraction for tourists, but are also especially critical for expatriate and local residents, arguably more so than in other places. With a lack of public open spaces, and the fact that temperatures are above 40 degrees Celsius, with high humidity for a good part of the year, the malls are the default public squares. Like other constructions in Dubai, a great many of these are of the 'iconic' nature – a mall with a ski slope, a Venetian-themed mall, a mall fashioned from the adventures of the medieval Arab traveller Ibn Battuta, and a mall fashioned as an Arab '*souk*' (market) with fake wind towers at the entrance. (The wind tower being the pre-oil era iconic architectural statement in Dubai, and an Iranian import.) A recent survey found that 30 per cent of UAE residents go shopping 'at least once a week', second internationally only to Hong Kong. An astonishing 84 per cent go shopping simply as 'something to do'. And they spend money while shopping – a lot. Another survey found that in the UAE, 60 per cent of family income was spent on consumer goods.[25] For expatriates, shopping is not just about immediate consumption, but is also a form of remittance, particularly for South Asian expatriates. People are expected not only to send back cash to their families, but also to purchase luxury items. Many find the cost of expected gifts is so beyond their budgets that they must take out loans.[26]

This culture of consumption has led to a boom in bank loans and credit-card usage among expatriate residents. Personal loans in the UAE are ubiquitous and necessary as landlords often demand an entire year's rent up front, and, until the economic collapse in late 2008, very easy to get, with banks more than willing to make loans far in excess of annual incomes for people earning as little as AED 3,000 per month. Those unable to repay their loans, including national citizens, often end up in jail. In 2007, more than 1,200 people in Dubai's central jail, or 40 per cent of the jail's population, were convicted for failing to repay loans for which banks demand little or no collateral, often secured only by an undated, signed blank check. And, once convicted, even when the person finishes his term, he cannot be released unless someone pays off his debt, leaving many to languish in jail. One police official said 60 per cent of the police force is busy chasing 'deadbeats'.[27]

Another critical base of the tourism industry is Dubai's hedonistic nightlife. The nightlife scene in Dubai has grown more diverse and sophisticated – as well as more base – to cater to all tastes; it is a tolerant oasis or den of sin (depending on your point of view) unparalleled in the Arabian Gulf. Before the late 1990s, what clubs there were did not cater to the younger well-heeled set of tourists and expatriates, as there were not many of them to cater to. But, as the population and economy have grown, and as the numbers of hotels and tourists have grown, so too have the number and quality of clubs, which in turn lure more tourists and expatriate residents from all over, not just Westerners.[28] A local journalist put it this way: 'We have nothing else going for us but our night life. Imagine if they arrested everyone who went to our clubs. Who would come and stay in the five-star hotels or even work in them?'[29] Without the nightlife, it is unlikely that so many Western tourists or professional expatriates would have come to Dubai in the first place and its development would undoubtedly have been much different.

The higher-end clubs today are regularly being written up in gushing or hypercritical travel pieces in newspapers and magazines around the world. Excess is generally the storyline here; playboys spraying Dom Perignon in VIP rooms of the hottest clubs and leaving Rolex watches as tips are the stuff that Dubai's nightlife legend is made of.[30] The Bentleys, Maybachs and Ferraris parked at the clubs are almost commonplace. A female manager of one of Dubai's biggest clubs, while watching approvingly as a second Maybach in fifteen minutes drove up, said of Dubai that, 'We're like the Miami of the Middle East. It's all about showing up in the best car, getting the best table and sharing the biggest bottle of Cristal with the best-looking girls.'[31]

These high-end clubs are in a way boringly generic – given the music and the crowd, you could be in any club in any global city. There is nothing particularly 'Dubaian' about them, but that is the point. Dubai is a city whose broad identity, given the over 90 per cent expatriate population, is rooted in a generic notion of upscale; it makes no cultural appeal to anyone in particular, and thus it can be appealing to everyone. There is little chance of feeling culture shock, as the culture on display is of a generic, global nature, like anywhere else. It is a city of commerce and consumption where ultimately money matters above all else.

The lower-end clubs are arguably more interesting. These clubs, the greater number lying in the 'old city' areas on either side of the creek in Bur Dubai or Deira, cater more to specific groups – Iranians, Filipinos, Africans – and many predate the economic boom of the 2000s. The most numerous of these are the many Indian 'dance' clubs (the *mujra* clubs mentioned in the previous chapter) where Indian female dancers show varying amounts of enthusiasm and skill on stage performing to Bollywood remixes. They do this for a leering audience of mostly middle-class, middle-aged South Asian men, with some younger, more working-class-looking South Asian men, a smattering of middle-aged nationals and Gulf Arabs mixed in, with the occasional white 'voyeur' (and me) peering in to see what the story is. While one or more women dance on stage, other dancers wait their turn on benches on the stage alternately looking bored or checking their mobile phones for text messages.

Aside from the high-end and ethnic clubs are the dance clubs that exist mainly to facilitate the trade in prostitution. As most hotels have a number of bars and clubs in them, they will have at least one club mostly for the trade. This is as true of the five-star international chains as the two-star dive hotels in Bur Dubai and Deira. These hotels have benefited greatly from the government purposefully turning a blind eye toward prostitution. An Indian travel agent in 1995 made the general point that 'Anything goes in Dubai as long as it's good for commerce. The authorities are very permissive.'[32] Nowhere is that clearer than in their attitude towards prostitution. Quite easily, if they chose, the authorities could shut these clubs down and drive a great deal of prostitution from the public view. Their permissiveness regarding prostitution can be contrasted with their 'zero tolerance' policy towards drugs, even prescription drugs, which are heavily policed. There are apparently limits to their tolerance to commerce.

Prostitution is not new to Dubai. A Westerner who lived in Dubai prior to its obtaining independence in 1971, but who would not authorize the use of his name, related to me what he remembered about the subject. It is worth quoting him at length:

Representatives of the local department of health were reportedly responsible for ensuring that the trade was confined to a specific area on the Deira [eastern] side of the 'creek'. In addition, the authorities were tasked with licensing the women and inspecting them on a regular basis so as to be able to vouch for their overall health and whether they were free of any infectious diseases. Whether the prostitutes' agents, sponsors and/or business partners were also required to register and adhere to a specific set of rules or regulations is something about which I was unaware and never inquired, but it would seem logical to assume that they were.

Part of such additional local lore as I recall being privy to hearing others discuss at the time was that the authorities took no moral position on the matter. They acknowledged that, because Dubai was a teeming port, a major transshipment centre, and the source of employment for thousands of unaccompanied foreign males, the practice was bound to flourish either below or above ground in one way or another. A major reason was that the ways in which foreign workers spent their leisure time, like their counterparts in other socially and religiously conservative societies the world over, were very limited.

For the emirate's overall general welfare and reputation, it seemed that enlightened self-interest impelled the authorities to allow the trade to exist, albeit in a regulated and relatively discrete manner. In any event, the regulatory representatives involved had the reputation of being exceptionally diligent. They gave every indication of being keen to ensure that, like other businesses, the business ought to be conducted as 'free' of legal and bureaucratic constraints as possible so long as it did not violate such prudent measures of protection as were stipulated, and they were determined to enforce, on behalf of the emirate's public health needs.[33]

What is immediately striking is how the local government saw prostitution as merely one more act of commerce. The notion of licit and illicit is not relevant; trade is trade and the government's role is to maintain as light a touch as possible to balance basic interests of the state with those of commerce, which in Dubai are often one and the same, as top government officials, including Sheikh Mohammed, are businessmen who are greatly involved in all aspects of Dubai's economy, like in the construction industry.

Today, prostitution in Dubai has spread well beyond the Deira area; the entire city is rife with the trade, with prostitutes walking the street and working out of apartment brothels, to a United Nations of prostitution working in almost every hotel in the city. The presence of prostitutes in Dubai, some have argued, is critical for luring business travellers, leisure tourists and of course sex tourists, many of whom come from the Gulf states, the UK and elsewhere in Europe. These travellers fly on Emirates Airline, stay in five-star hotels, eat at restaurants and shop in the malls. One observer writing in 2005 made the controversial assertion that 30 per cent of Dubai's economy was directly or indirectly based on vice.[34]

Prostitution does not stop even for the holy fasting month of Ramadan. A friend came to visit me during Ramadan in 2006 and we went to various hotels in and near the Golden Sands section of the Bur Dubai neighbourhood where I lived. (I did not know it at the time, but this tour of prostitution hotspots in that area is a favourite of many journalists.) All the clubs were open, the liquor was flowing, and the prostitutes were there in regular numbers. One Russian prostitute told my friend that some girls work during Ramadan and some do not. She had a national citizen pimp who demanded she work during Ramadan, though she generally did not work in the clubs as many other women do. The atmosphere is strictly business, as these discos do not play music during Ramadan, so there is no distraction, no façade that a man can be there for any other reason.

Since the late 2000s, as a response to pressure from human rights groups, the US State Department and equally if not more importantly from bad media publicity, the government has begun to take steps to curb human trafficking into Dubai (we will explore this in greater detail in chapter three). But given how widespread the prostitution trade is, and how nearly every hotel profits from it, any such action to curtail prostitution would likely have a tremendous negative impact upon the hospitality industry. It seems unlikely that the Dubai government would seriously threaten this arrangement.

PUBLIC RELATIONS AND PROFIT

As we have just seen, Dubai's image has been purposely created and maintained through its construction projects and tourism. These industries have grown so spectacularly mainly through direct investment by the government, generally through its sovereign wealth funds.

Sovereign wealth funds in the past few years have been making headlines because they control so much money – the Gulf states combined had almost *USD 2 trillion* in foreign assets in 2006 (when the price of oil was around USD 60 per barrel), though that shrank greatly by the end of 2008 as stock prices and oil prices plummeted. While these funds have been around for some time – the oldest is Kuwait's fund which dates back to 1953 – they became major players in global business in the 2000s as they ventured from safer investments, such as US treasury bills, to investing directly in major firms, such as Abu Dhabi's purchase of a 5 per cent stake in Citigroup for USD 7.5 billion in 2007, making it Citigroup's largest shareholder.

The Gulf states' sovereign wealth funds are largely funded through surplus cash out of their oil (and in Qatar's case natural gas) revenues, which they had in more than ample supply as the price of oil exploded from 2002–8 from less than USD 20 per barrel in 2002 peaking at almost USD 150 per barrel in July 2008. The biggest of these funds was Abu Dhabi's, estimated at up to USD 875 billion, followed by Saudi Arabia's at close to USD 230 billion and Kuwait's of USD 200 billion. Private investors in the Gulf additionally held USD 600 billion in foreign assets in 2006, with private Saudi investors actually controlling more wealth than their government's sovereign wealth fund, close to USD 340 billion.[35]

While bankers and others salivated at the possibility of accessing these funds' largesse, others in the West expressed apprehension over these funds because they generally come from undemocratic countries (with the exception of Norway) and because the management of these funds is opaque. Even the actual values of these funds are just educated guesses by financial analysts, as none of the funds gives much in the way of access to their data. Their managers routinely point out, however, that their goal is not global domination, but rather profit.[36] Still, many people worry that these governments are intent on controlling strategically important industries to nefarious ends, as we saw above with the outrage in the United States over DP World's play to take over the contract managing US ports.

Dubai's sovereign wealth funds are actually a mere pittance compared with Abu Dhabi's, and at their combined peak had less than USD 25 billion in assets. But size is not everything: Dubai has used its funds to great public relations advantage. Dubai has three holding companies that manage its wealth through ownership of various smaller companies: Dubai Holding (Sheikh Mohammed's personal vehicle), Dubai World and Investment Corporation of Dubai, the latter two owned directly by the government. There is a division of investing labour between them, and much overlapping, where they are in direct competition with each other. Some of these firms are outward looking and buy into big-name companies such as MGM Mirage (they of the casinos), Sony and Dreamworks. Others buy recognizable properties and assets like the upscale clothing store Barney's and the Essex House luxury hotel next to Central Park in Manhattan. (In a copycat plus oneupmanship move, Abu Dhabi bought the Chrysler Building, an art deco icon on Manhattan's skyline.) Still others like Dubai International Capital are more focused on financial investments primarily for returns (as opposed to branding), such as in banking and insurance-related businesses.[37]

While some companies are focused on the international scene, others are domestically oriented. Construction projects such as the Palms (there will be three), the World, the Universe, Dubailand – the list goes on and on – are the most obvious. As with many of Dubai's overseas purchases, these are primarily branding mechanisms first, and profit-making ventures second. Whether they return a profit is actually not altogether critical. Take for instance the hyper-luxurious sail-shaped Burj al Arab, the first and most iconic of the iconic structures of the past decade, built in 1999. Its cheapest hotel room rents for well over USD 1,000 per night, and still the hotel is rumoured to lose money. But that is not important: its value is in advertising Dubai, and to that end it has been enormously successful. Less flashy but just as central is Tecom, which manages most of the free zones, home to a great number of the international firms that operate in Dubai. The mushrooming of these free zones has attracted some of the biggest international firms, and smaller firms who do business directly with Iran and South Asia.

Possibly the most interesting of Dubai's investment strategies is Borse Dubai, the main attempt to make Dubai a regional, if not international, financial centre. Borse Dubai is the holding company for Dubai Financial Market and NASDAQ Dubai (formerly known as the Dubai International Financial Exchange, or DIFX). While DIFX had been in operation since 2005, they bought a stake in NASDAQ in 2008, and with it the name brand, to give it greater international clout among the important financial players and furthering Dubai's ambitions to become the premier financial centre in the region and a major global centre.

The free zone in which NASDAQ Dubai operates, Dubai International Financial Centre, has successfully lured major players in the global financial market since it opened in 2004. Dozens of banks and other international financial firms have set up shop here, including Morgan Stanley, Deutsche Bank, Credit Suisse, Goldman Sachs and so on. The rush of foreign firms – attracted by the usual free zone trappings of no tax, no restrictions on ownership, no restrictions on foreign exchange or repatriation of capital – became a deluge by 2008, as the credit crisis spread from Wall Street to London and further afield. Bankers (and real estate agents fleeing the crumbling property markets) from London and New York ended up in Dubai in droves, further fuelling already overheated rental and property markets, as well as rampant inflation (which we will discuss in more detail in chapter four).

As the global economic crisis deepened in late 2008, the value of sovereign wealth funds throughout the Gulf also declined significantly.[38] But since these funds were the invested profits from oil and natural gas sales, in essence excess cash, it has not adversely affected the economies in these states. Unlike sovereign wealth funds elsewhere in the Gulf, Dubai's are not funded by excess profits from oil, as Dubai has relatively little oil to speak of. Dubai's various funds operate like private equity firms, and have built their asset empires in that most modern capitalistic way – through debt, borrowing from local and international banks. Debt financed Dubai's boom, but that proved to be problematic as property prices 'fell off a cliff' once global finance dried up in late 2008, and more loans to individuals (for mortgages), companies and the government were not forthcoming.[39] Many economic analysts and rating agencies became nervous, as no one quite knew what Dubai's balance sheet actually contained. To calm the nerves of investors and banks, the Dubai government, breaking with its previous practice of secrecy on such matters, announced that it had USD 80 billion in debt (though the likely figure is much, much higher), USD 10 billion owed by the government and USD 70 billion owed by government firms, with close to USD 15 billion of this debt coming due in 2009.[40]

It was becoming clear in late 2008 or early 2009 that Dubai was going to need help from the much richer Abu Dhabi to address this. Here I need to take a moment to briefly clarify the relationship between the two. The UAE is a federation of semi-autonomous emirates. Abu Dhabi is the capital of the UAE and its richest emirate, and basically funds the UAE government (bureaucracy, military, etc.) Thus, Abu Dhabi is the most important emirate and basically gets to decide on major federal issues, with Dubai acting as a junior, albeit important, partner. The other emirates are largely bystanders and recipients of welfare largesse from Abu Dhabi.

For most of the time of the economic boom, Abu Dhabi had taken a more conservative and low-key approach to its development, in contrast with Dubai's flashy approach, which was necessary given its reliance on tourism. While Dubai became famous, Abu Dhabi became, well, simply wealthier. Many people inferred that Abu Dhabi was both jealous and annoyed with Dubai's fame and flash – as if this were a story of sibling rivalry. As Dubai's economic façade began to crumble, rumours began to fly that Dubai would get its comeuppance, that Abu Dhabi would demand its pound of flesh for saving it. One rumour, reported in *The Sunday Times*, was that Abu Dhabi was demanding a stake in Emirates Airline.[41] That would have put Dubai in its place, as Emirates is in some ways the poster child for the success of Dubai and the main competitor for Abu Dhabi's carrier, Etihad. In any case, this did not come to pass.

The notion that Abu Dhabi was annoyed with Dubai was further fuelled by the fact that Abu Dhabi was injecting funds to shore up its banks to prevent defaults, but not those of Dubai, early in 2009.[42] After a few months of speculation as to how Dubai was going to deal with its debt, and whether Abu Dhabi would be helping out, Dubai announced that it was going to sell USD 20 billion of bonds (only possible with Abu Dhabi's permission). The Central Bank of the UAE immediately announced that it would purchase the first USD 10 billion of bonds, which effectively solved Dubai's immediate financial crunch.[43] In December 2009, when it looked as if Nakheel and other major government-owned and -backed firms might default on debt repayment obligations, the government of Abu Dhabi gave Dubai another USD 10 billion.

CENSORSHIP AND 'BRAND DUBAI'

At the end of my short stay with Dubai's state security police, a senior, very stern officer told me I was being deported because 'the research you have been doing is creating divisions in UAE society and we will not allow it. You are asking too many questions about locals and non-locals. Why do you ask so many questions?'

At the time I thought that my questions were relatively harmless, but I had not understood that the mere act of asking questions was detrimental to the Brand. Dubai, like almost any other large corporation, puts a lot of time and effort into building up its image. Corporations for that reason generally prefer not to have people look too closely at their balance sheets or how their products get made lest something unsavoury comes out (balance sheets are fudged, toys have lead paint in them, etc.) and causes bad publicity or, worse, a drop in consumer confidence in the company, which could belie the image they have expensively built up through advertising. Dubai Inc. (as it is widely called) operates on the same principle.

Dubai's success story in large part rests on the careful maintenance of its image. While times were good throughout the 2000s, they could count on the international press (and of course the local press) to produce fawning reports on Sheikh Mohammed, various other business–political leaders (business and politics are basically the same thing in Dubai), and the myriad construction projects in Dubai. While some critical pieces were published, there were relatively few of them. This changed when the bottom started to fall out of the market in late 2008, and there were a spate of negative, hypercritical reports on cancelled construction projects, layoffs, jailings due to debt, worker exploitation and horrid living conditions, corruption and so on. There were so many negative reports coming so fast that even Sheikh Mohammed was moved to comment on them. Dubai's authorities had become so used to glowing press coverage, they were unprepared for this amount of critical reporting. Their response was essentially to 'cry foul' over the tone of reporting and then in 2009 to set up a public relations department, unofficially called 'Brand Dubai', to 'preserve and promote the image of the emirate by providing timely and accurate information to the local and international media'.[44]

International reporting is something that the authorities can try to affect, but in the end they cannot control the actions of reporters outside their borders. Even reporters working within Dubai's Media City free zone (where many Western outlets such as Reuters and CNN have their base of operations) are not subject to the same media regulations that companies operating outside the free zone are subject to. A major exception, however, are the third-world reporters, who are held to a different standard, seemingly because they are much less influential than Western reporters working for the Western media. For instance, in 2007 the Dubai government shut down Pakistani satellite channels Geo TV and ARY One World, which both operated out of Media City, at the request of President Musharraf because they held a critical stance regarding his regime.[45]

One method that many autocratic regimes use to silence dissent is to go after the dissenters. Dubai does this on occasion. For instance, a national citizen human rights activist and lawyer, Mohammed Al Roken, had his passport taken away, lost his university teaching position and is not allowed to write for local newspapers because of his past criticisms of the government. More recently a reporter for Bloomberg was detained by the secret police on his arrival in Dubai airport and was warned to 'be careful', a most unusual occurrence as he was both white and Western, and working for an international business news organization. While in Dubai he was followed and his hotel room searched. On his way out he was also detained for some hours, supposedly because of a story he was working on. A colleague of his said it reminded the harassed reporter of his time as a reporter in the Soviet Union.[46]

But this type of reaction on the part of the government happens much less than one would imagine for an autocratic regime, especially one so concerned with appearances. More often than not they simply censor the story. With print matter, all incoming books, newspapers and magazines have to go through the National Media Council, where an Indian man takes a black marker and literally blacks out offensive materials – mostly images that he deems to be pornographic and 'anything against Islam'.[47] Bookstores are given lists of books that are banned, so even if an 'improper' book somehow makes it through customs, it won't make it onto the shelves.

More important than print in this electronic age is the Internet, which is regulated through a highly sophisticated filtering apparatus (supplied by an American company) to block such things as anything remotely pornographic and any website ending in .il – that is, emanating from Israel. The Open Net Initiative considers the UAE (along with Saudi Arabia) to have the broadest filtering regime in the world, which in a way is not surprising, given Dubai's obsession with superlatives.[48]

While many websites get automatically blocked by the filtering software, a great number of critical sites are specifically blocked. For instance, one of the most popular blogs, 'Secret Dubai Diary', written by Secret Dubai, a long-time resident British expatriate, was blocked for a short while in 2005, unblocked, and then permanently blocked in 2008. Her blog often picked up and elaborated on locally reported news items, and was the site of heated, open and lively debates between expatriates and nationals – apparently a bit too open and lively for the state apparatus.[49] Another blog that was blocked in 2007 was 'Sex and Dubai', which was a little too 'spicy' for governmental tastes. Actually, it was rather amazing that it took so long for the government to block it, given its rather frank discussion of sex, and from a woman's perspective at that.[50] Another website, UAEPrison.com, which reports on a vast range of human rights violations within the UAE, is also (not surprisingly) blocked. Individual news items also ended up blocked, such as a widely read critical essay in the *Independent*.[51] While the *Independent* itself was not blocked, this particular essay was, though a month and a half later, it was unblocked. The author was told by authorities that he was banned, and that if he went back he would either be arrested or turned back at the airport.[52] It is not just bad news about Dubai that gets blocked from the Internet; even video from Iran of people protesting the election fraud in 2009 were censored.[53] Twitter, Flickr, Orkut, Friendster, Naseeb (a Muslim version of Friendster), and a whole range of other social networking sites have been blocked, unblocked and reblocked. Even the *New York Times* was blocked for a short while.

Regarding the local media, the government sometimes orders editors and reporters off of stories with ominous threats. A recent example in 2009 involved the Al Fajer Group, whose CEO is

Sheikh Mohammed's nephew. The firm and its marketing agency were accused by investors of fraud. Investors were shown photographs depicting three tower blocks as being actively under construction, which led many people to invest in them thinking these were actual buildings rather than merely planned properties. In actuality, there were no buildings, just holes in the ground. Before this scandal was reported locally, news agencies across the city were ordered not to report on it. One reporter said he had been working on an article when his editor ordered him to stop. The investors tried to hold a press conference, but that was cancelled at the last minute by the hotel, the government-owned Mina A'salam, due to 'health and safety reasons'.[54]

Media blackouts such as the above are actually rare in Dubai. However, reporters are feeling a chill, even as new media regulations, advocated by Sheikh Mohammed, have ended the possibility of reporters facing criminal charges and jail while doing their jobs. The UAE introduced a new media law in 2009 that the government promoted as a step forward in press freedom, but was roundly criticized by many reporters and free speech advocates within and outside Dubai and the UAE for excessively harsh penalties for unclearly defined transgressions. For instance, reporters face fines of up to AED 5,000,000 for 'disparaging' the person of senior government figures or royal family members, as distinct from criticizing their performance as officials. Writing 'harmful' or 'misleading' information about the economy can rate a fine of up to AED 500,000. While Human Rights Watch has praised the UAE for doing away with the possibility of jail, the new law actually hampers reporters and organizations through such large fines, which, as HRW puts it, can 'close down publications and bring individuals to financial ruin'.[55]

No one apparently is exempt from these penalties. One of the most recent cases in mid-2009 involved the Dubai-based

Arabic-language newspaper *Al-Emarat Al-Youm*, one of the most widely read papers in the UAE. The paper was ordered to halt publication for twenty days, and the editor-in-chief fined AED 20,000 as a penalty for running a front-page story in October 2006 accusing the Warsan Stables, owned by members of the ruling family of Abu Dhabi, of giving their horses steroids. What makes the case bizarre, and especially threatening to reporters in the UAE, is that Sheikh Mohammed owns the paper.[56]

Self-censorship

Because of the likelihood of direct censorship and threats by the government, most reporters save the authorities the trouble and censor themselves, especially from controversial topics such as the high level of prostitution, money laundering and terrorism.[57] A local reporter for *Time Out Dubai* laid out well the culture of self-censorship among reporters in Dubai:

> I hesitate to call myself a journalist. Technically, I am one, but I haven't broken 'news' since the day I took up my position on *Time Out* in Dubai. Still, I take comfort in knowing that most journalists in the emirate are equally frustrated working in a media industry that 'makes nice, not news' . . . If you flip through Dubai's newspapers and magazines, you won't find [any scoops]. Instead, you'll read about what the rulers ate and whom they greeted, and what record-breaking new venture the emirate has just embarked on.[58]

Of course you will find complacent reporting and puff pieces similar to those in Dubai almost anywhere in the world. But the difference is that even under the most repressive regimes you will find reporters challenging the authorities. In Dubai this does not happen as nearly all the editorial staff and reporters are expatriates, mostly British and Indian, few of whom come to Dubai for the chance to do groundbreaking investigative reporting. For the British the lure is a fast rise through the ranks (much faster than at home), higher pay and a luxury lifestyle. Indians and Pakistanis, who are generally paid less for the same work, though relatively much more than they would earn at home, are fearful of losing their visas. No story really is worth jeopardizing their lives and lifestyles in Dubai. The head of the National Media Council, the UAE's censorship body, said there was too much self-censorship by the media even though the government did not ban writings on such topics as labour issues or citizenship (a particularly touchy subject I address in chapter six). He felt that journalists lacked courage in approaching topics they think are banned, that they need to be more daring.[59] He did not of course mention the most basic reason why they are not daring, which is that pushing the journalistic envelope means essentially putting your residency at risk.

The new law will only deepen the culture of self-censorship. One reporter said 'Journalists already don't want to annoy the authorities because they have the power to shut the paper down or make life very difficult for you. The papers are paranoid and cautious about what they write . . . the vague language and fines won't improve this situation.'[60]

For the most part, Dubai's media environment, like its social environment, has the trappings of freedom. But, just as individual expatriates, reporters and editors (who are nearly all expatriates) understand roughly where the invisible and unspoken lines are and where they cannot cross, so journalists do not go anywhere near them. This is no different than the average expatriate who generally knows not to argue with nationals if they get into a car accident, not to engage in any activity that looks at all political, and certainly never to say anything critical of the royal family in any setting where someone may overhear. The general lesson here is do not be political or overly critical, and you can stay and enjoy the good life. And for nearly everyone involved – expatriates, nationals and rulers – this has proven to be a highly acceptable arrangement.

KEEPING EXPATRIATES IN LINE

While the Dubai government has taken steps to control the media for the main purpose of maintaining its image, an even more basic principle and concern for them is managing and keeping their massive foreign worker population under control. Even before the UAE became an independent state in 1971, foreigners outnumbered nationals in Dubai and Abu Dhabi, and the numbers of foreigners was rapidly increasing. The question from early on was how to keep these workers docile. The most basic factor limiting a worker's freedom is the sponsorship system, as we saw above. Every expatriate in Dubai is required to have a sponsor (their employer), and that expatriate's labour permit is tied to their sponsor, as is the worker's residency visa. Until recently, if a worker changed jobs or was fired or quit, he or she had to leave the country and would be banned for six months, then they could come back with a new job, new labour permit and new residency visa. For lower-level workers, this in effect means it is very difficult to change jobs as they cannot afford the costs associated with the loss of work and travel back and forth between countries. No matter the conditions of the job, workers are for all intents and purposes stuck. The effect of this is to guarantee discipline and docility among workers. Also, workers know that if they 'rock the boat' in any manner, they are subject to swift deportation. The notion of 'due process' has no place here.

Until recently, professionals also laboured under the same visa conditions, which essentially shackled them to their jobs, assuming they wished to stay in Dubai. A person who wanted to change their job needed to receive a 'no objection certificate' (NOC) from his employer, which many employers refused to issue. A person who was fired or quit his job lost their residency visa, which entailed an automatic ban from working in Dubai, though they were still allowed to enter Dubai on a tourist visa. There is one interesting caveat to this: adult women can be in Dubai as dependents of their parents or husband, while men beyond the age of eighteen must have their own visas. This means that women who work while being dependents do not have to be sponsored by their employer, which allows women much more freedom in the labour market – an unintended loophole and benefit for women in this patriarchal system. In fact, I met a number of women who freely changed jobs, often quitting after mere months on the job, with no repercussions. Women who were sponsored by their employers and men across the board (who are all sponsored by their employers, unless they are company owners themselves) had no such freedom.

This changed in early 2006 (though the policy was not really implemented until 2008) when the UAE Ministry of Labour announced that expatriates could change jobs without incurring a six-month ban even without receiving an NOC from their employers, so long as they had been employed with the same firm for at least one year, had no legal entanglements and paid a transaction fee of anywhere between AED 1,500 and AED 9,000. (Those with higher degrees of education pay substantially less, while those without bachelor's degrees pay substantially more. As these people tend to be in the lowest paid occupations and cannot afford the fee, they essentially are prevented from availing of this benefit.) An official at the Ministry of Labour said this new policy was to prevent sponsors from being vindictive and sabotaging an individual's attempt to change jobs. The official said that, as long as workers fulfilled their contractual obligations and had not broken any laws, they should be free to move on.[61]

While the *kafala* system is still firmly in place, it is undermined by the Ministry of Labour's policy of allowing workers to change jobs, and therefore sponsors, without the permission of the original sponsor. The result is a greater degree of freedom of mobility for professional workers. Interestingly, this change roughly corresponds with a greater influx of Western labour, and the greater international attention Dubai has received since the mid-2000s, though I have not come across any evidence to suggest that this has directly swayed official policy.

But, and this is a big 'but', policies and laws and their application are fluid. As the rule of law is what the rulers say it is (this is not a democracy, after all), laws and their implementation can change rapidly. It remains to be seen if this policy on labour mobility holds. In mid-2008, the Ministry of Labour did an abrupt about-turn, declaring that once again NOCs would be required to change jobs, and that six-month and one-year bans were reinstated. The one caveat was for workers in free zones.[62] In fact, in 2009, the number of people banned seemed to be increasing as companies were laying workers off in great numbers. As we saw above, an expatriate can buy his way out of a six-month ban, but for those who have lost their jobs this is obviously a steep price. The government was considering scrapping the ban altogether, but it remains to be seen if they actually do so.[63]

While workers in Dubai have to worry about their limited mobility in the labour market (and what mobility there is has to be purchased, unless working in a free zone), Bahrain in 2009 did something radical for the Gulf states – they scrapped the sponsorship system altogether. (Kuwait is also taking steps in that direction.) While it is too early to tell the impact of that move, it will have an immediate positive impact for workers. I say this with particular confidence as the announcement brought immediate outrage from business groups there.[64] Expatriate workers in Bahrain will be directly sponsored by and have visas issued through the government, rather than having to go through citizen sponsors, a change which is likely to lead to labour mobility and an upward trend in wages. But the government's motive is not simply to improve the lot for expatriates, but rather for its own citizens. Nationals throughout the Gulf (as we will see in chapter six) generally have much higher wage expectations than expatriates for the same work, leading companies to hire cheaper (and generally better trained and educated) expatriates. As wages for jobs begin to approximate wage expectations of nationals, companies will (in theory) be more disposed to hiring local talent, which will result in an increase in the proportion of nationals in the private sector and a corresponding decrease in the proportion of expatriates.

In Dubai, the Police Chief publicly called for the sponsorship system to be abolished in June 2009, but the Dubai and UAE governments have remained mute on the subject.[65] Given how the construction companies owned by Sheikh Mohammed and by the Dubai government are so heavily reliant on cheap, 'bonded' labour, it seems highly unlikely they will follow Bahrain's lead.

CULTURE IN A CITY OF TRANSIENTS

'Plastic' is a term often used to describe Dubai, meaning that it is superficial and devoid of 'real culture', from the buildings to the malls to the culture of consumption and even to relationships between people. This is in large part a result of the *kafala* system, which makes expatriates by definition transients, so the question of laying down roots and contributing to a local cultural life is moot. These people have come to work for limited periods, earn their tax-free incomes, enjoy the good life and then they will leave. This is not to suggest that expatriates do not bring culture; of course they do. Nor do I mean to imply that there is no local Emirati culture, quite the contrary. But Emirati culture is for the most part hidden from public view, and is not dominant in the public sphere in Dubai. It is when looking at Dubai as a whole that people mean there is no culture, that it is plastic. As I mentioned earlier, Dubai's public culture is a kind of lowest common denominator of global, generic forms, and its generic nature, as it appeals to no one in particular, can then appeal to all.

This lack of 'real' culture has also been the result of governmental neglect. Unlike the construction and tourism industries, where the government has been directly involved in their development at all levels as these industries bring fame and profit, the Dubai government had largely ignored the arts and taken little interest in developing an educational infrastructure of any quality. In fact until quite recently there was not even a department dedicated to the promotion of the arts.

This superficiality and orientation to consumerism does not escape the notice of residents. Some are embarrassed by it. Take for example, Hadley, a young Dubai-born and-raised British designer who left Dubai for university and then work in the UK. She returned to Dubai in 2005 because she missed Dubai and felt she could not culturally adjust to the ways of her British peers in the UK, where she felt out of place. Yet she complained to me that she felt on returning to Dubai that people were excessively materialistic compared to how people were before she had left. She said her British friends in Dubai, nearly all recently arrived, were concerned with little but clothes, cars and clubs. As she reflected on this, she became embarrassed as she told me of her most recent purchase, a convertible sports car. But then she saved face by saying at least she bought her car used, unlike her peers who were purchasing sports cars new for prices well beyond their means. Her point that many expatriates, especially Western expatriates, have a dedicated devotion to various facets of the leisure lifestyle is a point we will explore in detail in chapter four.

Noor, a young Jordanian woman who also grew up in Dubai, gave a slightly different way of looking at the plastic nature of Dubai and its people when she rhetorically asked herself if she would raise children there. To which she said she probably would not, as she felt that Dubai has no identity or culture, that basic- ally it is just not an interesting place. This is an especially telling statement given the incredible range of backgrounds of expatri- ates living in Dubai. While there is certainly variety of nation- ality, there is seemingly not as much of a variety of approaches to life. This is understandable and predictable given the pressure on expatriates of having to work and not fall foul of the authorities, to maintain their residence visas and not be deported.

The consumerist bent that many residents have is reflected in how they interact socially. Many people I interviewed lamented how so many expatriates are plastic, very surface oriented with no depth, and that this is reflected in the nature of friendships in Dubai. Deepak, a Dubai-raised Indian in his early thirties who went to university in the US and with whom I spent a great deal of time, had very few friends in Dubai in spite of growing up there, as he found it very hard to relate to other expatriates on a personal level, especially recently arrived ones. Even if you find people to be friends with – and this is true even for those who grew up in Dubai – many friendships are fleeting, as your friends leave. This in turn, for some people at least, affects their attachment to Dubai itself.

While some lament a perceived lack of social depth, others revel in the unbridled consumerist spirit in Dubai, and see no shame in it. For many, it is a respite from places with cultural 'depth' and they are perfectly happy to describe themselves as 'shallow'. The shallowness of Dubai can then be seen as a virtue, in the same way that a lack of democracy is an attraction for many expatriates from developing-world democracies. A young, single Lebanese-Canadian woman who had been in Dubai for three years summed up this feeling when she said, 'I didn't come to Dubai for anything "real". I've already lived in real places.'[66]

I do not mean to suggest that all or even most expatriates in Dubai are plastic or shallow – you can of course find people who are single-mindedly devoted to consumerism anywhere. My point is rather that the combination of the government building up the economy in the manner they have while ignoring or making the expression of non-commercial culture difficult and the temporary state of expatriates leads to a situation where superficiality of interaction is common.

Art

When expatriates I interviewed complained that Dubai was plastic and lacked 'real culture', what they meant in large part was that Dubai, until very recently, lacked avant-garde and non-commercial art. It had only a handful of galleries or museums, hardly anything in the way of arts instruction at any level, few music venues and little in the way of non-commercial activity generally.[67] There was no government support for the arts or artists. There were few national or expatriate artists living and practising in Dubai, and what artists there were were not connected to each other in the sense of an artistic community.[68]

For expatriates, being an artist is especially difficult as they must be working full time for a company or have their own business to have a residence visa.[69] Thus, the time for creative work becomes limited, so the possibility that one could be a stereotypical 'starving artist' or devote oneself fully to 'art for art's sake' proves difficult. Take for instance literature. The co-owner of a local bookstore chain made the point that, aside from a small number of nationals writing in Arabic, there are no writers chronicling Dubai's life in fiction or non-fiction as 'everyone is busy rushing around, madly earning and spending money'. And, because of censorship, you won't in any case find a critical take on Dubai from a Dubai-based writer.[70] Further, critical writings by an expatriate could lead to deportation.

By the mid-2000s, in spite of governmental neglect, a nascent art scene began to develop and, in Dubai fashion, quite quickly at that. This was in part linked to the incredible increase in the size and diversity of the population in the middle years of the decade – in 2005–6 the population grew by 25 per cent, from 1.1 to 1.4 million – and also due to the staggering wealth being created. Commercially viable art became very popular in a very short period of time. The music scene has boomed in recent years with internationally renowned Arab, South Asian, Filipino and Western singers and DJs coming to perform regularly, and the flourishing of music festivals dedicated to jazz and heavy metal.[71] Popular, profitable stage productions such as *Chicago* have found their way to Dubai. Around this time, the fine arts were also gaining traction in Dubai with a handful of pioneering galleries opening, showing mostly Middle Eastern, Iranian and Indian artists, such as The Third Line in the industrial Al

Quoz area, and XVA Gallery in the historic Bastakiya area on the Bur Dubai side of the creek. Within just a few years, the number of galleries operating in Dubai went from five to nearly fifty. Christie's and Bonhams auction houses, capitalizing on the success of the pioneering galleries that showed that there was a taste – and more importantly, a market – for high-end art in Dubai, have done nicely selling to wealthy Gulf residents (nationals and expatriates) since 2006.

Even art that has not fully emerged as 'mainstream' elsewhere when imported to Dubai takes on a commercialized air. For example, while I was living in Dubai, Ursula Rucker, a 'spoken word' artist (her poetry is read with musical accompaniment) from Philadelphia came to perform. In New York, where you commonly find it, spoken word (or slam poetry) is performed in places like the Apollo Theater in Harlem or the Nuyorican Poets Café (a contraction of New York and Puerto Rican), places accessible to the young and hip but lacking much cash. In Dubai, Ms Rucker performed in the very upscale Kempinski Hotel in the Mall of the Emirates, just metres from the ski slope. (While there was no cover charge, people in the crowd were seemingly very well to do.) In the Apollo or the Nuyorican, the performers have the crowd's undivided attention and critical appreciation. In Dubai though, Ms Rucker was met largely with indifference – those in attendance for the most part were busy posing, flirting and checking their mobile phones. And for those actually listening this proved difficult as her microphone was set so low that you couldn't hear her even if you tried. Art in this instance was merely a social setting, rather than something to be appreciated for its own value.

While people in Dubai were developing a taste for art at this time, the art, like Dubai's workforce, was largely imported. One thing that is striking about Dubai is how an organic 'home-grown' cultural life had until quite recently not developed, and the institutional infrastructure necessary for it – government funding, arts schools and programmes, museums and galleries, concert venues, etc. – has been largely absent. While there were national citizens and expatriate artists living and creating works in Dubai, it could not be described as a 'scene' in the way SoHo in New York City in the 1970s and 1980s developed a creative interactive scene of artists and galleries, or in music the way the Manchester Sound in the UK in the 1980s was an explosion of like-minded musicians. To put it in the form of a question, could a community of like-minded artists emerge and develop the deep kinds of interactions necessary to create an artistic community given the immediately pressing need for expatriates to maintain residence visas and given that it is unlikely that an artist could get a labour permit for being an artist?

The answer to this question just a few years ago would have been no, but today that is changing. This is partly due to changes in how artists approach art. The founder of B21 Gallery, commenting on the development of the local arts scene, said that artists around the time of the opening of these galleries were beginning to be slightly more daring, perhaps indicating a perception that censorship was being relaxed. He felt that things artists just a few years before would have been hesitant to express were beginning to find legitimacy in the quickly changing cultural atmosphere of Dubai.[72] The opening of these galleries in the middle of the decade also helped to spur the development of the arts scene in Dubai by showing art that had not been showcased before. Today, these galleries increasingly show work being made by artists living in Dubai. Another important venue for displaying locally created art is the 'fringe' Bastakiya Art Fair (originally known as the Creek Art Fair) started in 2007 by XVA Gallery, which attracts thousands of visitors.

An important part of the story of how locally created art is now emerging are the small number of artistic collaborative spaces opening up. Of particular interest is Tashkeel, started by Sheikh Mohammed's niece, Lateefa bint Maktoum. Her entrance onto the scene was important as it helped to galvanize the legitimacy of the idea of art as a profession (that is, as a viable economic pursuit) rather than a hobby for national citizen artists, especially for female artists, and, even more especially for their families who have a great deal of control over what career choices young adult women make.[73] And there are a growing number of Dubai-based artists – nationals (mostly women) and expatriates, many of whom are long-term residents – who are gaining international prominence showing in such far-flung locales as Brooklyn and Geneva, with critical attention being paid them in many leading arts periodicals and international dailies.[74]

While the arts scene is growing and the scope for freedom of expression has widened, the artists and galleries still have to be careful to take censorship into account, even if it has been somewhat relaxed in recent years. The obvious concerns are, not surprisingly, obscenity and profanity and insulting royal family members. But another one according to the former art editor of *Time Out Dubai* is 'confusing the public', a concept vague enough to keep artists from pushing the boundaries too far.[75] A Pakistani artist at Art Dubai 2008 broached this line (or perhaps another invisible line of censorship of things that cannot be done or said) when she displayed a stuffed camel squashed inside a suitcase. The camel, while in no way a sacred animal (such as the cow for Hindus in India), still holds a place of cultural importance for Emiratis. The first day of the fair the piece was shown and actually reported on in the local press. But by the second day the organizers had been ordered to remove it.[76]

Following on the heels of the mushrooming organic growth of the arts scene in a very short span of time, the government has of late entered the market to take on the role of leading patron of the arts, which benefits the art market but also acts as another means of advertising Brand Dubai. The first foray of the Dubai government into the arts was with the establishment of the Dubai International Film Festival (DIFF) in 2004, not surprisingly as cinema's potential as commerce and advertising is obvious. DIFF immediately proved a marketing success for Dubai by drawing international attention and attracting Hollywood and Bollywood luminaries as well as screening a wide array of international films. However, until very recently, there has been little home-grown work, though that is starting to change as there is a grassroots movement of younger Emirati filmmakers in the UAE coming into their own.

Aside from film, the government has been behind the curve in its support for the arts, probably from not appreciating the potential of the arts as commerce and as a branding device for Dubai. That changed quickly, though. Following on from the success of local galleries and the entrance of Christie's auction house, which showed how profitable and media-friendly high-end art can be, the government sponsored the Art Dubai Fair, which started in 2007 and has quickly developed into a regional centre of artistic gravity, attracting galleries from all over the Middle East, South Asia, Europe and the United States, as well as attracting collectors from all over the world. In 2009, the government also sponsored high-profile literature and poetry festivals (the former sponsored by Emirates Airline, the latter by Sheikh Mohammed), attracting renowned international talent, such as Frank McCourt, the controversial young Saudi best-selling author Rajaa al-Sanea and the Nobel prize-winning poet Wole Soyinka.[77] And, importantly, these festivals also attract a lot of international media attention, building up Dubai's brand name as a place of culture.

Dubai is not the only place in the Gulf taking the arts seriously, nor is it the first. The conservative neighbouring emirate of Sharjah, which has eschewed the glitzy Dubai development model, has developed a reputation as a hub for the arts for some years now, and has gained renown for the Sharjah Biennial, held since 2003, which now runs concurrently with the Dubai and Bastakiya Art Fairs. Qatar and Abu Dhabi are also making plays at branding themselves internationally as high-end arts centres. Doha (Qatar's capital) has the recently built Museum of Islamic Art, designed by I.M. Pei, as well as four new galleries under plan, all designed by internationally known architects. The intention is that Doha's corniche should be as much of a draw for art-loving tourists as Dubai is for what *The Times* calls the 'glitz-'n'-tits brigade'.[78] Abu Dhabi is raising the cultural stakes further. Currently under construction, on an empty island that will be a cultural centre, are franchises of the Louvre and the Guggenheim, a maritime museum and a performing arts centre. These are of course also designed by some of the most famous names in architecture.

Not to be outdone by these high-profile projects of his autocrat peers, in June 2008 Sheikh Mohammed unveiled plans for a Museum of Middle East Modern Art in Culture Village on the shores of Dubai Creek. Along with the museum, plans called for an amphitheatre, an exhibition hall and smaller museums displaying local and international art, as well as a shipyard for traditional dhow builders.[79] Culture Village, not surprisingly, is a mixed-use luxury development that has as its theme, well, culture. When the village was first announced in 2006, its main feature distinguishing it from other developments was that, instead of mere condominiums, it had loft condominiums.[80] The recent announcement of the museum will actually bring culture to Culture Village.

Higher education

Dubai's system of higher education has largely been shaped by the same factors we discussed in the previous section on art: its perceived lack of value as a branding tool, and the temporariness of the expatriate population. In the past few years, as with art, the government has begun to understand higher education's commercial and branding value, and thus has aggressively become active in this field. Until very recently, universities were not seen as a source of prestige and as a result there was little investment in or quality control over the higher education sector. In the 1990s, there were few universities in Dubai for expatriates to attend at all.[81] (Of the second-generation expatriates I interviewed, only a few had gone to university in the UAE, and they went to university in the mid-2000s.) There was no visionary plan in place to accommodate the higher educational aspirations of these children of expatriates as they are seen as temporary, both legally and socially.

This neglect of education extends even to national citizens in spite of the fact that the Dubai government provides free universal education at all levels and also fully funds nationals studying at private institutions and abroad. The UAE's own universities serving nationals (United Arab Emirates University, established in 1977, the Higher Colleges of Technology, 1988, and Zayed University, 1998, though in 2009 it began admitting expatriates) have long suffered from underfunding and a lack of quality control. While Sheikh Mohammed pledged USD 10 billion towards education in the Middle East in 2007, none of that seems to be geared towards developing higher educational institutions in Dubai itself.[82] This, however, is beginning to change as the curricula at UAEU and Zayed University are being redrafted along Western lines with Western administrators and to a large degree a Western faculty.[83] This does not necessarily make them better, but it does enhance their reputation, and it helped Zayed University to get accreditation from the US-based body, Middle States Commission on Higher Education.

Until 2008, when the expansive Dubai International Academic City (DIAC) was opened, from 2003 most universities in Dubai were housed in the diminutively named Knowledge Village, which one writer described as 'a sterile cluster of second-tier institutions'.[84] The village itself along with DIAC is owned by Tecom Investments (a subsidiary of Sheikh Mohammed's Dubai Holding), which leases its buildings to these institutions. Aside from government universities, nearly all other higher educational entities in Dubai – roughly forty today – are for profit, lured in large part by the tax-free environment in these free zones.[85] Many are franchises or joint ventures of universities from other countries – including India, Pakistan, US, UK, Australia, Canada and Russia – that offer a limited number of academic programmes, mostly business, engineering, tourism, information technology and the like.

The ethos of education as commerce in Dubai is clearly visible in the attitudes of high-level officials, who see education as a commodity to provide to customers. For example, the director general of the Dubai Knowledge and Human Development Authority had not heard of one of the institutions he oversees, a branch of the Birla Institute of Technology and Science, a private Indian university. But he was perfectly happy to have it as 'it's the No. 3 engineering school in India, so it means a lot to Indians. We have to cater to them.' The consumerist colouring of the educational system in Dubai is impossible to miss; a government official even referred to Knowledge Village as 'a mall for educa-tion'. Students too are clear about what they are getting from their educational experience. A student at Mahatma Gandhi University said, 'We're here to get our degrees and that's it. No one comes here for a social life. If you want a real campus expe-rience, go to America.'[86]

The for-profit aspect of higher education is not limited to the attitudes of the universities or the government; it extends to the faculty as well, nearly all of which are expatriates, even at the government universities. Like any other worker in Dubai, these expatriate professors are also on three-year visas, and by defini-tion are temporary workers. This can shape how they approach their jobs. Turnover at universities is high, in part because profes-sors are generally on three-year contracts, and also because they are lured to Dubai (and elsewhere in the Gulf) by very generous terms of employment (for Western passport holders; Asians and Africans are paid significantly less). Professors receive salaries comparable to or exceeding those at home (and tax free, which greatly increases their value), free housing, free trips home yearly, furniture allowance, and tuition at private schools for their chil-dren. One British academic who was formerly a professor at Zayed University felt that there is a mercenary attitude among many professors, leading them to do the bare minimum of work for their tax-free salaries, and that they are 'pretty lazy'.[87] Their temporariness also affects the quality of classroom content. Topics such as nudity, evolution, Israel and the status of expatri-ates need to be broached carefully, if at all. This in part explains why so few schools have faculty or courses in the humanities or social sciences, especially sociology and anthropology, where such topics might be discussed. The same professor made the point that national students can cause problems for professors, espe-cially students from prominent national families. Like any other expatriate, as we will discuss in detail in the coming chapters, they are always under the implicit threat of deportation, which necessarily leads to a degree of self-censorship.

Where Dubai's educational system looks like a mall serving an increasing number of expatriate students concerned with simply receiving a degree, others in the Gulf seem to take educational quality, or at least educational name branding, more seriously. As with art, Sharjah had developed a quality higher educational infrastructure earlier than elsewhere in the Gulf, including the well-regarded American University of Sharjah. Qatar has received a lot of attention for its Education City, which has been in operation for over ten years, and houses prestigious brand names such as Carnegie Mellon University, Northwestern University, Georgetown University's School of Foreign Service and Weil Cornell Medical College, as well as Virginia Commonwealth University and Texas A&M University. While taken together they rank high on the prestige scale, these university branches provide limited academic programmes and they service relatively few students, mostly Qatari nationals.

Abu Dhabi, however, is raising the stakes in education in the Gulf further with the entry of a full-scale sister campus of New York University on Saadiyat Island, which the Louvre and Guggenheim will also call home. NYU's president was convinced that Abu Dhabi would make an excellent setting for a full campus by an initial gift of USD 50 million and the undeveloped Saadiyat Island. The government of Abu Dhabi promised to pay for the construction of the university and help fund faculty and services at the Abu Dhabi campus, as well as provide more funding for NYU's New York campus.[88]

Seemingly in response, Dubai has also been working to upgrade its academic status relative to its peers in the past few years, with a number of graduate schools opening, such as the

London School of Business and Finance, Rochester Institute of Technology, the Dubai School of Government (which has a tie-in with Harvard University through the 'Dubai Initiative') and many others. Perhaps more important than graduate education is the entrance of Michigan State University (MSU) in 2008, which will anchor the new DIAC. Government officials hope that MSU will be the first of many universities to set up shop in DIAC, and they hope to have 25,000 students in various universities within DIAC by 2012. The executive director of Knowledge Village and DIAC said that he hopes 'even better American universities will follow'.[89] While this may be an unwitting (or witting) slight aimed at MSU, clearly Dubai is aiming to compete with Qatar and Abu Dhabi in branding itself in the education industry as it is in arts.

The other side of this equation is the benefits to be had by foreign universities that enter the Arabian Gulf market. While there is certainly money to be made by bringing educational ventures to the Gulf, some universities that are globally expanding are refusing to be taken in by the glitz of Dubai, or the promise of luxury and high culture elsewhere in the Gulf. For instance, Bard College, a small liberal arts school in upstate New York, has decided to undertake a relationship with Al Quds University, a Palestinian university in Jerusalem and the West Bank. Bard's president said that he was glad not to be following the example of larger universities building campuses in the Gulf, a development that he said was 'like investing in Monte Carlo or Liechtenstein to develop Europe'.[90]

* * *

The economic and social changes in Dubai over the past forty years have by any measure been staggering. What was until quite recently a regional trading port has morphed into a proper global city. Dubai's rulers have purposely branded it through iconic constructions and as the pre-eminent tourist destination of the region.

But the glitz and glamour papered over a culture black hole; that is, Dubai had little that most people would recognize as culture. I have argued that this changed only after the rulers saw opportunities of branding and profit to be made from art and education. I have also argued that Dubai's reputation as 'plastic' was a result of how it treated its expatriate population as transient, which in turn affects the quality and depth of relationships that expatriates have with each other.

The book to this point has sketched out the basic factors of Dubai's economic transformation and how this impacted upon cultural life. In the remaining chapters I specifically turn to look at how the *kafala* system affects living and working conditions for expatriates and nationals as well.

CHAPTER THREE

IRON CHAINS

THE BULK OF THE population of Dubai today has been imported to service the less than 10 per cent of the overall population that are citizens of Dubai, as well as the middle and upper classes of expatriate labour. The massive labouring class in this city consists of people in a wide variety of occupations: construction workers; lower-level service sector workers including store clerks, security guards, taxi drivers, hotel staff, restaurant workers, hawkers and car cleaners; domestic workers including maids, houseboys and gardeners; and of course sex workers. These expatriates know full well that in Dubai, indeed throughout the Gulf states, they are nothing more than labour, they are simply factors of production. As human beings they are socially invisible, interchangeable and ultimately disposable.

Once in Dubai, these workers often become modern-day bonded labour, tithed to their employers by the conditions of their labour permits and residency visas. As a result of their occupational immobility, they are exposed to a high degree of exploitation on the job. As discussed earlier, Dubai goes to great lengths to brand itself internally and externally, for the purpose of promoting commerce and building Dubai's reputation. Government offices at the level of Dubai and the UAE historically have taken a largely 'hands off' approach to dealing with issues of labour exploitation, and they have generally dealt with them as they become public relations issues affecting Dubai's prestige and image in the West. Thus, human rights violations seen in this light are not issues to be dealt with because individuals have basic rights that the state is duty bound to protect, but rather the reporting and discussion of human rights violations is itself insulting to Dubai's honour, its reputation.

Labour exploitation became a serious issue to contend with as a result of the economic boom of the mid-2000s, which increased exponentially Dubai's exposure in the West. As Dubai became a well-known entity for its consumer culture and property boom, its treatment of workers came under scrutiny in the Western media and in the reports of various human rights groups, especially those of Human Rights Watch. Bad international publicity does damage to the carefully constructed image of 'Brand Dubai' and therefore needs to be counteracted. Laws are passed and policies made to address the slights, though not necessarily to redress the underlying causes, the exploitation itself.

This chapter addresses the exploitation of labour in this light, looking at how the temporariness of workers shapes the conditions under which they work and live, and how the government reacts to this. We explore this by examining the cases of possibly the most exploited workers whose conditions have come under international scrutiny: construction workers, maids, prostitutes and camel jockeys.

CONSTRUCTION WORKERS

The great bulk of scholarly and media focus on labour exploitation in Dubai has centred on the condition of construction
workers, who account for roughly one-fourth of the population
of Dubai. Construction workers in Dubai regularly work six-day
weeks of eleven-hour days, and often another half day on
Fridays. They work in dangerous conditions with more than
seven hundred deaths on the job and ninety suicides per year.[1]
Not only do they work long, dangerous hours, they must also
contend with the heat, which in the summers often rises to
50 degrees Celsius. The government in 2005 instituted a ban on
outdoor construction work during the hours from 12:00 to
14:30, but enforcement was lax until recently as there are very
few inspectors to check up on construction firms, and many
companies regularly flout the ban, though most companies do
seem to be adhering to it.[2] The fines are relatively miniscule in
any case, with one company violating the ban twice, thus having
to pay all of AED 20,000 as a fine.[3] By the summer of 2009,
though, it seemed the government was taking its own directive
more seriously, conducting nearly 2,000 inspections in the first
week of July in Dubai and Abu Dhabi, and finding 73 firms in
violation of the ban.[4]

Human rights groups and activists have for years decried the
exploitative conditions under which these workers live and labour.
Chief among the complaints is that workers are not allowed to
freely associate or to bargain collectively.[5] But exploitative working
conditions and restrictions on unions are a common feature of life
for labourers globally. My argument here is that the conditions of
the visa system, which are unique to Dubai and the Gulf states in
terms of scope, define the parameters under which workers are
controlled and shape how workers live their lives.

As we discussed in the previous chapter, the *kafala* system restricts workers' mobility by tying their labour permits and residency visas to their employers. To further limit workers' mobility, upon arrival in Dubai employers seize their workers' passports. In the UAE employers consider this to be appropriate and necessary. They argue it protects against workers running off (absconding is the preferred term), and protects them against theft. An assistant director at the Dubai Naturalisation and Residency Department told Human Rights Watch (HRW) that employers 'should not hold passports', but he justified the practice saying 'sometimes workers lose their passports so the safest place to keep it is at the company offices'.[6] This happens even though the courts have ruled this practice to be illegal.[7] The illegal holding of passports (which, if you look at your own, says it is the property of your government, not yours) extends even to the UAE Ministry of Labour and, indeed, all other governmental ministries.[8] The need to socially control workers trumps the rule of law, even within the government itself. One large-scale study of Indian migrants in the UAE found that employers often refuse to release passports back to their workers because of minor labour problems or disputes regarding payment of wages. And they even found that 11 per cent of employers refuse to give workers their passports back in order to return home.[9]

Another method that employers use to keep workers under control is to keep the workers' pay in arrears.[10] It is an incredibly common and, again, illegal method, but an effective one to ensure workers do not leave. All the construction workers that HRW interviewed for a scathing 2006 report said their employers routinely withheld their wages, often for months at a time. Workers whose wages are withheld for even a month immediately fall behind on their payments they owe to the recruiting agents back home.[11] These findings were echoed in a

2009 HRW report on the conditions of labourers on Saadiyat Island in Abu Dhabi, home of the Louvre, Guggenheim and NYU.[12] In spite of governmental rhetoric attesting to improved conditions for labourers, the story remains the same.

Sometimes companies close down while still owing workers vast sums of back pay. For example, the Lebanese owner of the East Coast and Hamriah Company shut down his construction company and fled to Canada. His legal partner, an Emirati, was absolved of any liability. The judge was not sympathetic when approached by the workers who were owed back pay in amounts ranging from over AED 10,000 to 21,000. 'You want to take your money? Bring someone who will buy all the company's stuff,' the judge said.[13]

This particular case illustrates two important points. One is the relationship between national citizen partners and the actual expatriate owners. Outside of the free trade zones, all companies must have minimum 51 per cent ownership by national citizen partners. Usually the expatriate owners pay an annual fee to their partners for their signature and for the issuance of labour permits. The partners then sign a side agreement that limits their actual ownership, so that the partner does not partake of profits beyond his yearly fee, thus protecting the expatriate owner. This is a system beneficial to both, as the Emirati partner does no work nor puts up any capital, but still receives ample yearly compensation, and the expatriate owner has a national partner for protection and for issuing labour permits. The second major point to come out of this example is the partisan stance of the courts. If a company goes bankrupt, the creditors will have precedence to recuperate costs, and the local owner is absolved of liability. The workers, needless to say, end up with nothing.

Even when the workers' pay is not stolen outright, it is precious little. The issue of low salaries cannot be escaped when discussing the boomtown that Dubai has become. There is no minimum wage in the UAE, even though UAE Labour Law has required it since 1980. Unskilled construction workers are among the lowest paid workers in the UAE, generally earning in the region of USD 150–200 per month.[14] Workers sign contracts in their home countries and then have contracts switched on them when they arrive, often for half the wage originally agreed upon.[15] Once in Dubai, they are trapped, legally obligated to work for their employers in spite of any underhand activity on the employer's part, and financially beholden to agents back home who own their debt. Rises are miniscule, or sometimes non-existent.

The low wages are made even lower before the workers make their way to Dubai. The workers are expected to pay their own visa and travel fees – on average around USD 2,000 in 2006 – to recruiting firms before they leave their countries of origin. This practice is illegal, as UAE law prohibits companies from dealing with agencies that charge workers recruiting fees, but nonetheless is ubiquitous as the UAE does nothing to ensure compliance with the law.[16] This is the kind of money that unskilled workers tend not to have; they scrape it up through mortgaging or selling land, borrowing from relatives, or borrowing from money-lenders. Borrowing from moneylenders is especially hazardous. Three Bangladeshi workers told HRW they were paying 11 per cent interest *monthly* on their loans.[17]

Companies in the UAE, like most firms in most industries around the world, unsurprisingly attempt to limit the amount they pay their lower-end workers. A young female doctor blogging from Dubai wrote of a particularly cheeky example coming from the young wife of a 'prominent construction industry bigwig'. This woman told the doctor how her husband introduced a clause in the labour force's contract which allowed the company to deduct AED 75 from a worker's wage should the worker fail to report for duty and AED 45 in case of a fight. The woman said, 'According to our estimate, on account of the fights alone we should be able to save thousands on book by the end of the year.'[18] The doctor was not amused.

Workers seem to be treated as temporary and disposable because they are. In the UAE, indeed in all the Gulf states, workers are classified not as migrants, but as temporary fixed-contract labour. To underscore that temporary means just that, the UAE Minister of Labour in 2006 proposed that unskilled workers should be limited to six years' residence.[19] A year later, before a Gulf Cooperation Council (GCC) meeting, Bahrain's Minister of Labour also announced that unskilled workers should not be allowed to stay longer than six years at a time so that workers 'do not come to live here for long periods that might entitle them to the rights of immigrant workers under the UN conventions'.[20] Initially, the proposal was for all expatriate workers, but he clarified that he meant only unskilled labourers. For government leaders in the Gulf, this is a measure to protect the identity and culture of nationals throughout the Gulf, which is awash in a flood of expatriate workers, especially from the South Asian subcontinent. But many businesses were apprehensive, for the obvious reason that unskilled workers often graduate into skilled workers, who are then more difficult to replace. A spokesperson for the Al Habtoor Group, a prominent construction firm, called the proposal 'unwise as the country will lose its semi-professional and professional manpower. Besides, there will be financial losses.'[21] For labourers who are indebted to recruitment agents back home and whose families are dependent on remittances, this move would have been especially devastating. Fortunately for labourers and businesses, this proposal was not enacted, though it was revived in 2009, with calls to limit labourers to working a maximum of five years in any one Gulf country, though they could subsequently work in another.[22]

Most of the ways that employers control their workers are illegal under UAE law and court decisions, but have been common practice in the UAE for years. In the mid-2000s, the government began to take legislative and policy measures to support workers' rights, seemingly in response to unfavourable press and activism from without. One particular report by Human Rights Watch in 2006, *Building Towers, Cheating Workers*, was closely followed by the UAE government. In a press release on 11 November 2006 regarding the report, HRW wrote:

> On October 27, Human Rights Watch communicated its findings and recommendations to the UAE government in a letter. Shortly thereafter, on November 7, the prime minister [of the UAE, Sheikh Mohammed, also the ruler of Dubai] ordered the labor minister to immediately institute reforms based on Human Rights Watch's recommendations. Specifically, the prime minister's decree directed the labor minister to set up a special labor court to resolve labor disputes, increase the number of government inspectors, require employers to provide health insurance for low-skilled workers, and develop mandatory mechanisms enabling workers to collect unpaid wages. Human Rights Watch welcomed this swift response and inherent acknowledgement of the problem of abuse.[23]

This report was widely reported in the international and local media, and it seemed the UAE government intended to implement many of the proposals within the HRW report. But, by the time of HRW's 2009 report on Abu Dhabi's Saadiyat Island, hardly any of these proposals had been implemented, except for the special labour court, which was recently improved with the addition of a 'hotline' to report non-payment of wages.[24] Indeed, a 2007 draft labour law that would have codified many of the above proposals had been scrapped.[25]

The exploitation of labour has been part and parcel of the story of the development of Dubai – indeed of all the Gulf states. And workers had largely remained silent about abuses as their wages generally fulfilled their unwritten compact with the government – work and remit. But since 2005 Dubai has seen a large number of work stoppages that have garnered international attention. In 2005, *Gulf News* reported there were twenty-four strikes involving more than 7,000 workers over issues such as unpaid wages, differential wages between nationalities, overtime, long working hours, poor working conditions and accommodation.[26] From 2006 to 2008 there were various protests involving hundreds, sometimes thousands of labourers, most famously at the Burj Khalifa and Dubai Marina construction sites. But while the government has been painfully slow to take measures to improve the lot of labourers, it reacted quickly to the strikes. For example, on 11 March 2007, 3,500 workers from ETA Ascon went on strike demanding pay rises. It was a peaceful protest that ended at 11 a.m. that same day, and the workers went back to work. The following day it was announced that 200 workers were to be deported after many of the workers rioted, following a company announcement that they would be granted a pay increase of AED 2 per day. Three days after the reported riot, 65 workers had been summarily deported, without arrest, trial or due process of any kind. Further, the company, owned by the prominent Al Ghurair family of Dubai, was then given 250 additional work permits issued free of charge to replace the deported workers. The contrast between the swiftness of action the government takes here, when labour unrest threatens Dubai's image and construction, and the snail's pace at which the government acts to curb the exploitation of labour is telling.[27]

This labour unrest roughly coincided with the heightening of the economic boom of the mid-2000s, which did not have a positive impact on workers' wages, and skyrocketing inflation, which affected them negatively. Perhaps most importantly, as a backdrop to the strikes, the UAE dirham is pegged to the US dollar, which became increasingly weak compared with many other global currencies, including the Indian rupee and UK pound. What this meant for workers was that even if they were able to remit the same amount as they had been remitting earlier, it was worth staggeringly less due to losses in currency conversion. As the economy boomed and an ever-increasing number of luxury buildings went up, the workers lost ground in Dubai in terms of the increased cost of living expenses, and at home in terms of what their remittances actually became in their home currencies. By the end of 2008, the US dollar had rebounded relative to other currencies. But workers then faced an even greater problem – layoffs. As the construction industry went into meltdown, as in so much of the world, thousands of workers found themselves unemployed, which in Dubai means they get sent home. While concrete data on remittances from Dubai, the UAE and other Gulf states generally are difficult to come by, the World Bank estimated that remittance flows from the Gulf, which had grown by an astounding 38 per cent in 2008, would decline by 9 per cent in 2009.[28]

So the question arises: if conditions are so bad, why stay? The answer is fairly simple and twofold: workers arrive saddled with debt, and they need to support family back home. Whatever they earn, they remit the bulk of it. While there are a staggering number of newspaper and magazine articles about the exploitation of construction workers, they contain buried within their pages the basic truth for labourers, that it is the remittances to family (and to the agents to whom they owe thousands of dollars) that keeps them in Dubai. Again, this is the basis of the unwritten agreement between the workers and the state and is the reason for the strikes – that wages were no longer enough to pay off debt and to remit.

Living conditions

The temporary state of workers can best be seen in how they live outside of work, specifically in their housing accommodation. A great number of Dubai's construction workers and other labourers live in segregated labour camps. The largest of these camps, on the outskirts of the desert surrounded by barbed wire, is called Sonapur, a Hindi word which means, ironically, 'city of gold'. This city is home to around 200,000 people, and its population is growing. One Dubai tabloid made the not-outrageous claim that Sonapur is likely to become (if not already) the largest labour camp in the world.[29] As the number of Dubai's skyscrapers and malls grows, so does Sonapur. As the Burj Khalifa is now the world's tallest building, complete with luxury condominiums and an Armani hotel, so Sonapur mirrors it in grotesque grandiosity.

Sonapur is basically a dormitory setting for labouring men, where they share rooms (often twelve to a room), toilets and kitchens. Many of the compounds are filthy, through no particular fault of the workers. They have poor drainage and poor sanitation, and 'live with flies and stench as a result of large pools of stagnant sewage in their surroundings'.[30] The sewage in their midst is the result of overflowing septic tanks, which many camp owners in Sonapur choose not to dispose of properly.

After the release of the damning HRW report in November 2006, the Dubai government moved quickly to contain the public relations damage, announcing a series of reforms while at the same time questioning the validity of the report and the motivations of HRW. One of the government's pronouncements concerned the hygienic conditions of labour camps, 75 per cent of which were deemed to be below government standards by the government's Permanent Committee for Labour Affairs in late 2006. (Inspections in late 2008 found that 70 per cent of labour accommodations violated hygiene and safety rules.) But, like so many of the government's other pronouncements, this one rang hollow. The companies that let the sewage fester in the camps were obviously not moved by the government's new position, as the penalty for ignoring the new regulations was a not-quite-exacting fine of AED 2,000, but only after three violations. That makes it cheaper for companies to amass fines rather than clean up.[31]

The situation has changed little in the years since. An April 2009 report by BBC's Panorama programme found that the labour camps of one of the country's largest construction firms, Arabtec, were overcrowded and wretchedly filthy, with raw sewage leaking all over the camp, and workers having to lay down a series of stepping stones to get to and from their accommodation blocks. One toilet block had no water and the latrines were full of piles of raw faeces. Panorama had obtained documents written by Dubai authorities a month before their arrival that described the sewage situation at the site as 'critical'. The government's response to the critical situation was to fine Arabtec AED 10,000.[32]

The timing of the report came in the middle of a flood of other bad news reports that were hitting Dubai and proved to be another huge public relations blow. The UAE Ministry of Labour was forced to declare they would investigate the situation, but months later nothing about this had appeared in the press. Arabtec initially denied the report, blaming the workers for the filth, but then conceded that in fact their camps were overcrowded and not particularly hygienic. They also promised to upgrade much of their labour camp accommodation for their

60,000-plus workforce, and close down the filthiest one where Panorama had filmed. At least they claimed they would.

Even when employers are willing to house their workers decently, the government of Dubai makes it difficult. For example, John, a European expatriate in his late twenties who was born and raised in Dubai, and whose family owns a construction firm, told me they had put their workers up in a nice villa in Jumeirah. But officials from the municipality evicted them, forcing them to search for accommodation in a labour camp, a decided step down in quality, though not a step down in price. The Dubai government's 2006 crackdown on 'bachelors' living in villas in family-only designated neighbourhoods resulted in accommodation in labour camps becoming in even greater demand.

The workers housed in Sonapur and other labour camps may be the lucky ones of the labouring class as their housing, poor though it may be, is provided by their companies. Other low-wage workers have to pay their own way. The possibility of renting an entire flat, or even a room of their own in a flat or villa, is well beyond their means. Rents in Dubai, and elsewhere in the UAE, had skyrocketed from 2005 to 2006, increasing in some areas over 100 per cent in spite of rent increase caps, and continued to increase dramatically well into 2008 even while the property market began to crash. As rents went up, workers found it more and more difficult to find places to live, and the local papers were filled with horror stories of abominable living conditions. Workers are crowded eight or more into a room in villas and flats throughout Dubai. A national landlord (the owners of villas or flats outside of freehold areas are always nationals) charging AED 500 or so for 'bedspace' (i.e. space enough for a single bed) per worker can bring thousands of dirhams in rent per month *per room*. And as their tenants are 'merely' labourers, and have no tenancy contracts, there is no need for maintenance. Throughout many areas of Dubai you can see rundown and overcrowded villas and blocks of flats in filthy conditions.

As a direct result of such lack of maintenance, in 2008 a deadly fire broke out in the Naif Souq area in Deira, on the north side of Dubai Creek. Eleven South Asian workers were killed in a villa complex housing over 500 people. The Emirati owner and three Indians he rented the house to who had subdivided the property were arrested.[33] This event led directly to the government cracking down on the subletting and overcrowding of villas in its 'one villa, one family' campaign. This crackdown extended well beyond the villas that house dozens of workers in a villa built for a single family to affecting young professionals who choose to share villas for lifestyle reasons, as well as economic ones (we will return to this issue in chapter four).

While living in an overcrowded villa or flat can be filthy and dangerous, at least it is a proper living space, rundown though it may be. Other workers are not even that fortunate. One company housed 2,000 of its workers in cargo containers, 16 workers in each 300-square-foot container.[34] A separate container was kept exclusively for workers who became ill. Originally these workers were living in Sonapur, but were removed in favour of company staff. The sudden increase in rents in the mid-2000s led many people to search for even more creative solutions. Some people in Dubai and Sharjah had taken to renting car trunks for the night at the cost of AED 5 per night.[35] Even these are sometimes shared. The situation in Abu Dhabi was not much different, where hundreds of workers were living illegally in the attics of their stores as there is a severe lack of bachelor accommodation.[36] (In response to this housing shortage, instead of building up middle and low-income housing, the Abu Dhabi government invested in constructing a labour camp to accommodate 400,000 working men.) And even these situations may be preferable to that of a group of Indian workers who were recruited to work as grocery store clerks, cleaners and janitors. Upon their arrival in Dubai they were informed they were to work in construction. When they refused and asked to be sent home, they were immediately moved from their accommodation and forced to live in a tent.[37]

MAIDS

While construction workers literally make the good life possible for nationals and middle- and upper-class expatriates by building the country's infrastructure, maids are central to making the good life what it is in the house. An estimated 150,000 UAE families employ around 300,000 domestic workers while nearly half of the 300,000 expatriate families also employ domestic workers.[38] That makes roughly 450,000 maids in the UAE in 2006 – 10 per cent of the UAE's then 4.6 million population.

Many maids have good relations with their employers; they are treated as members of the family, are paid adequately and in a timely fashion, and have acceptable time off during the workday, a day off once a week, and holidays.[39] Some maids actually do quite well financially and choose to stay in Dubai for extended stays. For example, a fifty-three-year-old Filipina maid who cleans four residences said the money is good, and her customers are polite and appreciative. She even brought her adult daughters to Dubai to work as maids.[40] But people like her are the exceptions.

Like in many parts of the world, maids are some of the most vulnerable workers in the labour force. Their work hours are long, especially if they live with the family, often exceeding one hundred hours in the week without rest breaks, in addition to being 'on call' day and night to attend to the family's and children's needs while not even having days off. Their work hours often increase during Ramadan, as much entertaining of relatives goes on at night, and as the family fasts during the day, it is up to the maids to do that much more work.[41]

The working and social conditions of maids are of servitude – they are servants, household help – and must show social deference to their employers in a way that other workers do not. For instance, it is quite a common sight in malls in Dubai and throughout the UAE to see an Indonesian or South Asian maid treading behind her master and mistress pushing their child in a pram, where the maid's '*hijab* fully covers her hair, her eyes are lowered, and she does not look at or speak to anyone: not even the child, not even if it starts screaming or throwing a tantrum'.[42]

Maids are further victimized in various ways. Like construction workers, they often have their pay delayed, have various 'deductions' made, or sometimes are not paid at all. They are subject to regular verbal and mental abuse from employers, and often physical or sexual abuse. The US State Department's Trafficking in Persons Report (TIPR) for 2008 says that taken together these abuses often amount to 'involuntary servitude'.[43] Even the most egregious cases of abuse get punished very lightly, if they get punished at all. Recently a Filipina maid was tortured with hot coals and ice cubes as her employers, an Iraqi man and his Kuwaiti wife bragged to friends that he treated her like a prisoner from the infamous Abu Ghraib prison in Iraq.[44] The two were initially given three-year sentences, later reduced to six months followed by deportation.

The visa status of maids contributes to their insecurity. Maids who are hired legally are on two-year contracts, and, even more than other classes of lower-level workers, are truly bonded labour. No matter their complaints, they have hardly any rights in the

UAE legal system; as household labour, maids are not even given the bare minimum protection that construction workers are accorded, indeed are not even covered under the UAE's labour law. Like construction workers, they are often not paid for months on end, sometimes never, but it is an allegation nearly impossible to prove. Maids who attempt to escape from abusive employers find they have been labelled 'absconders' and thus are in violation of the law. The Philippines Consulate in Dubai in 2008 reported they received at least four runaways a week as a result of physical abuse, rape, and non-payment of wages.

While absconding maids are quite often victims of abuse and non-payment of wages, they are the ones who are treated as criminals. Government officials prefer to think of runaway maids as disloyal types looking for better wages, and as threats to national security. The Director-General of the Dubai Naturalisation and Residency Department emphasized how maids often run away from sponsors that treat them well, asserting they can easily get hired by expatriates who do not wish to pay sponsorship fees, roughly AED 15,000. He further warned the public not to employ a runaway maid, as 'she could be suffering from an infectious disease or she may have committed a crime or she is involved in some other dangerous issue'.[45] That abuse of maids is common, and is a very common cause of maids absconding, is an issue the official did not address. A housewife from the posh Jumeirah neighbourhood complained in 7 Days, a Dubai newspaper, about how she had hired two housemaids who had run away after very short periods of work, and after she had paid thousands in fees to sponsor them. She blamed families that hire illegal maids for the problem of absconding, not issues of maltreatment. 'Although many people lock up their housemaids, I have always given them enough freedom and I am paying for it today.'[46] To help the public deal with the problem posed by absconding maids, Gulf News published an article with step-by-step instructions telling sponsors what to do 'just in case your maid runs away'.[47]

The issue of the exploitation of maids, like that of construction workers, is one that the government deals with as a public relations issue in response to outside pressure. While the exploitation of maids in Dubai has been a recurrent theme in the media in India and the Philippines, the Dubai and UAE governments have never shown an interest in their welfare. It was only after the issuance of an HRW report on maids in various countries including the UAE in July 2006,[48] and around the time of the HRW report specifically dealing with construction workers in Dubai in November 2006, that Sheikh Mohammed announced contracts for labourers and domestic workers that would limit working hours, allow them to switch jobs with no obstacles, and ensure workers' salaries could not be held for more than two months by employers. He also proposed a medical insurance scheme covering all grades of workers and a specialized court to be created to deal with mistreatment cases.[49] Later, in January 2007, the Director-General of the Dubai Naturalisation and Residency Department, speaking of newly announced contracts for domestic workers, said 'the new contracts will limit their work hours in accordance with international principles'.[50] The new contract went into effect on 1 April that year and provided for some protection of domestic workers, but with no limits on working hours, no provisions for a rest day or overtime pay and no workers' compensation, mandating only unspecified 'adequate breaks' and one month of paid vacation every two years. Protection for housemaids still falls woefully short of that provided for all other categories of workers, and housemaids are not covered under a draft labour law proposed in 2007, which has still not been enacted.

The underpayment (and non-payment) and abuse of maids is an issue that sending countries have become more serious about.

Pakistan has for years refused to allow its citizens to come to Dubai as housemaids, causing some Pakistani expatriates in Dubai to chafe under what they perceive as an unfair denial of the use of their co-nationals' household labour.[51] In 2007, the countries that provide most of the housemaids to Dubai and the rest of the UAE – the Philippines, India, Sri Lanka, Indonesia and Bangladesh – negotiated monthly minimum wage requirements for their citizens in 2007 with the UAE government. Many employers of maids, nationals and expatriates, were upset about this, complaining that raising minimum wages and income requirements to sponsor maids would affect them adversely.[52] Even with this legal protection, many families still pay their maids far less than the legally required minimum wage.[53]

PROSTITUTES

While maids are central to maintaining the good life for well-to-do expatriate and national families, prostitutes provide the illicit basis of the good life for many other men – tourists and visiting businessmen, UAE nationals and other Gulf citizens, and of course expatriates. A large number, if not the bulk of prostitutes, have been trafficked into Dubai. The US State Department's 2006 TIPR stated:

> The UAE is placed on Tier 2 Watch List for its failure to show increased efforts to combat trafficking over the past year, particularly in its efforts to address the large-scale trafficking of foreign girls and women for commercial sexual exploitation. Despite a significant problem of sex trafficking, UAE authorities failed to take adequate measures to screen women found in prostitution in order to determine whether they were victims of trafficking, and to provide them with adequate care. Instead,

many victims are jailed along with criminals and deported. Prosecutions for sex trafficking are extremely low relative to the scope of the problem. The government should do more to improve screening for victims, encourage victims to testify against their traffickers, and provide them with alternatives to detention and deportation.[54]

This was an improvement from 2005. In 2005, the 2005 TIPR had placed the UAE in Tier 3, its lowest ranking for human rights violators (downgrading the UAE from a Tier 2 ranking the previous year). The director of the Human Rights Section of the Dubai Police was not impressed, indeed was defiant. The day after the 2005 report was issued, he said, 'We don't need outside organizations telling us what to do.'[55]

In spite of the bluster of some officials within the UAE, various governmental departments at the Dubai and federal level have begun a public relations campaign to respond to the international call to step up vigilance against trafficking. In 2006, Federal Law 51 was enacted, which criminalizes human trafficking. (In 2008 this was being publicized with advertisements in the airport.) Under this law a handful of cases have been prosecuted and a few convictions obtained. For example, in July 2007, an Indian driver and an Indian maid were given fifteen-year sentences for purchasing an Indonesian woman for AED 4,300 and forcing her into prostitution and then trying to sell her.[56] A few months later, in January 2008, two Indian men were given ten-year sentences for trafficking and running a brothel. Their victims were maids who had absconded from their sponsors.[57] The biggest bust was of 12 pimps and 170 prostitutes, mostly Chinese, along with 65 clients.[58]

While the government has begun to take steps toward policing the trade, it falls far short of systematically addressing the issue, and still seems more directed at prosecuting and deporting the prostitutes themselves rather than addressing root issues of trafficking and pimping. The legal system and police attitudes are such that the women are usually jailed and deported for prostitution and visa-related offences rather than being treated as victims of trafficking. In 2006, over 4,300 prostitutes were deported from Dubai, far overshadowing the small number of arrests and trials of traffickers and pimps and madams. The 2008 US State Department TIPR highlighted this trend, saying 'An active anti-trafficking committee chaired by a cabinet-level official coordinated the UAE's anti-trafficking efforts . . . Nonetheless, the UAE did not aggressively prosecute or punish acts of trafficking for forced labor.' However, the UAE has become more proactive, which the 2009 TIPR acknowledged when saying the 'government demonstrated sustained efforts to prosecute and convict sex trafficking offenders during the year and made modest progress to provide protections to female trafficking victims'. But, at the same time, it criticized the UAE for not acknowledging that others, such as labourers and maids, can be victims of human trafficking, and for doing nothing to help these people as they have entered the country voluntarily, and are of legal age.[59]

The sex trafficking trade has boomed internationally since the early 1990s, with great numbers of women being trafficked from South Asia, but also a large number from the former Soviet republics, Africa, China and elsewhere. E. Benjamin Skinner, in *A Crime So Monstrous*, a book on international sex slavery, estimates that by 2005 there were at least 10,000 sex slaves in Dubai.[60] The numbers today are likely to be far greater, given that the population and economy exploded in the period from 2005 to the end of 2008, corresponding roughly with a fivefold increase in the price of oil.

A common method by which women are trafficked is for women to be promised work as clerks or waitresses, often by those they trust. A *New Yorker* article about a Moldovan counter-trafficker described how one woman from Moldova had a job as a waitress in Lisbon arranged for her by her boyfriend of a year and a half. A friend of his met her in Lisbon and told her the job had fallen through and offered to take her to Dubai. She took him up on the offer and an Arab man met them at the airport. The next day an Uzbeki woman took her to an apartment, at which point she realized she had been sold as the woman gave the man money and took her passport. After a few years of working in discos as a prostitute, she managed to escape and went to the police, who arrested her. The Uzbeki woman declined to hand over her passport, and continued in her thriving business. The police released the prostitute after a month, then she went back to work as a prostitute, freelancing for herself. Later she quit sex work but was arrested in a police sweep for not having documents. After a year in prison, she was deported.[61]

In the same *New Yorker* article, Sharla Musabih who runs the City of Hope shelter in Dubai talked about two Uzbeki woman staying with her:

> They were given cheap, slinky clothes to wear. Stiletto heels. These are Muslim village girls. But what traumatized them the most was being held down and having their boss shape and pluck their eyebrows. For them, that's so humiliating. If they go home like this, everyone will know.

The women ran away, but their boss kept their passports as the police were too slow in attempting to track down their boss. Musabih hoped the women would stay long enough to testify against the traffickers. But they received a call from an official at the Uzbek consulate who convinced the women that Musabih had been paid USD 4,000 by the *New Yorker* reporter (he insists he did not pay Musabih). The two women went back to Uzbekistan soon after receiving the call.

Some women manage to escape their pimps but then decide to become freelancers, like the Moldovan woman above. Skinner wrote of a Romanian woman who was tricked into coming to Dubai with the promise of a waitressing job. She was forced into prostitution for a year with often violent clients and in return was given one meal a day, coffee and cigarettes. She considered running away to the police, but to do so would have been a death sentence for her three-year-old son in Romania. After a year, her madam said she was going back to Romania and would manumit her. She could have gone back to Romania as well, but she knew she no longer had a reputation back home, would never find legitimate work, or a husband to provide for her son. Despite being in Dubai illegally and without a passport, she decided to stay and continue being a prostitute. She told Skinner that now, 'I am for myself.' But Skinner noted that for this woman and so many others like her, 'There was no joy in freedom.'[62]

While the story for the bulk of prostitutes in Dubai, as elsewhere in the world as Skinner so painfully documents, is heart wrenching, this is not always the case. One filmmaker who made a documentary on prostitution in Dubai for an American public television programme said she expected to find that the women were 'broken'.[63] Instead, she found that many of these women referred to themselves as 'businesswomen'. She went to one particularly famous seedy hotel in the Bur Dubai area and watched the women from Ghana, Ethiopia, China, Uzbekistan, Moldova and so on negotiating their night's labour. A modicum of propriety is maintained at the clubs; bouncers walk around to make certain that none of the activities paid for actually take place there. All this occurs with the government's seal of approval – literally. All clubs that charge entry fees give tickets, which are stamped by the Dubai Department of Tourism and Commerce Marketing. Entrance fees usually include a free drink.

Still other women come to Dubai on their own and of their own accord with the intention of becoming prostitutes. For instance, the majority of young Iranian prostitutes in Dubai according to a recent article are there by choice, and they see the work as 'prestigious' and providing them autonomy and personal freedom.[64] Other women moonlight as prostitutes, earning much more than they do in their day jobs, which they keep for the legal status it confers on them.

As is the case with workers in Dubai generally, pay will vary by nationality. The filmmaker found that Middle Eastern sex workers were paid the most, then Eastern European and Africans, and the lowest paid were the Chinese. Various people told me that Moroccans, Iranians, Filipinas and Indians commanded the highest rates, followed by Eastern Europeans and Africans.

The fact that prostitution is so prevalent in Dubai has ramifications for all women, from maids to professionals. For one, there is an assumption that a woman by herself (or with another woman, or even with a man) must be a prostitute. This can be seen in subtle ways, such as women being asked for ID when going to a club in a hotel (men are almost never asked), to not-so-subtle ways. For instance, a Somali media executive told me how a white American friend of his once was out for a walk and a man in an expensive car with tinted windows drove up to her and asked, 'How much?' To which she had no reply. He then offered AED 2,000. To which she had no reply. And he kept increasing the offer until he reached AED 3,500. She excitedly reported back to her Somali friend that she had found out her street value was AED 3,500! Another woman, a Chinese-American expatriate waiting to enter a club at a posh hotel, was asked by a man 'How much?' Her husband, standing right next to her, responded, 'She's my wife.' The man gave the husband a 'dopey smile' and walked away.[65] The filmmaker discussed above, while she was watching the prostitutes in the club in the seedy hotel, was herself propositioned by one man who asked her, 'How much do you want?' She played along, saying '1,000 dirhams'. To which he responded, 'How much will you let me have for 500?' When she questioned him about his brash behaviour and his assumption that she was a prostitute, he unapologetically asserted that, 'Every woman in Dubai has her price.'

CAMEL JOCKEYS

Arguably the most exploited of all workers in Dubai, the UAE and the Gulf generally were child camel jockeys. The use of small children as jockeys – mainly from Pakistan, Bangladesh, Sudan and Mauritania (though of course no UAE national children) – dates back to the 1970s, the time of the first economic boom associated with the increased price of oil resultant from the 1973 OPEC oil crisis.[66] Many camel jockeys – really child slaves – were as young as two years old and so lightweight they had to be tied onto the backs of the camels. But after a number of fatal accidents, they were, with advances in technology, fastened on with Velcro.[67] They were purposefully underfed, received poor medical care, sometimes sodomized and generally abused.[68]

It is obvious why light jockeys were preferred – the camel goes faster without the additional weight. Younger ones were also preferred for a more insidious reason. Ansar Burney, founder of the Ansar Burney Trust, a Pakistan-based organization that worked for sixteen years to end the practice of child slave jockeys in the oil-rich Gulf states and is largely responsible for the emancipation of these child jockeys, makes the point as to why these children are preferable: 'When scared or in pain – they scream; and the louder the child screams in pain the faster the camel to which he is strapped will run.'[69]

The use of children as jockeys, not surprisingly, is illegal under various international conventions, and even under the UAE's own 1980 Federal Labour Code, which bans the employment of any child under the age of fifteen.[70] The Indian press had been reporting on the abuse of child jockeys for years, accusing jockey brokers of stealing children and parents of selling them.[71] In spite of this, the practice was widespread for an obvious reason stated plainly in the 1999 US Department of State *Country Report on Human Rights Practices for the United Arab Emirates*: 'Those who own racing camels and employ the children come from powerful local families that are in effect above the law.'[72] Many racing camel owners justified the use of child jockeys, saying the poverty from which the children came from was almost as fraught with risk as the races in which they rode. Racing aficionados justified it, pointing to the safety precautions taken, how an ambulance followed closely behind in each race. A nephew of the Ruler of Sharjah said, 'sure . . . there were many accidents. Many children died.' But the parents were paid a good price for their children's services. 'And the children will get paid – like any labourer in the market.' And like any labourer in the market, they were used for as long as they were useful, then sent back.[73]

Camel racing is not some illicit, underground activity. Racetracks are in plain sight in central locations with training done at various farms throughout the UAE, and with a great deal of involvement of the royal family as owners, participants and sponsors. While Ansar Burney and others such as Sharla Musabih (mentioned earlier in the chapter) worked tirelessly for years, it was the media exposure of this practice in the West that likely marked the end of the use of child camel jockeys. In 2002, in response to increasingly bad news reports highlighting the employment and dangerous conditions under which these children worked, the UAE government passed (redundant) legislation banning the use of children under the age of fifteen, or weighing less than 45 kilograms, though, again, the law was not enforced. But a few years later things really changed. For an HBO sports programme, which aired in the US in October 2004, Ansar Burney took a hidden camera into the camel farms where the boys were kept and showed the inhuman conditions in which the boys lived, how they were regularly beaten, underfed and made to sleep on the sand in the open. The camels had far better lives.[74] This programme personally embarrassed John Miller, the US Ambassador-at-Large for Trafficking in Persons, into dropping the UAE from Tier 2 to Tier 3 in the US State Department's 2005 TIPR.[75] Miller apparently 'exploded' when he saw the 'shattering undercover footage of enslaved child camel jockeys'. The previous year he had upgraded the UAE to Tier 2. He said of the upgrade, 'The UAE really sold the State Department a bill of goods.' On his own gullibility, he said, 'Of course, I'd made a mistake.'[76]

In 2005, the UAE government finally responded with concrete measures, rather than simply window-dressing legislation as they have largely done for others of the working class. The resultant crackdown on the use of child slaves as jockeys in the aftermath of the uproar after the airing of this programme was pragmatic – the UAE wanted to join trade pacts with the West. Labour issues (ban of unions, child labour, human trafficking, and so on) stood in the way. In early 2005, the UAE Interior Ministry placed notices in local papers which described child slavery as 'against our national interests' and stressed that it was a violation of the UAE's obligations under international treaties and obligations.[77] The stress here on national interests and treaties is telling of the government's view of these children, and of the human rights of workers in general: child slavery is wrong not for any moral reasons, but rather because child slavery stands in the way of achieving 'national interests'.

The UAE and Dubai governments have been lauded by UNICEF and others more recently for ending the use of child camel jockeys in 2005, replacing them with robots equipped with riding crops, operated by their owners who follow the camels round the track in their SUVs (Chelsea tractors), whipping them by remote control. Even after the accord, though, for a short period children were still being used. Ansar Burney witnessed a secret late-night race with young boys as jockeys on a visit to the UAE in November 2005. He pointed out that the UAE government estimated that there were about three thousand child camel jockeys in 2005 but said it was having difficulty finding them. Since May 2005, more than one thousand camel jockeys have been repatriated since an agreement was signed with UNICEF.[78] Burney asked the obvious question: where are the other two thousand children?[79] Since 2006, it seems that children have disappeared from the more public face of the sport as jockeys. The 2008 US State Department's TIPR states that 'there were no new reports of children identified as trafficked for the purpose of camel jockeying'.[80] Even so, a posting on Ansar Burney's website states that on 18 August 2007 they filmed children being used as camel jockeys in Dubai (though there is no video clip there, and no one responded to my request to furnish one).[81] Still, the government has begun repatriations and started paying reparations. These are relatively miniscule amounts by UAE standards, though sizable by the standards of the boys' countries (USD 1.43 million to 879 Bangladeshi boys, USD 220,000 to 91 Mauritanian boys). The funds have been administered slowly, though in typical Dubai style, with great public-relations fanfare on the part of the Dubai government.

* * *

Workers in Dubai lead highly exploited work lives, and are socially degraded. Their wages are poor, when paid, and their rights under the law are limited, and rarely enforced. That is the case for the more fortunate workers. Maids, illegal migrants and prostitutes have basically no rights at all and no recourse to the police or the courts. Their exploitation is only mitigated when it becomes a public relations issue, particularly in the West, at which point the government takes action to make it stop being a public relations issue.

In spite of this, people still come to Dubai in droves to work at these kinds of job. Some are unaware of what they are getting into, while others arrive fully aware. Dubai broadly represents a promise of upward mobility for these people – not in Dubai itself necessarily, but at home. While their existence in Dubai may have the look of bondage, and legally often is bondage, Dubai offers the hope that suffering there may be rewarded with riches accrued that will be more valuable back in their third world homes. In that sense, their cages in Dubai are gilded. The next chapter examines those truly living in gilded cages, the middle class and professional expatriates.

CHAPTER FOUR

LIVING IN 'FLY-BY' DUBAI

*'We live in a bubble, a kind of fantasy world of luxury living and, if
you want it, endless partying.'*

British expatriate lawyer in Dubai[1]

MICHELLE PALMER, A thirty-six-year-old publishing executive
who had been living in Dubai for three years, went to an
all-you-can-eat-and-drink Friday brunch in a posh hotel where
she met Vince Acors, a thirty-four-year-old businessman who was
visiting friends in Dubai. After twelve hours of heavy drinking at
various venues, these Britons strolled onto the beach and began
to fool around. They were stopped by a policeman for kissing in
public and let off with a warning. The same policeman came back
later to supposedly find them having sex. They were arrested.
Allegedly, she called the policeman a 'f****** Muslim ****' and
tried to hit him with her high-heeled shoe. They were found
guilty of having extramarital sex and public indecency, given
three-month jail sentences – later suspended – and then deported.

Needless to say, this episode caused a tabloid sensation both in the UAE and in the UK, spurring headlines like those in *The Sun* (UK), 'Boozed-up brunette banged up for bunk-up in Dubai' and 'Beach cop saw Michelle on top'.[2]

I bring up this story not for its sauciness, but rather for the light it shines on the cultural and social bubble many expatriates live in. This bubble is a consequence of state policy, which defines expatriates as temporary, as interlopers and as outsiders. Essentially, the state has struck an implicit bargain with its professional expatriates – do as you please, within reason, while you build up our economy. (Having sex in Dubai on a public beach, as the reaction at the time of many Britons in the UK and Dubai media seemed to indicate, is not within reason.) The bargain the state strikes with expatriates of other nationalities and class levels varies – for labourers as we saw it is work and remit, for Asian and Arab middle-class workers it is work tax-free and raise children in a better, crime-free environment than you would have in your home countries. For all expatriates, the bottom line is that you can stay in Dubai and live rather nicely, as long as you do not engage in any political activity and you make no claims on the state. (Or have sex on a beach.) Indeed, the trappings of civil society (with the exception of nationality-based clubs) are largely absent by design and by law, not surprisingly as they are democratic forces by their nature. Once again, the idea of impermanence is important here. Expatriate workers in Dubai are largely on temporary, renewable visas, a fact that works to underscore that they are by definition transient, economic mercenaries, not immigrants. That is, you may be *in Dubai*, but you cannot be *of Dubai*. And, for the bulk of expatriates, this is a perfectly fine arrangement.

The stereotype of expatriates globally is of white Westerners sent by their home office on short-term 'hardship' postings in places such as Jakarta, Beijing, Riyadh or Bombay. The stereotype is usually of a man who works at a very high-paying job, complete with villa, golf club membership, luxury automobile and free schooling for the children at an international school. His wife is a 'trailing spouse', who often gives up her career to support her husband's, and as a bonus gets the opportunity to live abroad. While the husband works long hours, her days are given over to coffee with other expatriate wives, shopping and trips to the spa and nail salons, with summers spent back home so the children do not forget from whence they came.

In the past twenty years or so, another type of expatriate has become prominent – the younger, single, temporary migrant (again usually, though not always, white and Western) looking for international work experience and professional advancement, and the adventure of living abroad. They are often recruited in their home country, or, increasingly, go to their destination and search for work there. While there are major differences in outlook and attitude between these two types of expatriate, they both tend to be socially insular, mixing with people 'like themselves' – other white, Western expatriates.

In Dubai, though, white Western expatriates are the minority among the expatriate population. The largest contingent of Westerners is the British, roughly 100,000 strong, the vast majority of whom are of recent vintage. Unlike other cities whose expatriate populations are mainly Western, in Dubai there is greater variation in national origins and class levels of expatriates, with the majority of middle- and upper-middle-class expatriates in Dubai being Asian (mainly Indians with large numbers of Pakistanis, Bangladeshis, Sri Lankans, Filipinos and Indonesians), Arab (Lebanese, Egyptians, Sudanese, Palestinians, Syrians and Jordanians – i.e. those not from oil-producing Gulf states) and Iranian. These non-Western expatriates have been present in large numbers since the first oil boom of the 1970s. Many of them are in Dubai today as a result of restrictive immigration policies post-2001 in the US and elsewhere in the West, but also, and perhaps more importantly, due to the fact that after 9/11 a great degree of Gulf capital, which had been invested overseas, was shifted back to the region. In large part this happened because of the opening up of the real estate market in Dubai in 2002 and the related heating up of Dubai's stock market, which created many local investment opportunities and also created a huge demand for labour at all levels.

Today, Dubai is the temporary home to roughly 150,000 Arab expatriates, and is the city of choice for Arab 'yuppies' (young urban professionals) who find their language skills in high demand in many sectors, including the high-end world of finance. They also find a liberal lifestyle appealing in a place where politics is unimportant, a draw for many.[3] Dubai is also home to another 100,000 or so Iranian immigrants (not counting Iranians who have become naturalized over the years – supposedly one-fourth of the citizen population is of Iranian descent), many of whom have had a big hand in the economic explosion in Dubai, particularly in construction and commerce, and control anywhere from 10 to 30 per cent of real estate projects and have tens of billions of dollars in assets in Dubai (numbers in Dubai, again, are highly speculative).[4] There are also close to 300,000 Filipinos throughout the UAE, mostly in Dubai, though the majority of them work at the lower end of the spectrum of the service sector. Indians account for the largest number of professional expatriates, and roughly one-third are professional white-collar workers.[5] A large number of these are younger professionals, many born and/or raised in Dubai.

* * *

For those who choose to make Dubai their temporary home, they enter into a Faustian bargain, where one gives up certain Western notions of freedom, like voting and democracy. But democracy in the twenty-first century is perhaps an overrated concept, and other notions of freedom may supersede political ones. At a friend's house early in my stay, I suggested that not having a democracy, not having certain civil liberties such as free speech might pose a problem. My friend's mother became indignant. She said, 'Look at India, where I come from. You call that democracy? What is your vote worth? Corruption is spread throughout the government and bureaucracy. No, I prefer it here.' I asked her if she had any fear that one day the authorities might say, 'OK, you may go now.' She grew even more annoyed and said loudly, 'No! They would never. We live here quite well. We love it here.' And she and her family do. They have lived in Dubai for more than thirty years, their business has thrived and they have become quite wealthy, and own a freehold villa in one of the poshest neighbourhoods in Dubai.

The freedom that people have living in Dubai is largely economic, as workers and consumers. When my friend's mother says they live in Dubai quite well, she means that their business can operate without a great deal of bureaucratic interference, their living standards are high, and they do not have day to day worries that the secret police are watching (though they very well might be). Like my friend's mother, expatriates for the most part are uninterested in democracy so long as they are living well.

The idea of living 'quite well' means different things to expatriates of different class levels and nationalities, and has been facilitated by the economic boom in the Gulf in the past decade. For non-Western middle- and upper-middle-class expatriates, Dubai offers the economic and social 'pull' of a Western standard of living without the downsides of the West, which for many equates with crime, drugs, social isolation and a sense that Western societies are generally too permissive. Equally import- ant are 'push' factors in their home countries, where upward mobility and business opportunities are often blocked due to reasons typical in developing countries, such as discrimination, lack of connections, heavy bureaucratic red tape, graft and so on. Political unrest at home, in countries such as Lebanon, Palestine, Pakistan, Iran and Somalia (among many others), also acts as a push for people to migrate to Dubai. The fact that it is getting more difficult in many ways to get to countries that in the recent past were more inviting to immigrants – especially the US, the UK, Canada and Australia – makes Dubai a logical choice, even more so than other Gulf states given the more open lifestyle choices that Dubai makes possible. One Egyptian professional summed up the push and pull factors to being in Dubai simply when he said, 'The Arabs have a future here. Where are we going to go back to? Egypt? Jordan? This is the future.'[6]

In addition to their own personal interests, people are moti- vated to migrate to support family back home. They earn not simply to maintain and improve their lives in Dubai, but also, like the labourers discussed in the previous chapter, to remit. They remit to maintain family members' lives back home, and they also save to build up their lives once they return to their countries of origin, building houses, paying for private education for their children, starting businesses and of course buying lots of 'stuff'.

It is not simply economic factors that compel people to migrate. Many, especially those young and single, migrate for the reason that they have learned that it is good to migrate; that is, there is a culture of migration in their places of origin that encourages people to migrate. For example, many Mexicans go to the US, Lebanese to the Gulf, and Indians to just about anywhere, as migrants are seen as qualitatively 'better' – they are seen as more enterprising, and, thus, desirable as mates back home.[7] Conversely, those who do not migrate are often seen as lacking drive and thus not desirable as mates. One nineteen-year-old Lebanese girl in Beirut said bluntly, 'The guys that remain in Lebanon are the stupid ones! You start to feel that the men who stay in Lebanon are the ones with no ambition in their work, and so you wonder, why are they still here?'[8]

It is understandable why people would leave developing countries for Dubai – their reasons are similar to why these same sorts of people migrate to Western countries, and Dubai does not need to work too hard to attract them. But the lure for white (and non-white) Western professionals to migrate to Dubai must be greater, and indeed it is. Their salaries are higher than they would earn at home, and across the board higher than those of Arab and Asian migrants for the same kinds of work. In many, if not most industries and firms, differential wages are often paid based on nationality, especially at lower levels of employment. A 2004 survey by *Gulf Business* laid out average wages for various white-collar positions and how they varied by nationality, clearly showing a wage hierarchy across nationality lines in all the Gulf states, in descending order from local Arab, to Westerners, to expatriate Arab and then the lowest paid, Asians (Indians, Pakistanis, Filipinos, etc.).[9] In 2007, *ArabianBusiness.com* conducted a survey of workers in the Gulf states and found similar results. In terms of average pay of professional workers, for example, they found that Indians earned less than half of what Americans earned (USD 45,000 for Indians, USD 96,000 for Americans).[10]

This pay discrepancy, however, is not necessarily the result of direct discrimination or planned wage differentials. For example, a British manager at a media firm told me that the company's budget for salary would determine who they could hire; a larger budget meant they could hire an American or British or Lebanese employee, a smaller budget meant they were likely to hire an Indian. Oftentimes though firms will directly advertise that they want a particular nationality. But, even if they do not come right out and ask, the salaries posted in the job advertisements are a good indication of the nationalities sought. So it not necessarily the case that firms directly discriminate against Asians by paying them less for performing the same work as others, but rather that Western or Arab employees will not work for wages as low as those an Asian will be willing to work for. The end result, though, is the same.

Equally, if not more important than higher incomes, many of these Western expatriates enjoy a level of luxury in their lives above what they experience in their home countries. For one thing, they can employ household help – something few can afford in London or New York City. There is the not-so-trivial lure of year-round sunshine, beaches, water sports and golf, and, of course, the bars and clubs. (It is not accidental that there are so few young, single Western professionals in puritanical Saudi Arabia.) There is also the possibility for many of purchasing luxury property. Further, in terms of professional development, working in the Gulf is now seen as a positive addition to a résumé (CV) – something that was not true until recently.

The good life generally is the big draw for this breed of professional expatriate, even those from non-Western origins. A young Lebanese woman made the point that:

Unrealistic things happen to your mind when you come here. Suddenly, you can make [USD] 5,000 a month. You can get credit so easy, you buy the car of your dreams, you shop and you think it's a great bargain; when you go to dinner, you go to a hotel . . . nowhere else can you live like this.[11]

LIVING IN A BUBBLE: 'HIGH-END' EXPATRIATES

Of the high-end expatriate professionals in Dubai, British expatriates are perhaps the most privileged and certainly the most visible – white upper- and upper-middle-class faces in a sea of Asians, Arabs and Africans – even though they account for a relatively small number of the total population of Dubai. These British residents (along with smaller numbers of other white expatriates from Canada, Australia, South Africa, the US and other Western countries) and their short-term counterparts, British tourists, have acquired a reputation for living in a way that is, to put it mildly, disdainful of local mores, in terms of their dress, their sexual activities, their alcohol consumption and their demeanour generally. Dubai, for all its famed openness towards alcohol and sex and dress, is still a fairly reserved place compared with Western cities. (Even prostitutes in Dubai, whether working the streets or hotels, often dress like shop clerks in other countries.) This should not be surprising given the general social conservatism, at least relative to Westerners, of its population that is mostly comprised of South Asians, Arabs (nationals and expatriates), Iranians, Filipinos, Africans, and so on.

In the wake of the sex-on-the-beach scandal briefly described at the beginning of this chapter, the *Daily Mail* noted the Friday brunch (Friday and Saturday are the weekend days) is the ideal place to observe British expatriates in their social element. A staple of the weekly social calendar of British expatriates in Dubai, these brunches range from sedate and family-friendly to sloppy, drunken affairs. A thirty-one-year-old British property consultant described one particularly excessive brunch at a high-end hotel as starting off 'quite sophisticated, but when it gets going that wears off and the spirit of Magaluf [a decadent area in Majorca] takes hold. People just want to have fun and get absolutely smashed.'[12] It should be noted that Friday early afternoon is also the main public communal Muslim prayer time (akin to Sunday mass). Obviously liquor-fuelled brunches and Friday prayers pose an uneasy social juxtaposition, as alcohol consumption, while legally allowed for non-Muslims in Dubai, is religiously and legally forbidden for Muslims.

The story of Michelle Palmer and Vince Acors highlights the bubble lifestyle of so many Britons in Dubai. This lifestyle has been interestingly documented by Katie Walsh, a British scholar who is one of the few people to closely study the behaviour of British expatriates in Dubai. Her research from 2002 to 2004, at the beginning of the economic boom, focused on recently arrived British expatriates, mostly young, single white professionals (she excluded Asian and black Britons from her study).[13] For one article she wrote, 'It got very debauched, very Dubai', Walsh conducted research in clubs and bars, but not the cosmopolitan clubs that cater to an upscale, young international clientele. Her clubs and bars in Dubai were frequented mostly by white expatriates (British, but also Australians, South Africans and Americans). These places at which the people she studied hung out, with the exception of one club, tend, as she put it, 'not to attract wealthier Asian and Arab transnationals, in contrast to more "ethnically" mixed bars/clubs, such as Sho Cho's'.[14] (Sho Cho is a swank restaurant and bar in the Dubai Marine Beach Resort & Spa, which, incidentally, was the last stop for Michelle Palmer and Vince Acors before they headed to the beach.) Walsh's research subjects, for the most part, preferred the company of others like themselves: young, fairly well-to-do whites. Though, to be fair to the white Britons living in Dubai, many do frequent the cosmopolitan clubs, and many do have an eclectic mix of friends.

For Walsh's Britons, Dubai is a liminal, in-between space, a place where 'real-life' is suspended. She asserts that single British expatriates leave the UK for Dubai to escape the 'domesticated intimacy of couple ties', but, at the same time, are often dissatisfied in Dubai because they see fleeting sexual encounters as their only option since dating, given the transience of the expatriates there, is difficult.[15] Further, her participant observation (the technical social scientific term for 'hanging out') suggested that, 'alcohol consumption amongst single Britons is often excessive', as

> single Britons in Dubai tend to go out more frequently [than in Britain] and throughout the week . . . in comparison to their peers in the UK, they are cash-rich, almost irrespective of their occupation: salaries are tax-free [and] companies might pay an accommodation allowance.[16]

The living arrangements of her Britons further encourage this behaviour. She writes that, 'single expatriates sometimes share large villas and may even live on compounds with several other groups similar in age, factors that encourage spontaneous after-parties'.[17]

For Walsh, then, many young Britons (certainly not all) migrate to Dubai primarily to drink a lot, and have a lot of casual sex. That they live with other young Britons who are interested in drinking and casual sex leads them to do more of both. Young Britons in Dubai are notorious for this kind of behaviour, mostly because they are so public about it, and, as they are white, they tend to stick out in a city where whites are a small privileged minority. Even the British tabloids have picked up on just how excessive many of these expatriates can be, with the *Daily Mail* calling them 'The degenerates of Dubai'.[18] This is not a new story, nor characterization. In a 1990 book, *Expats*, the author noted how a British journalist had called Britons in Dubai 'the cretinous flotsam of British society'.[19]

While the British are the public, sometimes cartoonish face of overindulgence, they are not alone in enjoying the good life, nor are they even numerically dominant among the well-to-do in Dubai. Dubai is home to a very large contingent of upper-middle-class young professional expatriates from a wide variety of nationalities who live their lives similarly, if not to the same degree of excess. Go to any high-end club or bar and what you see is an international yuppie crowd. While the story of drink and sex among Westerners is not particularly surprising, it is one found even among Muslim yuppies. Some young Arab professionals spend their first months in Dubai like freshmen in university in America. Freed from parental and societal constraints and oversight they gain weight, drink to excess (like many of the British) and stay out all night.[20] Hadi, a tall, stunning Dubai-born Palestinian man in his late twenties, put this in perspective for me at a Japanese restaurant/karaoke bar favoured among the younger, well-off expatriate crowd when he said that, like yuppies almost anywhere else, 'we work hard and we play hard'. Just as he said this, a young British woman in a mini-skirt flirted with him briefly and gave him her mobile number.

MIDDLE-CLASS EXPATRIATE FAMILIES

In terms of expatriate living, media attention has focused on either high-end, mostly British expatriates, or low-end hyper-exploited labour, such as construction workers and maids. But arguably the backbone of Dubai's economy since the first oil boom of the 1970s has been South Asian (especially Indian) and Arab middle-class workers and their families. South Asians, and to a lesser degree Arabs, have filled the bulk of lower-, middle- and even upper-level professional functions. They are skilled, educated labour, and are either willing or made to work for wages often significantly less than their Western counterparts, though much higher than they would receive in their home countries. While high-end Western professionals may come and go with economic booms and downturns in the Gulf and their home countries, a larger number of these Asian and Arab expatriate workers and their families tend to be longer term, putting their children in schools and putting down roots, tenuous though they may be. A 1982 article noted that Dubai's many middle-class Indian migrants expected to remain in the Gulf for many years, possibly for their entire working lives.[21] While there are some Westerners who have been in Dubai long term and have raised and schooled their children there, they are in much smaller numbers than South Asians or Arabs.

These families of expatriates come to take advantage of two promises that Dubai makes to them – upward mobility and family living. Upward mobility is more possible for migrants from developing countries in Dubai than in their home countries. While it is possible for labourers to move up, the more common story in Dubai is the upward mobility from educated middle class to upper-middle, or even upper class. For instance, compare the experiences of Ahmed and Ashgar, two brothers from Bombay who came to Dubai in their mid-twenties in the late 1970s on transfer postings from multinational corporations. Ahmed decided to follow other family members to the US while Ashgar decided he liked the family-oriented lifestyle and business opportunities in Dubai. Ahmed went on to live a typical middle-class immigrant existence in the American suburbs – comfortable job, good public schools for the children and the opportunity to send them to professional schools to catapult the children to an upper-middle-class existence. Ashgar, on the other hand, opened up an import firm and became a millionaire and his wife became a prominent lawyer. They hobnob with Bollywood celebrities and own a villa on Palm Jumeirah.

For Asian and Arab expatriate middle-class workers and their families, being in Dubai is generally a 'step up' from where they came from, in the sense of economic opportunities and lifestyle, in a way that it is not for Western expatriates. For expatriates from developing countries, their incomes are far greater and their style and standard of living easier and better in Dubai than at home. For Western expatriates, Dubai is a place for short-term financial and/or professional gain, and a place to try out a different lifestyle – essentially an extended holiday in a foreign but not so different locale where they can also earn money well in excess of what they received back home. But they come knowing they will not stay. For one, they ultimately do not belong in an Arab/Asian city, even with all the luxury amenities it provides. In the end, family, friends and their futures ulti-mately are in the West. Asians and Arabs, however, do not have such orientations. For Indian families, for instance, Dubai is generally welcoming, given that the biggest portion of the city's population is of Indian origin. In fact, many Indians refer to Dubai as the 'best city in India'. Indeed, there are many parts of the city where you are hard pressed to find non-South Asian faces. For Arabs, they find a much more efficient and liveable city than in their countries of origin.

While family may be the reason these expatriates ultimately return to their home countries, it is often family obligations that drove them to Dubai in the first place, the need to support family by leaving them. Many Asian and Arab middle-class expatriates (like working-class expatriates) regularly remit large portions of their salaries, which when converted into their home currencies have much more value than they would for a Westerner remitting (or saving) similar amounts. While they know they must eventually leave Dubai, either to go home or to the West, they are more comfortable staying in Dubai for longer stretches of time. Many have been in Dubai their entire working lives, and have raised their children in Dubai. Many of their adult children, second-generation expatriates, still live and work in Dubai as adults (more on them in the next chapter.) Still, Indians residing in Dubai know that they do not belong, that they cannot stay. Few think of themselves as permanent residents – they envision returning to India, or pushing on to the US, Canada, Australia or the UK.[22] For some, the impetus to return is the mandatory retirement age of sixty. For others, their long-term stays in Dubai are complete when their children finish high school. In any case, no matter how long they are in Dubai, their days by definition are numbered.

Family living in Dubai centres on educational opportunities. While middle-class expatriates, like expatriates of all levels, are there to take advantage of work opportunities and do enjoy the lifestyle, education of the children in Dubai holds a special place of importance. Vinod, an Indian tobacconist raised in Dubai, made this point to me, saying the education of his daughter was paramount to his being in Dubai. While he does not earn much as a tobacconist (just AED 3,000 per month), his wife had moved up the ranks from secretary to manager in a small firm. Her company gave her a housing allowance, and, importantly, subsidized the schooling of their daughter at an Indian-administered, British-curriculum school. If not for that, he told me, he would probably leave Dubai and 'go back' to Mumbai. It is worth noting that he thinks of Mumbai as home, though he has never actually lived there. This is something we will address in the next chapter.

The private educational facilities in Dubai cater to the expatriate communities (only nationals and Arab expatriates can go to the government-run public schools), with curriculum and examinations mirroring those back home – that is, American, British, Indian, Pakistani, Iranian, etc. schools. But school fees have increased dramatically in the past few years as a result of demand outstripping supply, and of increased rents that schools pay. In fact, inflation in the price of education was second only to inflation in the housing market – major factors in the cost of living for expatriates as salaries, while increasing on average, failed to keep up. Until 2007, schools were only allowed to increase fees by 20 per cent over a three-year period. But in 2007 they were allowed to increase fees in that year alone by 16–20 per cent, and fees increased 25 per cent for secondary education and 18 per cent for primary education in 2008.[23] One Indian-administered school had even received permission to raise its fees an astonishing 90 per cent over two years in 2009–10, leading hundreds of parents to publicly protest on the school's grounds, an unprecedented action.[24]

The cost of education to families is heavy. A third of the readers of *Gulf News* – most of whom earn between AED 6,000 and AED 15,000 monthly – spend upwards of AED 6,000 per month for school fees for their children.[25] As a result, many lower- and middle-income families are sending their children home for school, and many families are leaving Dubai altogether. The Dubai Chamber of Commerce and Industry found an 'unusually low' number of children between the ages of ten to nineteen in Dubai, especially among Asians, for whom the relative cost of education has grown much higher than at home. Related to this, the number of available places in schools is shrinking, forcing parents who otherwise might be able to afford schooling children in Dubai to rethink their options.[26] In 2009, the number of workers leaving Dubai – and with them their children – was set to increase even more dramatically due to people losing their jobs, and therefore their visas. Also, the government was about to increase the minimum salary required to keep one's family in Dubai from AED 6,000 to AED 10,000 per month, which would mean a huge portion of workers from India, Pakistan, the Philippines and other developing world countries would have to send their families home. Even those families who could afford to stay were beginning to send their children home for school. The combination of these factors looks likely to greatly reduce the number of children in Dubai's schools.

WHERE THEY LIVE

The chapter to this point has told the story of those who live in Dubai, and how they occupy themselves. This section looks at a critical aspect of living in Dubai that expands on a discussion from the previous chapter – where expatriates live and under what conditions. As Katie Walsh (whose work we discussed earlier in the chapter) rightly notes regarding British expatriates, their living arrangements tell us a lot about their lifestyles. At the top are the wealthiest of the expatriates who live in luxurious villas in posh neighbourhoods such as Jumeirah, Palm Jumeirah, Emirates Hills and Arabian Ranches. The British housewives in such areas have acquired the derisive moniker 'Jumeirah Janes' for their haughty attitudes and leisure lifestyles. As they have expanded into other residential areas, newer terms have been coined, such as Satwa Sallys, Mirdif Marys and Mollies and Marina Cinderellas. Walsh adds that the term 'Jumeirah Jane' implies other characteristics, such as a dependence on prescription anti-depressants, plastic surgery, or the sexual and emotional attention of a personal trainer or tennis coach . . . non-working expatriate wives are [stereotyped as] shallow, materialistic, status-conscious, vain, lazy, and neglect their children by leaving them with their maid.[27]

While this stereotype, like most stereotypes, tends towards gross exaggeration, it reflects the social disconnect of these women (there is no corresponding term for the husbands). They are highly visible, seen in malls, on the road in SUVs and in cafes, but remain socially aloof. Most importantly for the stereotype, they live apart from the non-upper class, often in gated communities, which they share with wealthy non-Westerners. Supposedly the American-style gated community is one of Sheikh Mohammed's prized Western imports.[28]

Returning yet again to the sex-on-the-beach story, we can see how living arrangements play a critical role for social life among the young professionals who have not attained the social or economic status of the Jumeirah Janes and their husbands. Walsh describes how the sharing of villas and flats, combined with excess cash among Britons of similar age and partying proclivity lends itself to debauched behaviour. Indeed, the mansion that Vince Acor's friends lived in (it is massive, as the photo accompanying the *Daily Mail* article demonstrates) was dubbed the 'Playboy Mansion'.[29]

This villa lifestyle, however, is coming to an end. In 2007, the government enacted a ban on unrelated people sharing villas, which they went about enforcing even more stringently in 2008. An Indian friend in public relations told me she had been living in a villa with four other British and South African young women who were all evicted in 2007. Luckily for her, shortly before they were evicted she had moved out into her own studio flat for the very reasonable price of AED 70,000 per year (USD 1,600 per month – my mortgage payment on a two-bedroom apartment in Brooklyn, NYC!). A year later, her flat would rent for AED 85,000.

The sharing of villas and flats is often out of choice, but also out of necessity. For one, it is very expensive to live in Dubai, so, unless one's company provides housing outright or gives a generous housing allowance, it is difficult for a single person, or even a couple or a family, to live by themselves. Further, landlords often demand the rent for the entire year paid up front, which often requires individuals to take out bank loans to pay their rent. The rapid increase in rents, which in many neighbourhoods had doubled, even tripled, in the period from 2004 to 2008, has led Dubai to become one of the most expensive global cities to live in. It reached the point where one report found Dubai's rental costs in 2007 to be on a par with Geneva, one of the most expensive cities in Europe.[30] A 2009 survey put Dubai as the twentieth most expensive city in the world, in spite of rent caps put in place in Dubai from 2006 through 2009.[31] This led to parallel rental markets – one for existing tenants and one for new tenants. Many landlords got around the issue of the rent caps by not renewing leases, often speciously claiming they needed the flat for personal use or saying the building was to be demolished (common, especially for older buildings in neighbourhoods such as Karama, a mostly Indian area with many lower- and middle-income residents). Once the old tenant left, the landlord was free to rent at any price the market would bear. The effect of rising rents has been that people are either spending much larger portions of their incomes on rent (many companies who paid housing allowances started cutting back on this expenditure), some move out of the city altogether to Sharjah or other emirates, and some have no choice but to find shared accommodation in flats. While rents had dropped dramatically in many areas in 2009, they were still unaffordable to many, and still higher than in the middle years of the decade.

The sharing of flats for the moment is still legal, and given economic realities, quite necessary. As with villas, many young professionals choose to share flats for the social aspect, a common practice in Western cities as well. Often, also as with villas, these flats will be shared by nationality. For instance, one flat I went to see was shared by three young, hip Lebanese fellows in their twenties. I responded to their advertisement for a flatmate, but they felt I was too old and did not quite fit their lifestyle. (I was thirty-seven at the time with a wife and child back in Brooklyn. While I do not think of myself as a complete social outcast, I have to admit that, yes, I was not cool enough, and certainly not young enough for them.)

Not all young professionals segregate themselves by nationality. Shariq, a Pakistani-British man in his early thirties had sublet a few flats in the Golden Sands block in the Bur Dubai area that he himself was renting. Essentially, he ran them as hostels, renting bed spaces and also small bedrooms to young professionals in their twenties looking for (relatively) cheap rent. I went to apply for a room and had to go through an interview process with a few of his international boarders (among them were a Sudanese, a Briton and a Fijian). While I thought my interview went nicely, Shariq regretted to inform me that the general feeling was that I was too 'posh'. Again, my age and being married with a child worked against me.

While the sharing of flats has a lifestyle dimension to it, nearly all expatriates who share flats do so out of economic compulsion, even those with relatively high incomes. While some would enjoy being in a more fun and social living environment, in the end it is often the need to find cheap housing quickly that drives people. They find their flats quickly online, through the classified advertisements of local newspapers, or through postings in supermarkets or even in telephone booths and on walls throughout many neighbourhoods. Since they have no tenancy contract, they often end up shifting flats many times within a year, as landlords and agents routinely raise rents. Even if they are willing and able to pay rent for an entire flat, many landlords and real estate companies refuse to rent flats to bachelors, especially South Asians, thus compelling them to find rooms or bed space in shared flats.

I ultimately found my flat through an advertisement in a local newspaper. My 'landlord' was Joseph, an Egyptian-American from Brooklyn who had a distinctive Brooklyn-Italian accent (due to growing up in Bensonhurst, a heavily Italian neighbourhood). Like Shariq, Joseph sublet rooms in multiple flats in the Bur Dubai area that he rented in his own name. He had been in Dubai all of three years and had become successful in the real estate game, charging transient workers a premium to have a room in a shared flat in luxury buildings with gymnasiums and swimming pools. My flatmates initially were a thirty-something white South African male on a six-month posting with an advertising firm, a mid-fifties white American male who never spoke to me, and two chain-smoking Pakistani junior bankers in their mid-twenties who shared the living room. In the four months I was living in this flat, the two white men moved on, to be replaced by a Turkish, American-green-card-holding architect and a Lebanese consultant doing business in Afghanistan, both in their thirties. I estimated that the rent Joseph was paying on the flat, given prices at that time, was AED 90,000 per year. I did not know how much the others paid (I paid AED 3,800 per month), but assuming the five of us paid an average of AED 4,000 each per month Joseph was getting AED 240,000 per year. Since he paid nothing for repairs or maintenance, he pocketed a profit of AED 150,000 per year. Also, as he had at least three flats (he was looking for more), he was 'earning' a handsome sum. Nice work, I thought at the time.

It is not only bachelors who share flats; even families are forced to share accommodation. Renting rooms to bachelors is one very common way to ease the financial pinch. Often multiple families share flats. One Filipino hotel worker lived with his wife in a three-bedroom flat in Satwa that they shared with two other couples, an arrangement that for them was only made possible because their employers gave them a housing allowance.[32] Without this housing subsidy, many white-collar workers in general would not be able to afford to rent in Dubai, no matter the sharing arrangement.

But a proposed restriction on the sharing of flats (along with the raising of the minimum income requirement for families) may lead to lower-income families in Dubai becoming an endangered species. In 2008 the Dubai Naturalisation and Residency Department announced that the renewal of residency visas for families was to be determined by deciding if the size of the family's accommodation matched the size of the family; for instance, an inappropriate accommodation would be a family living in a studio flat.[33] If this proposal were to be enacted, many families would have to move to other emirates (which would further drive up rental prices in those areas), or the workers would have to send their families home, or entire families would have to leave altogether.

GO HOME?

The rapid expansion of Dubai's population during the economic boom led to a dramatic situation where wages for the bulk of the middle class rose substantially but failed to keep up with price inflation in housing and education, as well as in other basics such as groceries and taxi rides. Inflation hit expatriates especially hard in terms of their remittances and savings. As the dirham is pegged to the dollar, and as the dollar was especially weak against other currencies such as the UK pound and Indian rupee, the value of remittances and savings converted in the home country currencies decreased substantially. (This issue of the decreasing value of remittances was the backdrop to many of the strikes described in the last chapter.) The housing situation especially reached a stage that could, without being hyperbolic, be described as dire. While higher-end professionals had to rethink luxuries such as beach club memberships and restaurant outings, lower-end bachelors were forced to rethink living in Dubai altogether.

A near-perfect storm of linked events had led to a situation where lower-end workers and their families were being pushed from Dubai. First, all the construction projects in Dubai are luxury developments, and no new affordable housing was being built. Second, what affordable housing there was rapidly disappeared as landlords dramatically increased rents, in spite of rent caps to protect tenants. The arrival of legions of Western professionals in 2007–8 who fell victim to the downturns in the construction, real estate and finance industries in the US and the UK further intensified the process of rental inflation. Third, entire older buildings in neighbourhoods such as Karama and Al Qusais were being torn down with little advance notice given to residents. Tenants who were paying incredibly low rents of, for instance, AED 12,000 yearly for a two-bedroom flat suddenly had to find accommodation at market rates – which for similar sized flats would be closer to AED 100,000. A further exacerbation of the inflated housing market is the destruction of much of the neighbourhood of Satwa, between Jumeirah and Bur Dubai, which is one of the few affordable areas left in Dubai and houses large numbers of Filipino and Indian bachelors and families. *Time Out Dubai* estimated that close to 100,000 people were going to be evicted to make way for the Jumeirah Garden City luxury development, though at the last minute the neighbourhood received a reprieve as the economic bust caused the plans to be put on hold.[34]

While expenses increased dramatically for residents – expatriates and nationals both – across the board, these were merely nudges and hints to reconsider living in Dubai. But in late 2008, partially due to the global economic meltdown and partially due to the incredible overheating in the local property market, Dubai's economic miracle came to a grinding halt. Elsewhere in the world, this meant that as industries suffered hits, jobs were lost. The same situation presented itself in Dubai, but with one major difference: losing your job means losing your right to reside in Dubai. Tens of thousands of jobs were cut, especially in construction and finance, including in government-owned firms. The Filipino population, estimated at 4.3 per cent of the entire UAE population shrunk by 20 per cent in 2008.[35] Swiss bank UBS's research estimated that Dubai could lose up to 8 per cent of its population in 2009, as close to half of Dubai's population is employed in construction and real estate. They estimated that 20 per cent of workers in those sectors alone could lose their jobs.[36] A later estimate predicted Dubai's population would contract by 17 per cent.[37]

As bleak as this may be for those who lose their jobs, and hence must leave Dubai, there is a silver lining in this black recessionary cloud for those who held on to their jobs – rents plummeted in Dubai in 2009, in some areas by almost half of what they were in 2008, at the height of the boom.

* * *

The 'gilded cage' of the subtitle is a direct reference to these middle-class and professional workers and their families in

Dubai. I have argued that their insular social behaviour, lifestyles and living conditions are a direct result of the temporary visa system, that no matter how long an expatriate lives and works in Dubai, he or she, like the labourers discussed in the previous chapter, is just a factor of production. What sweetens the pot for the middle class and professionals is the enticement of a quality of social and economic life that the state allows expatriates to have, something perhaps unavailable in a similar quantity or quality back home. Essentially, these people are little more than economic mercenaries. Their lives, almost by definition, are oriented to their own enjoyment (and that of their families), as civic participation is largely frowned upon and political activity, broadly defined, is illegal.

The next chapter looks at a subset of the people examined in this chapter – second-generation, born in Dubai expatriates. They provide an interesting case study. Born in Dubai, but holding passports of a country they may not even have seen, they are betwixt and between, not Emirati, nor socially of their countries of passport. We consider how the legally imposed state of temporariness affects the ways they go about living their lives.

CHAPTER FIVE

GUESTS IN THEIR OWN HOMES

My friend Wilbur had come from New York City to visit me while I was doing research in Dubai. We went to dinner at a swank restaurant in the Madinat Jumeirah mall, a fake Arab *souk* complete with non-functional, traditional wind towers. We met up with Vishul, a thirty-something analyst who was born in India and raised in Dubai but had studied and worked in the US for almost ten years before returning. Wilbur asked Vishul where he was from, to which Vishul answered, 'Delhi.' 'Delhi?' I said, taken aback since we had known each other for a few months and this was the first I heard that he thought of himself as not from Dubai. Vishul clarified, 'Well, Delhi, and I live in Dubai.'

Vishul's answer – I'm from Delhi and live in Dubai – is telling in that it illustrates a basic dilemma of expatriate workers, especially those born and/or raised in Dubai, that they are legally and socially not 'Dubaian'. They may live in Dubai, but, largely as a result of this exclusion, they usually do not consider themselves 'of Dubai'.

Legally, as a distinct category, second-generation expatriates do not exist. Like any other expatriate, they are in Dubai on three-year, renewable residency visas; some even live and work illegally in Dubai on tourist visas. These expatriates acquire no additional rights or benefits from being born in Dubai. No matter how long they and their families have been in Dubai, there is little chance of attaining citizenship, and there is no such category as legal permanent residence. A child born in Dubai has the nationality and passport, by default, of their parents. In fact, the visa system is so strict that a child born to a national woman with an expatriate father is considered an expatriate, though a child born to a national father with an expatriate mother is a national. Dubai's economic and social system rests upon this structural instability (or flexibility – I guess that is a matter of perspective), the fact that, no matter how long you have been in Dubai, you are treated like anyone else coming in today. You have no *right* to be there and you have no *inalienable rights*; you are there at the pleasure of the government, and they can revoke your *privilege* of staying there at any time.

To reinforce to expatriates how tenuous their status in Dubai is, the visa and work permit systems in Dubai, indeed in all the Gulf states, do not recognize the bonds of adult male children to their parents (women can stay on a parent's or husband's visa without having to get a labour permit binding them to their employer). What this means is that a boy who turns eighteen is no longer on his parent's visa; he can be sponsored by a school, but otherwise needs to be working and on a labour permit. The legal and social limbo that second-generation expatriates in Dubai find themselves in is an unintended consequence of the 'original sin' of their expatriate fathers and mothers, who nearly all came for better working conditions and family living, only to raise children who do not belong in Dubai, who cannot claim to be of Dubai, and yet are socially foreigners in their countries of passport.

THE POSSIBILITY OF CITIZENSHIP

To fully understand the precarious situation of expatriates in Dubai, and the ways in which their identities and migratory behaviour are structured, we must discuss just how unlikely citizenship is, and the degrees to which people fear banishment and deportation. To stay in Dubai permanently, an expatriate must acquire citizenship. Citizenship in practice, though, is very difficult to acquire, even for Arab expatriates. In the past, the UAE was somewhat open to granting citizenship, mainly to Arabs (including Sudanese) and Iranians, though some Pakistanis and Indians have also received citizenship. From the time of independence in 1971 through 1997, about 50,000 people had been naturalized, roughly 8 per cent of the citizen population.[1] In recent years it has been a de facto state policy in the UAE (and in the Gulf states generally) to reduce the granting of citizenship to expatriates.

Citizenship, when granted, is qualified. Naturalized citizens do not automatically become nationals – they generally do not possess nationality cards that are given to Arab families, and thus are not eligible for government benefits such as free education, land grants, housing, direct cash payments and other welfare benefits, though they do acquire UAE passports. Naturalization is contingent, and can be revoked, as can UAE passports (as one Jordanian expatriate told me how her aunt's was confiscated).

The requirements to be considered for citizenship are often thought to include thirty years' residence, being Muslim, Arab and an Arabic speaker, and having a clean police record, 'proper' academic qualifications and a 'healthy' bank balance – though it is at the government's discretion to give citizenship after a screening process, at which point personal influence (*wasta*) comes into play.[2]

While most expatriates I asked told me some version of the above, it is unclear whether this procedure is actually codified. Even government officials seem uncertain of the policy regarding naturalization. For example, in 2005 the director of the Dubai Naturalisation and Residency Department (DNRD) announced that expatriates *of any nationality* living in Dubai for twenty years would be eligible to apply for passports, and, if granted, would be issued a document that would allow them to be treated as UAE nationals.[3] The following day, the director retracted his statement, tersely saying about the issuance of passports, 'such matters are beyond the purview of the DNRD'.[4] One month later, the UAE Minister of Labour and Social Affairs proposed granting UAE citizenship to expatriates of 'high calibre' and 'highly skilled professionals' who could be key contributors to national development. The minister was quoted as saying, 'Why don't we avail [ourselves] of highly skilled professionals for our economy needs. We should attract them and even grant them nationality to benefit from their high qualifications.'[5] But in late 2007 the same minister ruled out any possibility of expatriates being awarded citizenship, no matter how long they have been in the UAE. Again, expatriates in the UAE are considered contractual workers, not immigrants. The minister's adviser emphasized this point, saying, 'That is the whole reason contractual labour laws are used, so workers fall under contractual law rather than immigration law.'[6]

While I was in Dubai, I met only one person, Hasan, a businessman in his mid-thirties, who had acquired citizenship, though some of the Arab expatriates I interviewed had family or friends who had received citizenship. Hasan was naturalized in

2003, along with his entire Sunni Arab Iranian family. Like other expatriates, his life was shaped by the conditions of the three-year visa, which changed when he became a citizen. He said,

> You know, I grew up here all this time knowing I was an expatriate. My dad never told us to prepare for citizenship, it just happened . . . I think what changed was subconscious: sense of security, a sense of living in this place and wanting to contribute to its long-term prosperity.

Hasan told me that, if he had not received citizenship, 'I think I would've moved. In fact, I actually immigrated to Canada, but then I never stayed. I landed and came back.'

While there are no publicly available records, it is unlikely that many who are eligible to be considered for citizenship get it. For Hasan, *wasta* (influence) eventually led to the family acquiring citizenship. Even with *wasta*, it takes time – his father lobbied his connections for nearly ten years. Others though, while 'qualified', are not so fortunate. I interviewed two Arab expatriates in their mid-twenties whose fathers had both worked in government ministries for almost thirty years. These two, Zaid (a Syrian) and Hussein (an Egyptian), also work in government ministries, though at low-level positions as clerks (neither has a university degree). Both their families have had their applications for citizenship under consideration for twenty years. They both held faint hope that they would acquire citizenship anytime soon, something they both desperately wanted.

The most commonly stated reasons given by government officials for denying citizenship, or even permanent residence, are the threats of cultural extinction and demographic imbalance posed by the possibility of absorbing so many expatriates into the pool of citizens. These twinned arguments have been repeatedly advanced over the years as the main reasons to deny expatriates any kind of permanent residency.[7] However, there are two major factors that are critical to the government's stance on naturalization which are left unstated, but which are central to the management of expatriates in Dubai. First, the government's legitimacy depends to a great degree on its ability to guarantee a high standard of living to nationals.[8] Allowing expatriates to become naturalized might lead to the state having to spread its welfare largesse among a much larger pool of recipients. Secondly, the three-year visa system provides a simple and effective mechanism of social control over expatriates. The system as it stands requires all expatriates to have a sponsor, their employer, for their visas, and is a particularly effective threat that works well to keep all levels of expatriates in line.

For the vast majority of second-generation expatriates I interviewed, citizenship is a non-issue. They accept, however grudgingly, their second-class status in Dubai. They live their lives in a place where they are always in a liminal or in-between state, where their existence is defined by a permanent condition of legal and social precariousness. And these expatriates for the most part are comfortable with this.

FEAR OF BANISHMENT

As a means of social control, the three-year visa system works effectively through the possibility that the visa may be revoked. There are two main fears that all expatriates must at some level consider: being summarily deported, and not being allowed to remain in Dubai when they get older. The fear of not being able to stay in Dubai when they get old is a concern of second-generation expatriates, as there are few elderly expatriates in Dubai.

The one reality all expatriates must face is compulsory retirement at age sixty. When an expatriate reaches this age, he is no longer issued a three-year work permit and residency visa. He can apply for a shorter one- or two-year visa, but these are issued on a case-by-case basis, or he can stay if he owns a company. This restriction on the issuance of visas past the age of sixty necessarily affects how people see their relation to Dubai. John, a European-Canadian expatriate in his late twenties working in his father's construction company, said simply, 'In all honesty, no one expects to retire here; everyone expects to go where they're from.'

While the possibility of not having their visas renewed past the age of sixty is not immediately pressing for the second-generation expatriates themselves, as the oldest person I interviewed was thirty-seven, it was pertinent for their parents. A few of the parents of people I interviewed had already gone back to their home countries, and a few more had migrated to Western countries permanently. Others were reaching the point where they had to decide in a short time where they wanted to go. Still others were able to postpone this decision indefinitely as they were investors in companies, and eligible to stay in Dubai on that basis, or had been granted special permission by the government to continue working on shorter-term visas.

The possibility they one day might be made to leave Dubai before they reach retirement age is one that most people I spoke with acknowledged, but, as a practical issue, surprisingly few were troubled. Manoj, an Indian entrepreneur in his mid-thirties, put it this way:

I don't know what difference it's going to make in your day to day life, you know? Even permanent residency can be . . . I mean this is not a democracy . . . what difference is that going to make?

While many people expressed nonchalant views similar to Manoj, others were more apprehensive about the possibility of deportation. For example, Prince, an Indian corporate headhunter in his early twenties, said he doesn't live in Dubai, but, rather, is 'squatting'. He said he always felt uneasy,

> simply because you don't know what can happen tomorrow, simply because the nationals run this place, and what they say is law. You can't live in a country knowing in some sort of subconscious level that you aren't safe here. I don't mean that you are going to be mugged in the street. It's that you can't make this your home.

The reality of deportation in Dubai is that it happens frequently enough that it shapes people's behaviour – they are more cautious about staying out of trouble with the police, they make certain not to engage in behaviour that might look political, and they avoid criticism of the ruling family and nationals in general. But I was surprised to find during the course of my research how people took the possibility of deportation in their stride. This is largely because deportation is often not permanent. People routinely overstay visas, lose their jobs or fail to get 'no objection certificates' from their employers when changing jobs. All of these can lead to temporary deportations and bans, but, once they have left, they can reapply for a visa. John casually made the point that, 'You can get banned for six months, but you can still come back on a visit visa. It's normal for people who live out here. Especially from our generation.' I asked him if he ever feared being deported, and he said, 'No, we've never really been worried about it.'

Whether or not these expatriates feared deportation, they were quite cognizant that the laws are often applied in an ad hoc manner, not surprising given that the UAE is a kingdom, a young country, and has a still developing legal system. This works to create carefully managed attitudes towards impermanence in the minds of workers. They are always mindful of what they say; this is especially true for expatriates from developing countries.

RELATIONS WITH NATIONALS

I went to an Iranian restaurant on the busy main street in Satwa at three in the morning with my friend Thomas, as we were unable to find anywhere to smoke *sheesha* at that hour. He ordered for us and had a long conversation with the waiter, who was a bit thrown that he was not a national, and was impressed with how he spoke Arabic with an Emirati accent. I was impressed that Thomas spoke Arabic at all as he was the only second-generation non-Arab expatriate I had met who had any competency with the Arabic language.

Thomas is an Indian Catholic in his early thirties, and has had experiences with nationals that were unique for any expatriate, especially an Indian, and are worth recounting in detail:

> I assimilated into the [Emirati] Arab culture when I was twelve. My best friends were my Arab friends. For two years, I only hung out with Arabs. I wore Arab clothing, I would go to Arab functions, I would celebrate all the Arab holidays. I would spend weekends at my Arab friends' houses, I would eat with their parents . . . I flew falcons in the desert, I went hunting – these are things that very few people outside the Arab community could or would have ever done . . . The reason why [many people think nationals are] not cultured is that they've never been invited inside the Arab community. And that was just a stroke of luck. Typically I wouldn't

have been either. Just because I moved to Jumeirah [in the 1980s] and hung out with Arab guys who I became friends with, who were like, 'Come over, play board games with me.' Slowly you eat lunch with them, slowly you go away for a picnic with the family one weekend, you know. Before you know it, you're in. And that's where the culture is. People think that when they come to Dubai, they're going to see culture like, 'Oh, I'm going to see old buildings, I'm going to see how glass was made, like in Syria.' No, there is none of that culture here, and there never will be. The culture here is within the community, the interactions and experiences you have with the local people.

When talking of assimilation, or in this case, non-assimilation, we must define our reference point – to what culture/people might these immigrants be assimilating? Dubai presents an interesting and opposite case to most places where people migrate to: the Emirati national citizen population is a small minority who are under siege from an ever-increasing foreign majority, and find that their culture is diminishing in importance in public spaces.

This 'siege mentality' of nationals has heightened as a result of the post-2001 economic and population boom in Dubai, leading many nationals to withdraw socially and geographically from expatriates. However, this was not always the case. John, the European-Canadian expatriate working in his father's business, pointed out how relations between expatriates and nationals had changed. He said,

Even running around in the desert near our places we used to hang out with the local kids. But now if you hang out with local people it's probably business . . . Back in those days, there were loads of tents everywhere; they'd just welcome you. 'Come in, sit down.' All the locals offered you food, so welcoming. That doesn't really exist anymore, because there's so many expatriates out here, they [nationals] have started to shut themselves off. So that culture existed back then, it was great, it was really nice.

Arab expatriates, not surprisingly, often had close relations with nationals, as did many Westerners. Part of this is due to lack of cultural distance – Arab expatriates share language, religion and other common cultural traits. Part of this is due to social equality – Westerners (read whites, especially British and Americans) are at the top of Dubai's status hierarchy with nationals, with expatriate Arabs not far below.

Two Arab expatriates I interviewed who had the closest relations with nationals were Zaid and Hussein, the Syrian and Egyptian expatriates I discussed above. Both were in very similar situations. They were in their early twenties, both working for government ministries, and both wore the *khandoura*, or *dish-dasha* as it is often called, the long robe favoured by Emirati and other Gulf Arab men, which young men often wear with baseball caps. Zaid and Hussein felt themselves to be fully invested in Emirati society – most of their friends were nationals, and they spoke Arabic with an Emirati accent. Their fathers had both worked in government ministries for most of their adult lives. Both said they would not mind marrying into an Emirati family, or having their sisters marry into Emirati families, except that their relatively low economic position (both earned roughly AED 4,000 per month [USD 1,090], far less than half what a local would earn in the same position) made the prospect of marriage nearly impossible for the near future. While they dressed and spoke like nationals, and in spite of cultural traits they shared with nationals, they were in fact not nationals. They were merely expatriates.

Almost all the other Arabs I interviewed had some degree of social relations with nationals, though none were as socially immersed as Zaid and Hussein. While they may have had friendly relations with nationals, it seemed not to go much beyond that, unless they marry into national families. For instance, Noor, a twenty-five-year-old Jordanian expatriate whose uncle (one of the first Arab doctors in Dubai) received citizenship in the 1970s (unlike her own father), said all her cousins, second-generation citizens, are like nationals and even married to nationals. Noor, on the other hand, by her own reckoning, is not like a national, and she faces the same issues resulting from impermanence that every other expatriate faces. Formal, legal citizenship, then, is important. At the end of the day, no matter how close they may be with nationals, expatriates are still just expatriates.

Though nationals may have accepted some Arab and European expatriates into their social world, most Indians never feel that invitation. Thomas thought there was a lack of confidence on the part of Indian expatriates, that they interacted with nationals with fear. This is not surprising given the social imbalance between nationals and Indians, who mostly occupy lower rungs on the employment ladder, though many, including the bulk of parents of expatriates I interviewed had high-level occupations or were successful entrepreneurs. Deepak, an Indian in his late twenties in the insurance sector, and son of one such high-level expatriate, reflecting on this social gulf said, 'We just looked at them [nationals] from a distance . . . I don't think they really liked foreigners, and I don't think they were genuinely rude, but . . . [they treated] Indians like servants.'

Looking at the experience of immigrants globally, it is not unusual to have limited social experience with 'natives'. But, in Dubai, it is the norm that Indians generally have nearly no social engagement with nationals beyond business and bureau-cratic dealings. Thomas and Deepak were the only South Asian expatriates, including Muslim South Asians, I interviewed who had any social engagement with nationals at all, unlike Arab expatriates. At first glance this seems sensible: Arab expatriates and nationals share many customs, religion (though many Arab Christians have good relations with nationals) and language. However, there is a great deal of cultural affinity between nationals and Indians as a result of a long historical relationship. Many nationals are conversant in Urdu, are fluent in Indian cultural forms through a history of business and other dealings predating the discovery of oil, and have a love of Bollywood films. So, then, it is not culture per se that links Arab expatriates and nationals and distances Indians expatriates from nationals, but rather an historical, demographic and social progression that leads to the boundaries between Arabs and nationals being blurred, and between Indians and nationals being more defined. These differences reflect the fact that Arab expatriates rank higher in the local status hierarchy than Indians. Interestingly, I found in my interviews that this social gulf between Indians and nationals was not present to the same degree between Indian and Arab expatriates, who socialized with each other more easily. This makes sense as Dubai-born Indian and Arab expatriates share the most important identity marker in Dubai: a state of temporariness.

An interesting in-between case is that of Hajira, a Somali nurse in her late twenties. She went to government schools with local girls, and many of her best friends were nationals. Even though she was not a native Arabic speaker, she was classified as Arab and thus eligible for public schools, though she had to pay school fees, whereas schooling was free for nationals. She said she preferred nationals as friends to other Arabs. But she felt a rift develop between her and her local friends after the first Gulf War. In the late 1990s, after she graduated school and did her nursing programme, and worked as a nurse, she saw further tensions develop over what she saw as discriminatory practices that rewarded local girls for simply being local. As an adult, her social relations with nationals had ceased.

While many expatriates had social relations with nationals in the pre-2001 economic and population boom, today these ties seem to be waning, as John pointed out above, in part due to demographic shifts, in part due to geographical segregation as many nationals move out of neighbourhoods like Jumeirah and Bur Dubai, where they lived near expatriates, to neighbourhoods in the further reaches of the city with low concentrations of expatriates, or even out of the city altogether.[9] Essentially, nationals increasingly define themselves as Emirati and distance themselves from all expatriates, including other Arabs and other Muslims, as the expatriate population explodes.

WHAT IS HOME?

One question that I asked almost everyone I interviewed was 'Why are you here?' It is a simple question, but a loaded one. It assumes that you need a reason to be in the place you live. I would never ask that question of someone born to immigrant parents in New York City or London for the simple reason that it is obnoxious and assumes the person somehow does not belong there. But for expatriates who have been in Dubai all their lives it is a perfectly reasonable question to ask, as they are, by definition, transients.

Scholars of assimilation typically examine relations between immigrants and 'nationals' whose families have been there for generations, as I briefly did in the previous section. The purpose of examining this dynamic is to act as a measure of assimilation, by which most scholars mean the degree to which immigrants identify with and are accepted by the nationals, or 'host society'.[10] My reading of this is that the idea of host society is a stand-in for the concept of home. The question of assimilation then is, how do you fit into your home, the place where you live?

But 'home' and 'host society' are not necessarily the same thing. For example, in a study of second-generation immigrants in New York City, researchers found that many of these young adults thought of themselves as New Yorkers without necessarily identifying themselves as being of their parents' nationality or as 'American'.[11] They are not New Yorkers in the sense of New Yorkers who are also 'native' Americans. They are a new and distinct breed entirely, not necessarily 'American' nor of their parents' place, but rather uniquely made in New York.

In Dubai, I found a similar dynamic. Many second-generation expatriates define themselves as Dubaian because they live in Dubai, grew up in Dubai, and have a feeling that it is their place, contradicting the official interpretation of expatriates as guest workers and thus temporary foreigners. In the government's view, only local citizens are Dubaians; the rest are interlopers who cannot claim Dubai as their home. Indeed, as I pointed out above, these expatriates are legally invisible, in the sense that they gain no benefits or recognition for having been born in Dubai. This necessarily affects how expatriates will view Dubai.

Dubai is home

It is a very bold statement for an expatriate to say definitively that Dubai is home. These people are certain their tenure in Dubai will be permanent. Likewise, they are equally certain about their relationship to their country of passport: they know they do not or cannot belong there.

Acquiring citizenship, as I discussed above, is the most defini-
tive way to cement Dubai's status as your home. Citizenship ties
Hasan, the Iranian who became naturalized, to Dubai. He immediately felt a sense of security and a desire to contribute to
Dubai's benefit. While his is a kind of second-class citizenship –
in that he is not eligible for welfare largesse from the state – he
feels a connection to Dubai; he is a Dubaian even though he has
little in the way of relations with nationals beyond business and
bureaucratic dealings, does not dress like a national and does not
even speak Arabic.

Citizenship, however, is not necessarily the ultimate basis of
feeling attached to a place. Many expatriates I interviewed felt
more than just that they lived in Dubai, but that they deserved
to remain there. A common sentiment/question among many
second-generation expatriates was, 'How can I be considered a
foreigner when I have lived here and contributed as much or
more than nationals?'

On a second-generation expatriate's blog, I asked somewhat
seriously, somewhat tongue-in-cheek, 'How do you deal with a
place that treats you as disposable? How can you continue to love
a place that has little but contempt for you?' One blogger who
calls himself 'localexpat' replied,

> It's like being a geopolitical orphan with this being the only place
> you know of and, more importantly, feels like home. What else
> can we, the local expatriates, do? To a certain extent it does feel
> like a relationship where you are showering the other with your
> love only to be bitch-slapped in return. But what else can an
> orphan do?[12]

The reality is that expatriates generally cannot become
'Dubaian', not legally and not socially. Still, many expatriates

who feel a great sense of attachment to Dubai resist this exclusion. Faiz, a Sri Lankan lawyer in his early thirties, wondered if the nationals' views of second-generation expatriates would change if they realized that they are not 'mercenaries' like their parents, that they have more of an emotional stake in Dubai.

For many expatriates from developing countries, their attachment to Dubai was also defined in large part as a reaction against their country of passport, a place few wished to live in. For example, Sushil and Vinod are brothers in their mid-twenties who were illegally working as freelance graphic designers. They spent a lot of time in India as children and young adults, mainly because of their mother's poor health, and because of visa troubles that got them banned from Dubai for stretches at a time. While they extolled the many virtues of Bombay, and said they felt like 'locals' whenever they go back, they also felt that they could not, in the end, make do there. The work environment is too hierarchical and status conscious, with too many people asking what firms you worked at and what college you went to. Also, they felt there was no scope for freelancing, and they hated the idea of working for someone else. Plus competition in Bombay is fierce, and wages are much lower than they would be willing to work for. Dubai for them provided a freedom and scope for opportunities in their work lives that India simply could not match.

Dubai is not home

As sure as these expatriates above think of Dubai as home, there are just as many, if not more, Dubai-born and -bred expatriates who know that Dubai is not home, that they are neither of nor from Dubai. This is not surprising given the terms of residency. I was often told that since people can never put down roots in

Dubai they do not even bother trying. So people psychologically, culturally and emotionally keep a part of themselves at home or wherever it is they are ready to move to next.

Pritim, an Indian in his early twenties who was preparing to leave for postgraduate studies in the US had an interesting take on the idea of home:

> Dubai's home in the sense that the streets are familiar, I know where to get stuff. I have friends over here, that sort of thing. But, at the same time, it's not home in the sense that I don't belong over here; I'm not going to be quote unquote 'one of them'. In a sense I don't really have a home, because there's no place where, you know, they accept me and I accept them.

While many people rejected the idea that they were of/from Dubai as the basis of their identity, some squarely identified with their country of passport. One person like that with whom I spent a great deal of time was Vinod, my tobacconist, who was born in Dubai thirty-five years ago, went to Indian schools in Dubai throughout, and went to India for university. He strongly identified with India, often talking of how he wanted to move back to Bombay (he refused to call it Mumbai, its relatively new official name), and always talked about Dubai as the place he resided in, nothing more. He even married a woman from India. When I asked him why a woman from India and not an Indian woman from Dubai, he was indignant and said simply, 'Why not?! I'm Indian!'

Vinod was somewhat unique among the expatriates I interviewed in his 'Indianness', and his desire to go back to India – none of the other second-generation expatriates from developing countries I interviewed felt so strongly about returning to their country of passport. Many of the other Indian expatriates I met who did not feel Dubaian did not feel Indian either, and did not see themselves ever living there.

Tahniat, a half-Pakistani, half-Bangladeshi woman in her late twenties, summed up the quandary of the uncertain space that expatriates occupy. While she is very attached to Dubai, she had apprehensions when talking about her living situation. She said that her parents go back to their home countries once in a while to visit and eventually will return. But for her and people of her situation, they generally think of Dubai as home, but then they have to hold themselves and say, 'Listen this is not your home, don't get too comfortable here, because there's always the chance that you have to pick up your bags and leave one day'.

Dubai is 'kind of' home?

While many feel strongly that Dubai is, or is not, home, most of the people I interacted with had mixed feelings. They are obviously *in* Dubai, but not sure if they are *of* Dubai. Jinu, an Indian in her early twenties who had recently graduated from university in Australia, emphasized this sense of uncertainty. She told me that when she is in Australia she feels like she is from Dubai, but when she is in Dubai she does not really know where she is from.

Similar to the experience of many second-generation immigrant New Yorkers mentioned above, some expatriates advocated a third type of identification of second-generation expatriates as not nationals, but not foreigners either. For instance, Muhammed and Levant, Turkish brothers in their twenties, had recently returned from university in the UK. Muhammed made the point that they are more like people who grew up in Dubai from places such as France or India or Brazil than they are like people in Turkey. He said in Turkey they do not get treated differently, but he feels that they do not fit in so well. And also because they have a bit of an accent when they speak Turkish, people think they grew up in Germany.

So they are foreigners in Turkey, their country of passport, and also they feel like foreigners in Dubai because of their lack of citizenship, but also because of the rapid pace of change in Dubai. In the few years they were away the city had changed so much that they felt like tourists. Even so, they are comfortable with being foreigners in Dubai, as everyone else is a foreigner in Dubai. Muhammed said, 'Here everyone's already out of their home country. You will never meet anyone who says, "Yeah, my grandfather lived in that house there." They'll probably say "My grandfather is from another continent." '

Similarly to the Turkish brothers, John, the European-Canadian we met above, makes the point that Dubai is home, but he is not of Dubai. 'We've become completely used to it, that we're not from here. But it's our home. It'd be strange for someone like you to understand, where you have rights where you're living and you've made your home. For us it's just normal.'

Still, these expatriates generally understand that their home might not want them. I asked Hajira, the Somali nurse, about this and she said, 'I'm telling you I love this country. It's my country. But if my country doesn't want me, what do you want me to do? They can tell me, *khalaas* [finished], go.'

STAY OR GO?

Prince, who we met earlier, was born in Dubai and had never left the UAE until just before we met in 2006. In spite of his only ever having lived in Dubai, and having never travelled abroad, he told me, 'the fact is, for me, Dubai is a pit stop, a place where you come, make a good amount of money and you get out.'

How can a place where one is born and raised be just a 'pit stop'? Interestingly, Prince's attitude is common among expatriates born and/or raised in Dubai. One thing that surprised me was not simply how common international migration among these people was, but rather how they accepted the reality of going between multiple countries to live and work with such mental ease. They live with the possibility, though of low probability, that their visas could be cancelled, and they may find themselves deported. Given that these expatriates are by definition transients, they are all faced with the question, should I stay or should I go? On the one hand, living with the (at least in the abstract) possibility that you could be deported from a place you have lived your entire life is, at minimum, troubling. But, on the other hand, this uncertainty forms the basis of a worldly attitude among these people. If the time comes, most are prepared to go.

It was hard for me as an assimilated child of immigrants in the US to understand this because, when you are in a place where you (at least legally) belong, the thought of picking up and moving to another country is a heavy decision. There may be all kinds of discrimination and other issues, but, in the end, it is your home, warts and all. Additionally, it is a place from where you do not expect to be expelled. Plus, for a Westerner, where would you go that affords you better social and economic opportunities? Leave Canada to live and work in Egypt or Bangladesh? Maybe for the adventurous few, but the traffic is heavier the other way.

But in Dubai people seem to be 'free' of that weight of staying. They do not have ties to this place that immigrants in other countries do. Dubai does not create ties to them, does not acknowledge them. Again, there is no citizenship by birth for expatriates, there is no acknowledgement legally or socially of their standing. They are on temporary work visas, like anyone who just steps off the plane today. This ties in with the insistence of the UAE government (and of the Gulf states in general) that expatriates are not migrants but temporary labour. The distinction is crucial. Migrants have a stake in a place; temporary labourers do not. And the labelling often becomes a self-fulfilling prophecy.

A major difference between these expatriates and other global migrants regarding migration choices and strategies is the sheer scale of migratory behaviour – most of the people I interviewed had studied and worked abroad before returning and many people had come and gone multiple times. Again, expatriates make up more than 90 per cent of Dubai's population, and they are likely to migrate. While their individual decisions to migrate are voluntary (unless deported), they have a predisposition towards leaving, which is undergirded by the three-year visa policy of the state.

Why come back?

Pamila, an Indian advertising professional in her early thirties who had lived in the US and UK for university and work, had a simple but telling answer to the question, 'Why come back?' She told her mother in Dubai, 'Mom, I'm going to come back to Dubai.' Her mother said 'Why, are you stupid?' To which she said, 'No, Dubai has this pull, and I want to be back there.'

In spite of the uncertainty they may or may not feel regarding the visa situation, these expatriates have responded to this pull, and have chosen to come back to Dubai. Close to two-thirds of the second-generation expatriates I interviewed had completed university in the West, and, of those, most had worked abroad as well. But they had all returned. The benefits of being in Dubai generally outweigh the precariousness of living on three-year visas that conceivably could be cancelled for any reason. In Dubai the professional expatriate returns to find family, a booming job market (until late 2008) and a lifestyle that, in many ways, is better than how they would live in the West or in their Asian or Arab countries of origin.

The 'good life' that Dubai offers was a common theme I kept coming across. This good life is especially built upon the prevalence and affordability of personal household services of maids, nannies, 'houseboys' (grown men, actually), gardeners, cooks and drivers. These people are paid third-world wages, while the majority of second-generation professionals I interviewed generally earned as much as their counterparts in Western countries, and tax-free at that. These personal services are made even more affordable as more than three-quarters of the second-generation expatriates I interviewed lived with their parents. They nearly all had domestic help. Being upper-middle class in Dubai means a much more comfortable style of life than that of a similarly situated person in the West. In short, if you have money, Dubai is easy living.

But that is the key: to have money. Levant, the Turkish business consultant, stressed this when he said, 'Our family is pretty well off here; we can have a really good life. These people with lower incomes, they have it really hard. If we [he and his brother, Muhammed] were on our own and with a little lower income, it might be better to be in Europe.'

Family, as Levant and most others pointed out, is, not surprisingly, another important reason to return. Even though these expatriates and their parents are there temporarily, by definition their ties to each other transcend this legal limitation. For instance, Tahniat said, 'For me, my attachment being here is my family. I haven't exactly come here – I didn't come back for any career move. It was purely family.'

In addition to family and an easy style of living, the job market, which had been greatly expanding since the beginnings of the post-2001 economic boom, drew many people back to Dubai. Gloria, a graduate student in London, whose British father and Indian mother still live in Dubai after thirty years, understands why many do return (even though she said she would not). She pointed out that returning is largely seen now as being totally acceptable, and not necessarily a failure, depending on whether the person's new job is good or not. She thought this was due to Dubai's new status for other people around the world as a place to go and work. This was a recent shift in attitude. Until the early 2000s, it was standard for second-generation expatriates who were not 'IDB' (in daddy's business) to leave Dubai permanently. Gloria put it eloquently: 'If people did come back to Dubai to work after studying abroad, they were scorned for not being able to make it in the real world and having to come back to rely on daddy's contacts to find a job.'

Why leave?

In spite of having returned, most people I interviewed had been considering leaving Dubai at some point in the near future, or a little further down the road. For all the compelling reasons that people gave for coming back and staying in Dubai, others gave equally compelling reasons why they were contemplating leaving. Their reasons are in many ways the mirror opposites of those who intend to stay: lack of family and friends, lack of job opportunities and discrimination in the workplace.

A common theme that emerged from my interviews was that, for many people, even though they were happy enough to be in Dubai, they were fully prepared to leave, as the root structure of family and friends was not deep enough to keep them. For example, I asked Pritim, who had tired of Dubai and was leaving permanently (he hoped) for the US, 'Is it hard to pick up and go?' To which he replied,

> Uh, that's a good question . . . Many of my closest friends have moved away. A lot of my friends in Dubai are newer than my old friends who moved out, so that kind of affects things as well. Why? It's not as hard to leave newer friends as it is to leave older friends . . . My dad has a business, but there's no pressure that I have to take it over. I have memories over here, but, you know, you can make memories somewhere else.

Unlike Pritim, Tahniat has deeper roots in Dubai. Even though she came back for family, and loves the lifestyle, she still thinks of Dubai as a temporary place. She told me about how many of her friends have circulated in and out of Dubai, going abroad to university, working, then coming back. 'Why come back?' I asked.

> I personally believe that a lot of us cannot survive anywhere else, as we are just too 'spoon-fed' here and we cannot adjust to 'real life'. So this is an easy option. Dubai is a situation where it is booming and you can save a lot of money and then go other places.

I asked, 'So are you thinking of going to other places?' Contrary to the idea that she cannot adjust to 'real life', she replied, 'Yes, it has always been at the back of my mind to get a job offer somewhere else.'

Where will they go?

Expatriates in Dubai from developing countries regularly told me that having a Western passport or residency greatly enhances their sense of security. It makes international travel easier, and it opens up work options. Of the second-generation expatriates I interviewed, about half had passports or residency from the US, the EU, Australia or Canada. These expatriates, whether privileged and/or lucky enough to have Western residency, oriented their lives in varying degrees in relation to three, and sometimes four, countries.

For expatriates from more modest means or those without prior residency in the West, the transnational life of the upper-middle class was not something they could live. Their immediate option beyond Dubai was to return to their developing country of origin, something very few found enticing. For them, the hope of migration to the West represented an escape from the uncertainty of life in Dubai.

For some, the route to the West was through marriage. Hajira, the Somali nurse, was looking online for love, partly because the time was right (she was in her mid-twenties), but mostly for escape from her tenuous existence in Dubai. She no longer had her local friends from school (she went to schools for nationals throughout), and her father and brother had already left, the former back to Somalia, the latter to the UK. She had expressed a particular desire to migrate 'somewhere in North America, where nurses are really paid like hell'. (In Dubai, they are paid very little – Hajira earned AED 2,000 per month.) Before I left Dubai, she had met a Somali man online who was a Canadian resident, married him and left for Canada. Ritu, an Indian designer in her mid-twenties, was similarly looking at marriage as her way out of Dubai. She told me that if the right guy came along and wanted to leave, she would go. A few months after we met, she did exactly that – got engaged to and quickly married an Indian-American and left immediately for the US. Her boss was greatly annoyed. This pattern even extends to men. Vishul who we met at the beginning of the chapter had tried to stay in the US after spending ten years there for his studies, then working on an H1-B visa.[13] He was forced to return after failing to acquire a green card. After he returned to Dubai, he dated then married a European national, and now lives in London.

For others who do not already have the security of Western residency or family network connections in the West, whether they are privileged or not, Western residency serves as a contingency plan, a strategic backup in case they have to leave Dubai. One of my first interviews was with Sunil, an Indian MBA student at an Ivy League university who was in Dubai doing an internship at an investment firm. We spoke at length about the possibility of his staying in Dubai to work, or of staying permanently in the US. When we left the coffee shop, his mother met him and reminded him to finalize his Canadian papers by the next day to guarantee his soon-to-be acquired Canadian residency, though he had no immediate intention of settling in Canada.

Even for people who have no immediate intention of leaving Dubai, many have made backup residence plans in Western countries, just in case.[14] I found during the course of my research that this was a quite common practice. Some, like Sunil, have actually done it. Of the people I interviewed who did not have Western residency, three-quarters expressed a desire to acquire Western residency, primarily in Canada or Australia. It is interesting that so many people were concentrating their efforts on obtaining Canadian or Australian residency, as they perceived these countries to be more inviting to immigrants than the US or the UK.[15] A local paper reported on the phenomena of Canada as a backup plan, citing a year-long survey conducted by the Canadian embassy in Abu Dhabi, which found that 98 per cent of applicants for immigrant visas were planning to return to the

Gulf almost immediately after landing in Canada, like Hasan had done before he acquired citizenship.[16]

Having residency in a Western country provides a safety net, the answer to the question of what happens if these expatriates do get kicked out of Dubai. For the vast majority of the Arab and Indian expatriates I met, going back to their countries of origin to settle was not a palatable option for them financially, occupationally or socially. Of the people I interviewed only three – two brothers from Mangalore, India, and the tobacconist from Bombay – were comfortable with the possibility of returning to their country of passport to settle. For the rest of the expatriates I interviewed from South Asian or Arab countries, 'home' was a nice place to visit, but not to work or live. Haya, an Egyptian nurse in her mid-twenties, put it most succinctly when I asked how it would be if one day her visa was cancelled and she had to go to Egypt: 'God, don't say that! I would love to visit Egypt, but visiting is good. Enjoy it and then come back.'

*   *   *

The story here has been how the government's three-year visa policy plays a central role in shaping the ways second-generation expatriates in Dubai relate to the host society and how they define the idea of home. Expatriates are unable to assimilate legally and for the most part socially. At some point nearly all expatriates, including those born in Dubai will have to leave, and this affects how they approach the idea of leaving home.

In spite of the existential angst or justifiable fears that many suffer as a result of their state of permanent impermanence, they all go about living their lives, and for nearly everyone I interviewed, it is a very nice life. I was actually jealous of their lifestyles and often thought about how I could get myself to Dubai to live the good life.

The previous three chapters all concentrated on how the temporary visa system affects short- and long-term working-class and professional expatriates. But the system of having 90 per cent of the population on temporary visas also shapes how national citizens go about living their lives. This is the subject of the next chapter.

CHAPTER SIX

STRANGERS IN THEIR OWN LAND

THROUGHOUT THIS BOOK I have argued that the key to understanding the intertwined stories of Dubai's history, economy, and culture has been its treatment of expatriate labour as temporary. This visa regime also shapes the working and living situations of nationals, and it also has unwittingly created an identity crisis they are trying desperately to come to grips with.

Until now, nationals have been a fleeting presence in the book. I have barely mentioned them with respect to the construction of Dubai's consumer culture, social life and living conditions, and work. The near absence of nationals from the narrative is due in large part to the state essentially treating 'average' nationals as unimportant for Dubai's development, contrary to public pronouncements. By this I mean that they have little presence in the economic or cultural spheres, and certainly not in politics, given that Dubai and the UAE are run by monarchies not beholden to the views of their subjects. It is not an exaggeration to say that nationals are, to a large degree, passive observers and beneficiaries of what Dubai has become.

WORK

It is now nearly forty years since the UAE became an independent nation. In a very short time they have built an educational infrastructure for national citizens that has produced a basic alphabetical literacy rate of 93 per cent.[1] The UAE has also been steadily increasing its numbers of high school and university graduates, though the quality of their education through the high school level is questionable, as, for instance, at UAE University, 90 per cent of first-year students require one or more years of courses in basic maths and literacy.[2]

Since at least the late 1990s, a great gender discrepancy has arisen, with women having achieved greater levels of educational attainment than men in high schools and universities. Today, the ratio of women to men in higher education is three to one. In Abu Dhabi half of the men drop out before they finish high school and in universities women are known for working much harder than men. This discrepancy is due in part to many men having other employment opportunities available to them, including the military, the police, a family business or the government, which allows them to bypass university education. Other men just do not want to spend so much time in school.[3]

While the sheer numbers of educated nationals – especially women – are increasing, they have not become the skilled national workforce that the rulers of Dubai and the UAE envisaged. Dubai needed to increasingly import foreign labour at all levels from the 1960s onwards as its citizen population lacked sufficient numbers and sufficient expertise to build up various sectors with their own labour, and increasingly for lower levels, nationals came to see construction and lower-level service work as undignified and beneath them. With the second oil boom of the 2000s, the dependence on expatriate labour increased even more markedly.

As a result, a two-tiered labour market has arisen in Dubai and largely throughout the Gulf: the private sector, which is staffed almost completely with expatriate labour, and the public sector, where nearly all employed nationals work, but which is still staffed with 90 per cent expatriate labour.[4] Far and away, nationals prefer to work in the public sector, as working here is basically a form of governmental subsidy to national citizens. Government jobs generally pay well, often exceeding similar positions in the private sector. This is especially pronounced at lower levels, where the wage for nationals is much greater than an expatriate would earn for the same work in the public sector, and far more than for the same work in the private sector. Working hours are much shorter than in the private sector, vacation days are greater in number, pensions are generous, the workload is easy, and government jobs are seen by Emiratis as more prestigious than private sector jobs. And, importantly, there is tremendous job security.[5]

Given such incentives for nationals to work in the public sector, it is a wonder that any nationals bother with the private sector at all. (Indeed, only 13,000 nationals were employed in the private sector as of 2009, or 0.4 per cent of the private sector work-force.[6]) As an illustration of this point, a European expatriate manager I interviewed told me a story of one extremely talented young national university graduate he recruited to work for him. The manager gave the young man a job with a great degree of responsibility and autonomy – something most new recruits in the labour market can only dream of. After six months, however, he resigned. When the manager asked him why, the young man replied that the manager was working him too hard and for too many hours, and that he had gotten a job in a government ministry that paid just as well with much shorter hours, and far less responsibility.

Many companies are not keen on hiring nationals because they are seen as lacking the requisite academic and technical skills, and companies stereotype nationals as lacking drive. Even if they do get jobs in the private sector, there is little in the way of motivation as it is very difficult to fire a national worker.[7] In a recent study, private sector employers in the UAE, Saudi Arabia and Bahrain reported that a quarter of national employees fail to show up for work regularly, and many quit in less than a year due to 'boredom'. In fact, it is very common for firms to hire national workers as 'window dressing' to show that they have national workers. Some companies do not even bother these employees, letting them stay at home and be 'ghost workers'.[8] In another recent survey, 12 per cent of expatriate CEOs said they wanted to hire nationals regardless of their qualifications, simply to have them on their books.[9] This benefits the employee, as he gets money for nothing, and it benefits the employers, as hiring nationals facilitates their ability to acquire more labour permits to hire expatriates who do the actual work. This story of non-working national workers is one that has not qualitatively changed in years. One scholar writing of the Gulf generally said that in the 1990s, 'the typical incentive to work, the need to earn a living, is not necessarily applicable to nationals, who often receive an income without working, or without working particularly hard'.[10]

Another issue contributing to the small numbers of nationals working in the private sector is salaries that nationals expect are far in excess of what a company can hire a Filipino or Indian expatriate to do, so nationals in essence price themselves out of the lower end of the labour market. At the higher ends of the market, nationals often just do not have the academic or technical skills that firms need. This is a situation that has remained basically unchanged since even before the first oil boom.[11] Partially as a result of the combination of lack of appropriate skills and an unwillingness to take jobs that either pay too little or that are seen as being 'beneath them', and as the welfare state is so generous, there is no absolute financial need to work. Many nationals would rather be unemployed than take a job they do not want in the private sector. This should not be surprising, given that over half of the recipients of social security benefits are of working age, and that the average national male receives roughly USD 55,000 worth of social security benefits a year.[12] As a result, the official unemployment rate among UAE nationals was very high, around 17 per cent before the economic meltdown of late 2008.

The lack of commitment and qualification of national workers is a constant worry for the government, but in a way shows just how successful the government's policy of importing expatriate labour to do work at all levels has been in developing their economy and society. The government has been able to provide a welfare system for its citizens far in excess of what nearly any other state can provide. The downside in Dubai, and in the Gulf generally, has been that governments provide possibly too well, and in recent years officials in various Gulf governments have recognized this. The late president of the UAE, Sheikh Zayed, worried about the work ethic of Emirati youth, commenting in a 1995 speech:

It is of paramount importance that the UAE's unemployed youth be oriented towards work, so that they can be made aware of the physical and mental ability to earn their own living . . . I cannot understand how a physically fit young man can sit idle and accept the humiliation of depending on others for his livelihood.[13]

Sheikh Mohammed echoed this point in 1996, complaining of 'voluntary unemployment' among nationals, a situation that was wrong given that the UAE was providing all its sons and daughter opportunities that had been unattainable just a generation before.[14] A decade later, while noting that 54 per cent of social-security beneficiaries were of working age, Sheikh Mohammed wondered, 'How can we integrate these people into the development process and transform them into productive and effective members of society?' He further made the link between not working in the labour force and not working in the home: 'The number of domestic help in some families exceeds the size of the family itself. Most families maintain a number of domestic help which is beyond their actual need.'[15]

Where Sheikh Mohammed dances around the work habits of young nationals, others are more direct and cutting. For instance the Bahrain Labour Minister called nationals in the Gulf 'lazy' and 'spoilt'.[16] A well-known Emirati columnist took it one step further in an interview where he echoed and harshly amplified Sheikh Mohammed's point, saying of his compatriots, 'People here are turning into lazy, overweight babies! The nanny state has gone too far. We don't do anything for ourselves! Why don't any of us work for the private sector? Why can't a mother and father look after their own child?'[17]

Emiratization

In 2006, the (then) UAE Minister of Labour announced that all expatriate secretaries in the UAE were to be replaced with nationals. There was a public outcry about this, with much discussion of how nationals would do no work, and companies would have to retitle and keep these expatriate secretaries (at far lower salaries than those of nationals) to do the work, even though the minister made it clear that he would not allow this. Nationals never took these jobs, the expatriate secretaries were never let go, and the whole plan ended up a colossal failure. At the same time, the minister proposed that all expatriate human resources managers and public relations officers should be replaced with nationals. This too failed. (An attempt to Emiratize taxi drivers in Sharjah in 2009 was an even bigger failure, with only one national showing even a passing interest – not surprising given that taxi drivers work twelve-hour days, seven days a week.[18])

A year later, Sheikh Mohammed gave a public dressing-down to the Minister of Labour for this failure, not because not enough nationals were filling these positions, but rather because the minister was aiming too low. Sheikh Mohammed said the reason for the failure was that the minister 'ignored the nation's priorities'. Regarding secretarial jobs, he said 'We need to have UAE nationals in more important roles and responsibilities.'

The minister, having been properly chastened, tried to lay out a Plan B. He said, 'Emiratization of some of the job categories will be revised accordingly, especially for human resources, as we might set a condition that the foreigner cannot be the manager, or we might think of a shadowing programme through employing an Emirati in every human resources department'.[19] Both of these propositions are so vaguely phrased that they seem to be off-the-cuff remarks, rather than clearly thought out policy statements.

These programmes of 'Emiratization', or quotas, are intended to nationalize sections of the workforce in government and in the private sector to jumpstart workforce participation among nationals. The programme of Emiratization started with the Committee for Human Resources Development in the Banking Sector, which was established in 1997 and called for 4 per cent Emiratization yearly in the banking sector. The push to encourage nationals into the workforce broadened with the establishment of Tanmia (National Human Resource Development and Employment Authority) in 1999, which works to coordinate national job seekers with the private sector, and broadly aims to reduce unemployment and to enhance work skills of nationals. In the banking sector especially, Emiratization has been successful. By 2008, the percentage of nationals employed by banks stood at 32 per cent, short of the 40 per cent goal, but still seemingly impressive.[20]

More than ten years on now, these various programmes that fall under the rubric of Emiratization (which is handled by a handful of ministries at the federal and Emirate governmental levels) have had variable success at getting nationals into the private sector. But, even where Emiratization is successful in initially getting nationals into the private sector, they do not necessarily stay there. Tanmia found that 27 per cent of nationals hired by banks left within six months, and on average spent only nineteen months employed at a given bank, compared with sixty months for the average expatriate. Further, hiring nationals is very expensive, and greatly affects the banks' bottom lines. One study of banks in the UAE found that the two banks with the lowest Emiratization rates also had the best cost-to-income ratios.[21] While it is expensive for private firms to employ nationals, due to low productivity and high cost of labour, it is still a cost they must bear to do business. In effect, it is a not-so-hidden tax.

While the governmental push for Emiratization is strong, there is ambivalence at the top. Sheikh Mohammed, while he

171

believes that nationals should be employed at the highest levels, at times seems to regard the use of quotas as a bad idea. For instance, in 2007, he said, 'It is very easy to impose Emiratization. We can do this at any time, but what would we gain if we did not provide our youth with the best knowledge, skill and expertise commensurate with these jobs?'[22] That same year he pledged to reduce hiring quotas to encourage nationals to increase their qualifications.[23] That never happened.

While the government has actively been attempting to match private employers with national jobseekers, a major roadblock has come from a lack of interest on the part of nationals themselves. For example, at a job fair organized by the Dubai Government National Human Resources Department, only seven nationals out of 451 who were contacted came to meet managers from insurance companies.[24] Again, because the welfare state is so generous, nationals can be very picky about taking jobs, as they essentially do not need to work, which greatly affects how they approach work and working. A human resource manager at a government-owned energy firm said of nationals applying for jobs with him, 'Unfortunately, the first thing most nationals ask us about is how much the package is. They rarely ask us who we are, the scope of our work, our vacancies, career progression or training.' His colleague said of her compatriots: 'Many UAE nationals apply to work here, but the hours scare them, even though the package we offer tempts them.' She further added that graduates who were serious about applying did not have the right skills – even though they hired mainly engineers, most of the résumés she received were from business administration graduates.[25]

Recently, newspapers have presented anecdotal evidence that women are showing an increasing interest in working in the private sector, a seemingly positive sign, especially given the wide discrepancy in educational achievement between men and women. But a recent study on Emiratization found no significant difference between men and women regarding their attitudes towards working in the private sector: both equally disdained the idea for the longer working hours and lower (initially, at least) pay to be had there. Neither men nor women are willing to part with the better benefits and easier working life of the public sector.[26] Indeed, women, who account for 30 per cent of employed nationals, occupy two-thirds of all public sector jobs.[27] Thus, the nationals most ably situated to gainfully work in the private sector generally show little interest in working there.

These notions of nationals as 'hardly working' workers are pervasive, and derisively commented on by many expatriates, so it is not surprising that Emiratization has had limited success in the private sector. But this is not simply a case of expatriate bosses discriminating against national employees – government officials and nationals in position to hire other nationals voice the same concerns. Surprisingly, government ministries, government firms and private companies owned by Emiratis (actual ownership, not legal paper ownership) have been slow to hire other nationals. Of 65,000 employees in different ministries in the federal government, only 28,000 were Emiratis. Dubai Aluminum Company, a government-owned firm, reported that only 24 per cent of their workforce was comprised of nationals. In Sheikh Mohammed's Tecom, 30 per cent of their workforce is comprised of nationals. At one of Sheikh Mohammed's investment firms, Tatweer, of approximately 1,100 workers in late 2008, only 100 were nationals. And at the Al Futtaim Group, one of the larger, non-governmental firms owned by a prominent national family, the Emiratization manager reported that, of their new hires for 2007, 6 per cent had to be nationals. He proudly reported that they had almost met their target in the first quarter of the year.[28] We can infer from this that the overwhelming majority of his hires are expatriates. Even at the highest levels of many state- or ruling family-owned firms, such as Emirates Airline and Sheikh Mohammed's Jumeirah Group, many expatriates are in the highest positions.

It is telling that national employees do not numerically dominate in governmental and private firms owned by nationals. It would be reasonable to expect that here preferential hiring of nationals would be pronounced. But this is not the case. In fact, it may even be that nationals themselves (as employers) are standing in the way of effective nationalization of sectors of the workforce. A recent study found that Emirati employers are less likely than expatriates to hire nationals. Emirati managers were more concerned than expatriates about how hiring local staff would affect their businesses, with 86 per cent stating that the lack of skills, education and experience would keep them from hiring nationals (as opposed to 61 per cent of expatriate managers). And 28 per cent of Emirati managers were fearful of having a 'bad experience' with an unproductive national employee, as opposed to just 10 per cent of expatriate employers.[29]

While certain governmental departments are actively trying to involve nationals economically and socially in their own country, at the highest levels it seems that they are willing to continue to allow nationals to be passive observers and beneficiaries of Dubai's development. Even with the efforts of groups like Tanmia to train nationals and match them with employers, and with the cajoling and shaming of unemployed nationals by Sheikh Mohammed himself, as long as the benefits of the welfare state are so generous, there will be a large percentage of nationals content not to work. And there is a basic structural reason for the overly generous welfare state, which is summed up bluntly by the former UK ambassador to the UAE: 'The social contract is that you get given things by the sheikh and in return you give the sheikh your allegiance.'[30] If the sheikhs fail to thoroughly provide for their subjects, their subjects might openly question their rule, which could lead to social unrest or worse, as can be seen in Bahrain and Saudi Arabia in the past two decades as the rulers there have broken this social contract.

It is often assumed that this attitude towards work among nationals is untenable, that the government sector is saturated, and, with high unemployment and a burgeoning young, increasingly educated population soon to be of working age, that a social crisis is imminent. Young nationals will find themselves educated but unemployable, especially as the government may not be able to absorb them and the private sector will not want them. This is a fear shared by all the Gulf governments. But there is a basic assumption here that is faulty: that nationals need to and should work as a goal in itself. But why work if you don't have to? Many nationals will not take jobs that are beneath them, or feel they will not like, and, as stated above, often quit when they are bored. As long as the government coffers keep getting refilled, there is no need to work. And even with Dubai's debt in 2009 standing at 107 per cent of GDP (that is, they owed more money than they brought in), welfare programmes are not being cut, as most of the programmes are funded through the federal government, whose budget comes almost exclusively from Abu Dhabi. Basically then, Abu Dhabi gives 'welfare' benefits to Dubai and all the other emirates for their public expenditure, as well as giving benefits directly to all the individual nationals in all the emirates. So the need to work in the UAE is not a question of basic needs, as all their basic costs are taken care of. Working, then, is more an existential need, one of personal fulfilment. Given that, it is actually surprising that the employment rate is as high as it is.

In a way, this concern over the lack of nationals in the private sector in particular, and of unemployment generally, is much ado about nothing. The high rate of unemployment that consumes many government officials, economists and pundits of various stripes obscures the scope of the problem, as there were only 14,000 nationals registered as unemployed as of 2009.[31] The government can easily afford to support them. In a more basic way, this is a discussion over who runs the country. As Sheikh Mohammed pointed out, nationals should be in jobs of importance. Indeed, many nationals are CEOs of major companies, but only because the law requires companies that operate outside of free zones to have nationals as CEOs. Tellingly, only one of the twenty-eight members of the Dubai Financial Market General Index in 2007 had a national as their chief financial officer, a position requiring extensive knowledge of accounting and compliance, something few nationals have.[32] The obvious inference from this is that nationals are marginal in their own country, not just demographically but, more importantly, socially. The threat then is not an economic one, but rather a more basic threat to defining exactly who they are.

'DON'T YOU WISH YOU WERE EMIRATI?'

As I pointed out above, the primary factor shaping how nationals approach work is the incredible scope and amount of welfare benefits that nationals receive through the UAE and Dubai governments. These include free schooling in public or private schools up to PhD level anywhere in the world, free plots of land, interest-free loans to build a house and payments to nationals to marry other nationals, among others.[33] In addition to providing government jobs (which often require little work or effort and thus can be seen as a form of welfare), the government also provides many nationals the opportunity to collect rent as landlords and as 'paper' business partners.[34] For nationals with low incomes, the government provides even more subsidized housing. For instance, the Dubai government has recently built 2,300 'affordable' houses for nationals in various Dubai localities. Each house is valued (in April 2008, before the housing bubble burst) at roughly AED 2 million, and the average plot of land is nine thousand square metres.[35] For low-income nationals who are not given villas, the government has also started to build apartment blocks in outlying neighbourhoods. All apartments in these residential complexes have either three or four bedrooms plus a servant's room.[36] (A servant's room is a must because, as the UAE-based sociologist Rima Sabban put it, 'a porter at the school, a poor woman on welfare, can afford to hire an Indian migrant to [be a maid]'.[37]) For those nationals who do not or cannot work, the UAE Ministry of Social Affairs provides generous charity to widows and divorcees, orphans, disabled people and families of prisoners, with aid starting at AED 4,700 per month up to AED 40,000 per month, depending on the number of family members.[38]

Aside from the national in the previous section who railed against the 'nanny state', most nationals generally are quite happy with this arrangement. As a twenty-three-year-old worldly national male argued:

> This is the best place in the world to be young! The government pays for your education up to PhD level. You get given a free house when you get married. You get free healthcare, and if it's not good enough here, they pay for you to go abroad. You don't even have to pay for your phone calls. Almost everyone has a maid, a nanny, and a driver. And we never pay any taxes. Don't you wish you were Emirati?[39]

Because these benefits are so extensive, the government has, not surprisingly, greatly limited the possibility of naturalization, in the process drawing a clear line between nationals and expatriates. The legal and social division between nationals and expatriates has been of great concern for the state and its national citizens for many years now, especially so since the first oil boom when the expatriate population began to far exceed that of nationals. And since the number of naturalized citizens is so low, as the number of expatriates has grown tremendously over the past few decades, the ratio of nationals to expatriates has correspondingly decreased to the point where nationals are, according to some national analysts, an endangered (though pampered) minority in their own country – roughly 15 per cent nationwide, and possibly as low as 3 per cent in Dubai.[40]

This has led nationals to consciously think about issues of identity in a way they never had to before. This concern over identity among nationals is to a large degree a result of nationals and expatriates being segregated in schools, neighbourhoods and the workplace. While this has been commonplace throughout the UAE's history, in the past there was more of a chance for social interaction as there was more of a demographic balance between nationals and expatriates, and the overall population and geographic dispersal was much less. Many of the second-generation Arab and Western expatriates I interviewed, as we saw in the previous chapter, had national friends and had regular social interactions with nationals. But, as the population has boomed, and as nationals have moved to areas where they are the exclusive residents, even for these people social relations have largely ceased. To put it another way, even if nationals were extremely outgoing and sociable with expatriates, a great number of expatriates would not have close social relations with nationals as there are just not enough of them, at less than 10 per cent of the population, to go around.[41]

Concerns over the presence of so many expatriates leading to loss of national culture, assimilation, Westernization and so on have been voiced in the UAE and elsewhere in the Gulf for many years.[42] This fear has reached such a crescendo that the President of the UAE and Ruler of Abu Dhabi Sheikh Khalifa bin Zayed Al Nahyan declared 2008 'National Identity Year'. In April 2008, a National Identity Conference was staged in Abu Dhabi which garnered heavy national and even international attention, with dozens of articles being published around that time sounding the alarm over threats to Emirati identity.[43]

We don't speak Arabic – blame the maids!

One example often given as evidence for the supposed crisis of the state of Emirati identity and culture is the declining significance of the Arabic language in public life, and the declining fluency of younger nationals in written and oral Arabic. For example, instructors in the Arabic department of Zayed University complain that students are barely literate in Arabic, and how it is becoming a second language to them. But few nationals are fully fluent in English either, so 'there is a growing feeling that a population of linguistically rootless people is being created'.[44] Indeed, a study by Abu Dhabi's Policy Agenda in 2003 found that 25 per cent of national males and 20 per cent of females were illiterate in Arabic, a problem most pronounced among the young.[45] Here the problem is assumed to lie within the schools as a result of poor or non-existent Arabic language instruction, the effects of English-language media and parents who do not make their children speak Arabic more often. Perhaps the biggest scapegoats for this are the poorly paid, overworked and often-abused maids, who are mostly Asian and non-Arabic speakers. A 1995 survey found an average of two foreign servants per national family, and four years later another survey lamented that a third of national families were 'totally dependent' on Asian housemaids for child rearing.[46] The same is true today.[47] A high-ranking official at the UAE Ministry of Culture, Youth and Community Development emphasized how this has led to a lack of 'cultural and Arabic language awareness' among younger Emiratis, as domestics are fully responsible for the upbringing of the children.[48]

If it is true that children and young adults speak Arabic less and less well, the cause is more likely that there is no reason to speak it at work or at school, places where English often predominates – a by-product of the globalization that the UAE rulers have actively promoted for years. A common complaint is that these younger nationals speak a mix of Arabic and English. Rather than blaming maids or teachers, a more likely explanation is young people who speak a mix of Arabic and English do so because their peers do too. This is quite similar to young people in India speaking 'Hinglish' (Hindi and English) or Latinos in the US who speak 'Spanglish' (Spanish and English).[49]

The emphasis today on Arabic language and culture leads many national intellectuals to accentuate the affinity of Arab expatriates with Emiratis. For instance, Jamal Al Suwaidi, director-general of the Abu Dhabi think tank, the Emirates Centre for Strategic Studies and Research, felt that the UAE 'should try to bring in more [workers] from the Arab countries because they share the same language and a similar heritage'.[50] Likewise, Khalfan Musabih, cultural adviser at the Sheikh Mohammad Bin Rashid Foundation, felt that Arab expatriates who have lived in the UAE for a long time have a sense of belonging since they share a common culture.[51]

While they may share some similar cultural markers of language, religion, food and so on with Emirati nationals, Arab expatriates – Lebanese, Syrians, Palestinians, etc. – are not and cannot generally become nationals, as we discussed in the previous chapter, and thus cannot fully have a sense of belonging, as they do not properly belong to the UAE. This, of course, makes any attempt to inculcate a sense of belonging among expatriates moot, as they are nothing but guest workers, or the children of guest workers. No matter the cultural similarities with nationals, Arab expatriates in the end are simply expatriates, no different than Indians, Britons or Chinese. And, in fact, they are more problematic than these other expatriates as their claims on the state and nationality through the argument of cultural similarity could be seen as more legitimate than those who do not share these cultural markers, thus threatening the boundary between expatriates and nationals.

Essentially, the debate over the importance of the Arabic language and Arab cultural forms actually tells us little about identity. Many expatriates speak Arabic, but that does not make them Emirati. Conversely, Emiratis who do not speak Arabic, or speak it poorly, do not lose their status as Emiratis. They are Emiratis because they have been defined thus.

Marriage

Since the first oil boom, national leaders and intellectuals have also been fixated on the 'problem' of marriages of nationals with foreigners. Marriages between nationals and foreigners are not new to Dubai, and they were not uncommon in the pre-oil period, unsurprising given Dubai's centrality in trade in the Arabian Gulf and Indian Ocean region. At the beginning of the oil boom in 1973, Sheikh Zayed commented on these mixed marriages, saying they were having a negative effect on society and were to be discouraged, and reasoned that national men did so to avoid paying an exorbitant *mahr* (dowry payment from the groom to the bride).[52] In addition to the rising costs of weddings, since the 1980s girls were being educated in much higher numbers than boys, leading to an obvious mismatch for these educated young women, as there are far too few educated men.

By 1989 the rate of marrying foreigners had supposedly risen to an incredible 47 per cent of all marriages, mostly to 'Asians' (presumably Indian and Pakistani Muslims).[53] This spurred the UAE government to start a 'marriage fund' in 1992, which provides up to AED 70,000 for couples on low incomes to get married (which many nationals feel is woefully inadequate). The UAE also famously sponsors mass weddings, where anywhere from a handful to hundreds of men participate in these public wedding ceremonies (women have their own separate private ceremonies). Since the advent of the Marriage Fund, the rate of out-marriage to foreigners has actually decreased, from 47 per cent in 1989, to 37 per cent in the mid-1990s, to 26 per cent in 1999 and holding steady through 2006.[54]

Even though the rates of marriage to foreigners has declined, there is a near-hysterical fear of cultural dilution due to men marrying foreign women and the resultant (supposed) negative effects on children. These fears pale in comparison to the possibility that national women will marry expatriates. The government strongly discourages marriages between female nationals and male expatriates. In fact, Amnesty International recently reported a case of a UAE national who married a foreign male while abroad without her family's permission. She was detained for eight months when she returned to the UAE in November 2007, treated poorly in prison, and then threatened with prosecution for adultery, a capital offence. She was returned to a relative and eventually left the UAE.[55]

For national men and their children, many of the supposed problems are manageable, as descent and inheritance are paternal. Let me reiterate a point I made earlier – a child whose father is a national but whose mother is an expatriate is by definition a national, while a child whose mother is a national but whose father is an expatriate is an expatriate. They may have the exact same 'cultural' backgrounds, but the difference is in the way the state defines them, which is through descent.

This disinheriting of the offspring of expatriate husbands and national wives is new, dating to the early 2000s. Until as late as 2000, all children born to any national were also nationals. What that meant was that women who could not find or did not desire a national husband could marry an expatriate (almost always an Arab Muslim). So if national men were unable to marry national women because of the cost, national women could still marry. In fact, many teenage national girls at this time before the law changed were reluctant to marry national men, finding them conservative, while finding expatriate Arab men more considerate as husbands. One teacher in Dubai said of his students, 'It amazes me how cynical my female students are about marriage. They often say they want to marry a non-national. They do not want to be second wives; they want to be the first wife.'[56]

As a result of the redefining of descent, the numbers of marriages of national women with expatriates has dropped – in 2000–2007 only five hundred national women married expatriates, and with that a supposed rise in the number of unmarried, or unmarriageable women.[57] One solution that some propose, like the teacher above, is that national women should be amenable to being second wives. This would help to solve the issue of the cost of the wedding: a second wife is of lower status, and therefore unable to command as high a bride price as a first wife. The problem here though is that, at least according to a recent survey of university students, the majority of young Emirati women would prefer being unmarried to being second wives.[58]

* * *

The discussions about identity among nationals tiptoes around the broader issue: not whether nationals are losing their identity or culture, a dubious claim, but rather that their social significance in their own place is declining in the public sphere. The identity 'crisis' is not simply a matter of demographics; if all the expatriates were labourers and maids, it is doubtful that there would be such psychological angst. The need to distinguish between nationals and expatriates is heightened because there are more expatriates who are, *socially and economically*, relatively equal to nationals. Labourers and maids, while physically close, are socially and economically subordinate.

Until the latest economic boom, nationals as a group were socially superior to nearly all expatriates, but more recently the social status of nationals vis-à-vis other expatriates has declined. Nationals are well taken care of, but, for many, that is not enough. This tension is heightened due to the realization that welfare benefits may shrink in the future, and that the government sector is saturated and nationals will probably have to enter the private sector in large numbers, though how that will happen is uncertain as nationals largely do not have the qualifications or attitude toward working that would allow them to succeed in the private sector. Given that political dissent is not allowed, complaints over threats to identity and culture posed by the presence of so many temporary expatriates are one way that displeased nationals can voice disapproval of the government's policies in a safe manner.

Again, it is the policy of the government, i.e. Sheikh Mohammed and the other ruling sheikhs, that allows so many expatriates to come. Couching their words in terms of culture and identity allows nationals to indirectly criticize the rulers (including Sheikh Mohammed for marrying a foreigner as his second wife – Princess Haya, daughter of the late King Hussein of Jordan), without the rulers losing face.

And, when the complaining is done, nationals are largely resigned, and generally at least minimally pleased, at the presence of expatriates, without whom Dubai's development would not have been possible. As the worldly young national quoted earlier put it, 'We see the expats as the price we had to pay for this development. How else could we do it? Nobody wants to go back to the days of the desert, the days before everyone came.'[59]

CHAPTER SEVEN

THIS IS THE FUTURE?

I WAS STANDING on the helipad of one of the (then) new swank high-rise apartment buildings in the Dubai Marina with my friend Vishul. We took in the panoramic, night-time view of Dubai, looking north on Sheikh Zayed Road towards the 'older' parts of the city, looking across the highway to the Burj Khalifa construction site and south towards Jebel Ali Port. Vishul turned 360 degrees and jokingly exclaimed, '*This* is the future!'

The purpose of this book has been to document and analyse this future, unmoored from and unhindered by 'tradition'. For Dubai to be what it is, the meeting ground for work and play for much of the world, requires the Puritan ideals of mainstream Sunni Islam to be suspended, even during Ramadan, so as not to inconvenience residents and tourists (especially Westerners) too much. The only compromise and nod to the fact that Dubai is very close to the epicentre of Islam is that live music is banned for the holy month of Ramadan, and alcohol cannot be served until the fast has been broken after sunset. But not to worry – this is a city of commerce where business goes on as usual and the prostitutes are still at work.

This future Dubai crafted for itself was a sort of utopian vision of economic and social freedoms, where workers gladly trade away political rights in search of the good life. Over 90 per cent of Dubai's population is composed of temporary expatriates, who are by definition short term even if they end up being long-term residents. Dubai caters to them and placates them through a kind of 'immediate gratification culture'. This is a path the rulers purposefully decided to take two decades ago to create wealth, as, unlike their immediate neighbours, they could not rely on oil to make them wealthy. I have argued that this policy decision to cater to expatriates, and national citizens, as consumers goes some ways to explaining why Dubai was seen until very recently as 'plastic', and why the arts and education sectors in Dubai are so underdeveloped relative to sectors such as construction, tourism and nightlife. This consumer culture fuelled Dubai's fame, which in turn helped to create its fortune.

* * *

This future came to be as the result of an influx of an army of temporary workers over the years whose lives are regulated by the *kafala* system, where workers come on short-term visas that are sponsored by their employers, essentially bonding these workers to their employers. This worked well enough while the economy boomed – people came in droves from all walks of life from the ends of the earth to perform all manner of work to live their personal version of the Dubai dream. While the dream soured for many, especially for construction workers and housemaids, for others Dubai was as promised. Since the bulk of immigrants came as self-conscious economic mercenaries, the limitations of the short-term visa regime were an acceptable trade-off.

In the recession the shortcomings of this system were duly exposed. Because expatriates' residence visas are tied to employment, as workers were being laid off in large numbers they had to leave. While the government and many employers gave workers more time to find alternative employment, this had negligible impact as there was little employment in Dubai to be found. As a result of the down job market, analysts predicted that for 2009 Dubai's population would decrease by as much as *17 per cent*.[1] (At the time this book went to press, more exact numbers, rather than projections, were unavailable.)

In the midst of the bust, a few of the Gulf states were beginning to rethink the necessity of the *kafala* system. Bahrain was the first to initiate radical change, discarding the sponsorship system altogether in August 2009. Expatriates will now be 'sponsored' directly by the government, and their visas will no longer be tied to a particular job. Following Bahrain, Kuwait announced that expatriates would be able to change jobs after three years without the sponsor's approval, or after one year if the sponsor does not object. This is perhaps a first step towards the abolition of the *kafala* system altogether, which a Kuwaiti minister, using language that Human Rights Watch would approve of, called 'modern-day slavery'. The minister elaborated, saying

> The decision will undoubtedly help remove the misery of the expatriate community, who have been suffering, on a daily basis, from repugnant and inhuman attitudes by some companies known for trafficking in humans and for engaging in the sordid business of selling foreign labourers.[2]

Perhaps more important is a proposal that came from the Saudi representative to the International Labour Organisation in July 2009. He suggested that long-term expatriates be given permanent residency, even nationality, and be exempt from having to renew their visas every few years. These longstanding expatriates would then no longer be at the mercy of their sponsors for visas, and presumably for their businesses.[3]

The policy changes in Bahrain and Kuwait and the Saudi proposal for permanent residence (if enacted) represent a monumental shift for the region. The basic premise of this book has been that the *kafala* system colours everything in Dubai. Such radical changes would affect the ways expatriates and national citizens live their lives. Expatriates would have freedom of mobility in the labour market, and would no longer have to fear deportation should they lose or quit their jobs. This would probably lead to higher wages, especially at the middle and lower end of the job market, where most workers are from the developing world and paid accordingly. These countries also hope that high unemployment rates among national citizens will be reduced, as the financial costs of hiring and training nationals will become more in line with that of expatriates, making nationals more attractive to private-sector firms. The Saudi proposal would especially be welcomed by the tens of thousands of long-term expatriates and their children in the Arabian Gulf, many of whom would prefer to stay rather than return to their countries of origin, particularly South Asian and Arab expatriates.

Conspicuously though, the silence of officials in Dubai on the possibility of such changes has been deafening. This is not surprising given that government-owned companies in construction, hospitality and other sectors employ tens of thousands of workers at all levels and their coffers are enriched through the depressed wages of these workers. While the social openness

Dubai undertook as its avenue to wealth is liberal relative to its neighbours, its attitude toward the visa system is quite conservative.

* * *

Sheikh Mohammed has gone to great lengths over the past two decades to transform Dubai from a trading port into a global city. He wanted Dubai not simply to be wealthy, but to be internationally famous. He and others in Dubai have put a great deal of energy and resources into creating Dubai as a brand. Dubai's brand image was built largely on its iconic constructions, and the idea that it was a consumer's paradise, with tax-free incomes, more shopping malls per capita than almost anywhere else, and few restrictions on hedonistic behaviour for residents and tourists alike.

While Dubai attracted a great amount of awe for its iconic constructions and fabulous (read Western) lifestyle, at the same time it came under scrutiny for a litany of human rights abuses of construction workers, maids and prostitutes. The government has in recent years attempted to redress many of these concerns. But, with the exception of the plight of young camel jockeys, which they addressed only when it became widely known in the West, the manner in which Dubai's government has approached these abuses looks largely like an attempt to mitigate bad publicity rather than attack the root problem of the exploitation itself.

The international press, which during the boom years was largely smitten with the economic and social freedoms that Dubai offered, discovered in the recession that began in late 2008 that Dubai was actually an autocracy. The idea of Dubai as an open playground for Westerners and as the land of opportunity for third-world migrants was supplanted by stories of debtor jails for professionals with unpaid credit card and mortgage debt, with even high-level executives fleeing Dubai to escape the threat of prosecution for collapsed businesses. Stories of the exploitation of labourers became more pronounced. The economic boom was found to be built on huge amounts of debt, which might have sunk Dubai had Abu Dhabi not come to its rescue.

Dubai's economic woes were symbolically laid bare with the public unveiling of the Burj Dubai. At the moment that the building was inaugurated, it was announced on the spot that this epic monument to Dubai and Sheikh Mohammed's aspirations was now the Burj Khalifa, renamed for Sheikh Khalifa bin Zayed Al Nahyan, ruler of Abu Dhabi and president of the UAE, who, significantly, was not in attendance. Whether the name change was demanded by Abu Dhabi as a sign of deference, or suggested by Sheikh Mohammed, is known only to those involved.

There has been speculation that this renaming of the most iconic of Dubai's structures suggests that Abu Dhabi – which is, famously, much more socially conservative than Dubai – will extend its control beyond matters financial. It is just as plausible, however, that Abu Dhabi's ruling class sees Dubai's brand and role in the UAE as complementary to their own, and will let Dubai continue on its chosen path. Another possibility is that, rather than Abu Dhabi seeking to exercise influence over Dubai as a result of these bailout loans, Dubai will become more conservative in the future (financially and socially) as a result of the lessons it has learned from this recession.

Only time of course will tell how this all plays out. Dubai's economy will certainly recover to some extent, though it may take a long time to reach again the peaks of the recent boom, if indeed it ever does. Whether Dubai's utopian brand image will recover and whether its rulers will tackle the issues I have detailed in this book is something that is in their hands.

* * *

The story of Dubai's expatriate population may end up being replicated beyond Dubai and the Arabian Gulf countries. While Bahrain and Kuwait are in the process of abandoning the *kafala* system, Western countries are increasingly adopting labour policies similar to those of Dubai and the other Gulf countries. While guest worker programs for working-class labourers in Europe go back roughly fifty years, now professionals may find themselves living under similar visa regimes.

The UK, for instance, overhauled its visa system in 2008, recognizing different tiers of immigrants. Tier 1 visas for highly skilled professional migrants do not require a sponsor, but Tier 2 General visas, which allow skilled workers to stay for a maximum of three years plus one month, are tied to the worker's employer, as in Dubai. While after five years a Tier 2 worker can apply to make his or her status permanent, the sponsoring business must certify that it still requires the worker. If an employer does not sponsor its employee for permanence, that worker and their family will have to leave. Moreover, in 2009 the government was considering banning access to citizenship for skilled workers from non-European Union countries who arrive on 'intra-company' transfers.

The US similarly has a program that limits the ability of professionals to stay: the H-1B visa program for mostly IT professionals, whose visas are tied to their employers. They can stay up to six years, so long as they are employed, then they must leave. They are allowed to apply for permanent residency, but there is no guarantee they will receive it. At its peak in the early 2000s, roughly 200,000 people a year were coming on this visa category, though the number of visas being issued yearly has dropped to its original 1999 level of 65,000.

The US has for some years also toyed with the idea of a wide-ranging guest worker program for lower-skilled workers, echoing the Bracero Program, which brought temporary Mexican agricultural laborers from 1942 to 1964, but was ended in part because of widespread abuse of workers. In 2006, Congress proposed a plan – which in the end was not enacted, but still has many supporters – to create a permanent guest-worker program that would admit 400,000 more workers a year.

At the time of the debate over the immigration bill in 2006, the *New York Times* columnist and Nobel Prize-winning economist Paul Krugman wondered about the 'Dubai effect' of an expanding disenfranchised workforce. He felt it would be a betrayal of the US's democratic ideals and lead to an even more entrenched caste system of labour, whereby the interests of these temporary workers would largely be ignored, their rights circumscribed and their wages under pressure.

If this comes to pass Dubai may not end up being such a unique case after all, but rather a harbinger of how migrants may increasingly in the future be treated in Western countries, and an indication of how they may respond.

NOTES

PREFACE

1. Robert Worth (2009) 'Laid-off foreigners flee as Dubai spirals down', New York Times, 11 February 2009, http://www.nytimes.com/2009/02/12/world/middleeast/12dubai.html (accessed 13 February 2009).

2. Maria Abi-Habib, 'Dubai Bailout from Abu Dhabi Is Cut in Half', *Wall Street Journal*, 18 January 2010, http://online.wsj.com/article/SB10001424052748704541004575010930199296878.html (accessed 23 January 2010)

3. Syed Ali (2007b) 'You must come with us', *Guardian*, 12 November 2007, http://lifeandhealth.guardian.co.uk/family/story/0,,2209519,00.html (accessed 25 July 2009).

4. See the comments to my blog post, which was the basis for my *Guardian* piece: Syed Ali (2006) 'Five guys in white come to my door, and I get a new iPod', *Dubai Notes*, 11 November, http://bklyn-in-dubai.livejournal.com/5259.html.

5. Arif Sharif (2008) 'Dubai can't find the taxis to make its skyscrapers commodious', *Bloomberg*, 14 July, http://www.bloomberg.com/apps/news?pid=20601109&sid=aUYy8mpe6e6o&refer=home (accessed 17 July 2009).

6. Shubhajit Roy (2007) 'Are you an American scholar? You aren't welcome in India', 11 February 2007, *Indian Express*, http://www.indianexpress.com/news/are-you-an-american-scholar-you-arent-welcome-in-india/23071/ (accessed 22 February 2007).

INTRODUCTION

1. Other cities in the Arabian Gulf, such as Abu Dhabi, Doha and Kuwait City, also have majority expatriate populations. But outside the Gulf no other city comes close. For instance, Singapore, which is famed as a haven for expatriates, has an expatriate, non-resident worker population of 'only' 20 per cent.

2. See, for example, Christopher Davidson (2005) *The United Arab Emirates: A Study In Survival*, Lynne Rienner, Boulder, CO; idem (2008) *Dubai: The Vulnerability of Success*, Hurst, London; Aamir Rehman (2008) *Dubai & Co.: Global Strategies for Doing Business in the Gulf States*, Mc-Graw Hill, New York; Ahmed Kanna (ed.) (2010) *The Superlative City: Dubai and the Urban Condition in the Early Twenty-First Century*, Harvard University Press, Cambridge, MA.
3. This can be seen through a rough indicator of current research, presentations at the major Middle Eastern Studies Association's annual meeting in the United States, where scholars from all over the world come to present their latest research on the Middle East. An examination of the papers presented in the past few years shows that surprisingly few deal with economic, political or social aspects regarding Gulf countries. For example, out of 207 sessions at the 2007 MESA conference, only two dealt directly with Gulf issues. Likewise at the 2009 conference, out of 230 sessions and 935 papers there were only a handful of papers that addressed Gulf matters.
4. Saskia Sassen (2007) *A Sociology of Globalization*, W.W. Norton, New York, p. 29.
5. Ashfaq Ahmed (2008) 'Expats make up 99% of private sector staff in UAE', *Gulf News*, 7 April, http://gulfnews.com/news/gulf/uae/employment/expats-make-up-99-of-private-sector-staff-in-uae-1.96744 (accessed 27 June 2009).
6. George Soros (1998) 'Towards a global open society', *Atlantic Monthly*, January, http://www.theatlantic.com/issues/98jan/opensoc.htm (accessed 29 June 2008).

CHAPTER ONE: THE ROOTS OF DUBAI

1. Fatma Al-Sayegh (1998) 'Merchants' role in a changing society: The case of Dubai, 1900–90', *Middle Eastern Studies*, vol. 34, no. 1, p. 87–102, 90.
2. The passing of the pearling era today is remembered and memorialized nostalgic- ally, but, once the sheikhdoms of the Gulf had other sources of employment and wealth, no one who had worked at sea in the pearl fisheries regretted its passing. Life on the boats was squalid, and the food was nasty – dirty sodden rice and maggoty dates were what the pearl fishers had to eat for months on end. See Peter Lienhardt (2001) *Shaikhdoms of Eastern Arabia* (ed. Ahmed Al-Shahi), Palgrave, Basingstoke, UK, p. 152.
3. Ibid., p. 123.
4. Michael Field (1985) *The Merchants: The Big Business Families of Saudi Arabia and the Gulf States*, Overlook Press, Woodstock, NY, pp. 61–4; Abdullah Taryam (1987) *The Establishment of the United Arab Emirates, 1950–85*, Croom Helm, London, p. 21.
5. Christopher Dickey (1990) *Expats: Travels in Arabia from Tripoli to Teheran*, Atlantic Monthly Press, New York, pp. 40–1.
6. Warren Richey (1982) 'Tiny Dubai, an Emirate trade hub, beset by area rivalry', *Christian Science Monitor*, 9 December; John Duke Anthony (1975) *Arab States of the Lower Gulf: People, Politics, Petroleum*, 1975, The Middle East Institute, Washington, DC, pp. 159, 168.
7. Field (1985) pp. 61–4.
8. Richey (1982); Alan Cowell (1988) 'A barometer of riches: How now the dhow?' *New York Times*, 27 October.
9. Christopher Stewart (2008) 'The axis of commerce', *Portfolio.Com*, September, http://www.portfolio.com/news-markets/international-news/portfolio/2008/08/13/US-Trades-With-Iran-Via-Dubai (accessed 12 May 2009).

10. Ibid.
11. Though the British never directly ruled Dubai or the other emirates, they controlled their foreign relations and defence, and did have a great deal of say and influence over internal affairs. This was a relationship beneficial to the rulers, who begged the British to stay in the late 1960s after the British announced they were ending their military involvement in the Gulf. See James Onley (2007) *The Arabian Frontier of the British Raj: Merchants, Rulers, and the British in the Nineteenth Century Gulf*, Oxford University Press, Oxford; idem (2009) 'The Raj reconsidered: British India's informal empire and spheres of influence in Asia and Africa', *Asian Affairs*, vol. 40, no. 1, pp. 44–62; Graeme Wilson (1999) *Father of Dubai: Sheikh Rashid bin Saeed Al Maktoum*, Media Prima, Dubai, also available at http://213.132.44.227/english/dubai/fatherofDubai_winds1.asp (accessed 18 June 2009).
12. John Duke Anthony (1975), p. 159.
13. Wilson (1999), also available at http://213.132.44.227/english/dubai/fatherof Dubai_ruler1.asp; http://213.132.44.227/english/dubai/fatherofDubai_ruler2.asp (accessed 17 June 2009).
14. The story of Mumbai's underworld, and its connection with Dubai is a fascinating one, and is masterfully told by Suketu Mehta (2004) *Maximum City: Bombay Lost and Found*, Penguin, New Delhi.
15. Jim Krane (2009) *City of Gold: Dubai and the Dream of Capitalism*, St. Martin's Press, New York, pp. 105–11.
16. Matthew Maier (2005) 'Rise of the Emirates empire', *Business 2.0*, October, http://money.cnn.com/magazines/business2/business2_archive/2005/10/01/ 8359251/index.htm (accessed 10 February 2009).
17. Sandra Dallas and Drusilla Menaker (1996) 'The mall of the Middle East', *Business Week*, 25 November.
18. *Business Times* (1994) 'Dubai: A curious blend of old and new', *Business Times* (Singapore), 17 September.
19. Lekha Rai (1996) 'Dubai shopping festival', *Advertising Age*, 9 December.
20. Shahid Ali Khan (2000) 'Saudis biggest spenders at Dubai shopping festival', *Saudi Gazette*, 14 February.
21. Yaroslav Trofimov (1995) 'United Arab Emirates Inc.', *Jerusalem Post*, 15 June 1995.
22. Ibid.
23. Susan Horner and John Swarbrooke (2004) *International Cases in Tourism Management*, Butterworth-Heinemann, Oxford, pp. 140–1.
24. Sethuram Dinakar (1999) 'The Russian crunch has Dubai crying . . . But the mob is still moving goods', *Business Week*, 8 March.
25. Kathy Evans (1992) 'Lazy days on the beach and stunning starlit desert nights', *Guardian*, 2 December.
26. Kathy Evans (1994) 'Dubai: State of sin', *Guardian*, 26 November.
27. Mark Hodson (1995) 'Shop of the desert', *The Sunday Times*, 3 December.
28. *Travel Trade Gazette* (2000) 'Dubai's star still in the ascendant', *Travel Trade Gazette UK & Ireland*, 17 July.
29. Joan Henderson (2006) 'Tourism in Dubai: Overcoming barriers to destination development', *International Journal of Tourism Research*, vol. 8, no. 2, pp. 87–99.
30. See Anh Longva (1997) *Walls Built on Sand: Migration, Exclusion, and Society in Kuwait*, Westview, Boulder, CO; Andrzej Kapiszewski (2001) *Nationals and Expatriates: Population and Labour Dilemmas of the Gulf Cooperation Council States*, Ithaca Press, Reading, UK.

31. Karen Attwood and Haneen Dajani (2008) 'Passport holders sell visas illegally', *The National*, 2 July 2008, http://www.thenational.ae/article/20080702/NATIONAL /688537372/1105/ (accessed 22 June 2009).

32. See Frauke Heard-Bey (1982) *From Trucial States to United Arab Emirates*, Longman, London, p. 411, note 17.

33. Liesl Graz (1992) *The Turbulent Gulf: People, Politics and Power*, I.B. Tauris, London, p. 188.

34. Myron Weiner (1982) 'International migration and development: Indians in the Persian Gulf', *Population and Development Review*, vol. 8, no. 1, pp. 1–36, 11.

35. Anthony (1975), p. 163.

36. Graz (1992), p. 165.

37. Wilson (1999), also available at http://213.132.44.227/english/dubai/fatherof Dubai_oil.asp (accessed 17 June 2009).

38. Rayeesa Absal (2007) '342,000 illegal immigrants took advantage of amnesty', 14 November, *Gulf News*, http://archive.gulfnews.com/indepth/amnesty/main_story/ 10167345.html (accessed 22 June 2009); *Indian Express* (2007) 'Over 1 lakh Indian illegal workers avail UAE amnesty offer', 4 September, http://www.indianex-press.com/news/over-1-lakh-indian-illegal-workers-avail-ua/214337/ (accessed 17 July 2009).

39. Weiner (1982), p. 13.

40. Akbar Ahmed (1984) ' "Dubai Chalo": Problems in the ethnic encounter between Middle Eastern and South Asian Muslim societies', *Asian Affairs*, vol. 15, no. 3, pp. 262–76, 269.

41. Weiner (1982), p. 6.

42. Andy Sambidge (2009c) 'UAE raises minimum salary limit for expats with family', *ArabianBusiness.com*, 2 July, http://www.arabianbusiness.com/560719-uae-to-raise-minimum-salary-limit-for-expats-with-family (accessed 3 July 2009).

43. Graz (1992), p. 198.

44. Henry Russell (1995) 'Jousting for jobs: You want to work in Dubai? So does everyone else', *Resident Abroad*, April, pp. 26, 28.

45. Dickey (1990), pp. 171–2.

46. Ibid.

CHAPTER TWO: BECOMING A GLOBAL BRAND

1. The other two were Saudi Arabia and Pakistan. All three, however, officially withdrew their recognition after the 11 September 2001 attacks.

2. Steve Coll (2004) *Ghost Wars*, Penguin, New York, pp. 446–50.

3. Kim Sengupta and Daniel Howden (2009) 'Pirates: the $80m Gulf connection', *Independent*, 21 April, http://www.independent.co.uk/news/world/africa/pirates-the-80m-gulf-connection-1671657.html (accessed 22 April 2009)

4. Barrett, Raymond (2009) 'New Jack Emirate: A key to understanding the history of Dubai's seamy underbelly', *Foreign Policy*, April, http://www.foreignpolicy.com /story/cms.php?story_id=4897 (accessed 14 July 2009).

5. John Cassara (2006) *Hide and Seek: Intelligence, Law Enforcement, and the Stalled War on Terrorist Finance*, Potomac Books, Washington, DC, p. 149.

6. Coll (2004), p. 152.

7. Hassan Fattah (2006) 'Emirate wakes up famous: Thank you, America.' *New York Times*, 2 March, http://www.nytimes.com/2006/03/02/international/middleeast/ 02dubai.html (accessed 3 June 2007).

8. Aamir Rehman (2008) *Dubai & Co.: Global Strategies for Doing Business in the Gulf States*, McGraw Hill, New York, p. 223.

9. The Real Nick (2009) 'The Real Nick's really visionary strategic plan to property investment', *Some Like It Not*, 7 April, http://some-like-it-not.blogspot.com/2009/04/real-nicks-really-visionary-strategic.html (accessed 15 April 2009).

10. Steve Rose (2005) 'Sand and freedom' *Guardian*, 28 November 2005, http://www.guardian.co.uk/artanddesign/2005/nov/28/architecture (accessed 22 June 2008).

11. Phillip Kennicott (2007) 'Arabian heights: Oil-rich Dubai raises its international profile with towers meant to be icons: But icons of what?' *Washington Post*, 28 October, http://www.washingtonpost.com/wp-dyn/content/article/2007/10/25/AR2007102501225.html (accessed 12 November 2007).

12. Fred Bernstein (2008) 'Reaching for the clouds in Dubai', *New York Times*, 8 August, http://www.nytimes.com/2008/08/10/arts/design/10bern.html (accessed 13 March 2009).

13. Sonia Verma (2009) 'Sun, sea and sewage in the playground of the rich in Dubai', *The Times*, 29 January, http://www.timesonline.co.uk/tol/travel/news/article 5607619.ece (accessed 22 February 2009).

14. A Saudi scholar who heads a think tank in Dubai estimated that the true cost of desalinating one litre of water is USD 1.50, which is then subsidized with the cost to consumers being only USD 0.50. See Emmanuelle Landais (2009) 'Experts seek to address water usage, scarcity challenges at special forum', *Gulf News*, 23 March, http://archive.gulfnews.com/nation/Environment/10297759.html (accessed 24 March 2009); Aftab Kazmi (2006) 'Dubai's water resources "insufficient"', *Gulf News*, 5 July, http://archive.gulfnews.com/articles/06/07/05/10051564.html (accessed 24 March 2009).

15. Leo Hickman (2008) 'Chilling developments in Dubai', *Guardian*, 18 December, http://www.guardian.co.uk/environment/2008/dec/18/artificial-beach-dubai-environment (accessed 25 December 2008).

16. Phil Clark and Anna Winston (2008) 'Mayne warns Dubai set for "ecological disaster"', *Building Design: The Architect's Website*, 10 October, http://www.bdonline.co.uk/story.asp?storycode=3124669 (accessed 14 November 2008).

17. See their website, http://www.dynamicarchitecture.net/home.html (accessed 5 February 2009). The brochure can be downloaded, or viewed as a short film on the site's front page.

18. MENAFN (2008) 'UAE: Foreign firms, individuals main buyers of Dubai properties', *Middle East North Africa Financial Network*, 27 May, http://menafn.com/qn_news_story_s.asp?StoryId=1093198097 (accessed 12 February 2009).

19. Parag Deulgaonkar (2009) 'Residence visas to boost property market', *Emirates Business 24|7*, 18 February, http://www.business24-7.ae/articles/2009/2/pages/02182009_fd18091bd07443628a393b46dcdf4544.aspx (accessed 14 April 2009).

20. Bassma al Jandaly (2008) 'Short-term visas for realty buyers in Dubai', *Gulf News*, 24 June, http://www.gulfnews.com/BUSINESS/Real_Estate_Property/10223343.html (accessed 22 February 2009).

21. Deulgaonkar (2009).

22. *The Economist* (2008) 'A new itinerary', 15 May, http://www.economist.com/business/displaystory.cfm?story_id=11374574 (accessed 12 April 2009).

23. These figures are from the Dubai Department of Tourism and Commerce Marketing. For statistics on hotel and hotel apartment stays, see http://

dubaitourism.co.ae/EServices/Statistics/HotelStatistics/tabid/167/language/
en-US/Default.aspx (accessed 27 February 2009).

24. 'Joseph Mortimer (2006) 'From Russia with love', *Arabian Travel News*, 3 December,
http://www.itp.net/news/494288 (accessed 3 March 2009).

25. Annabel Kantaria (2008) 'Expats in Dubai: Shop to stop dropping as Dubai
summer hits its height', *Daily Telegraph*, 1 August, http://www.telegraph.co.uk
/expat/4205374/Expats-in-Dubai-Shop-to-stop-dropping-as-Dubai-summer-
hits-its-height.html (accessed 21 January 2009).

26. Subramani Dharmarajan (2008) 'Unbearable demands: Broken promises', *Xpress*,
23 October, http://www.xpress4me.com/news/uae/dubai/20010165.html (accessed
4 November 2008).

27. Barbara Surk (2007) 'Jail time is cost for not paying debts in Dubai', *The Seattle
Times*, 12 June, http://seattletimes.nwsource.com/html/nationworld/2003744014
_debtors12.html (accessed 14 April 2009).

28. Dubai also draws a large number of young Iranian tourists who fly in for the week-
ends for the nightclubs. But the young tourists are not all hedonists – some come
to take a seminar on 'regime change' back home. See Ivan Watson (2007) 'Iran's
neighbour Dubai a place of intrigue', *National Public Radio (US) Morning Edition*,
9 May, http://www.npr.org/templates/story/story.php?storyId=10089956 (accessed
13 March 2009).

29. 'Charles Runnette (2007) 'Confessions on a Dubai dance floor', *New York Times*, 25
March, http://travel.nytimes.com/2007/03/25/travel/tmagazine/03talk.dubai.t.html
(accessed 20 January 2009).

30. Charlie Norton (2007) 'Dubai: If you're not loaded and decadent, you can't come
in', *The Sunday Times*, 10 June, http://www.timesonline.co.uk/tol/travel/article
1878608.ece (accessed 8 January 2008); Runnette (2007).

31. Runnette (2007).

32. Trofimov (1995).

33. Written communication received from the source indicated on 13 January 2009.

34. William Ridgeway (2005) 'Dubai: The scandal and the vice', *Social Affairs Unit*,
5 April, http://www.socialaffairsunit.org.uk/blog/archives/000345.php (accessed
18 September 2008).

35. Kito de Boer *et al.* (2008) 'The coming oil windfall in the Gulf', McKinsey Global
Institute, January, http://www.mckinsey.com/mgi/publications/The_Coming_
Oil_Windfall/index.asp (accessed 2 November 2009). See also Diana Farrell and
Susan Lind (2008) 'The new role of oil wealth in the world economy', *McKinsey
Quarterly*, January.

36. Emily Thornton and Stanley Reed (2008) 'Who's afraid of Mideast money?'
Business Week, 10 January, http://www.businessweek.com/magazine/content/
08_03/b4067042272294.htm (3 accessed July 2009).

37. For an intricate roadmap to Dubai's corporate model, see Phillip Lotter and Tristan
Cooper (2008) 'Demystifying Dubai Inc.: A guide to Dubai's corporatist model and
Moody's assessment of its rising leverage', *Moody's Investors Service*, October.

38. Brad Setser and Rachel Ziemba (2009) *GCC Sovereign Funds: Reversal of Fortune*,
Council on Foreign Relations, New York.

39. William Pesek (2009) 'Dubai's edifice complex is falling on hard times', *Bloomberg*,
6 February, http://www.bloomberg.com/apps/news?pid=20601039&sid=aYDcH7_
GEdkc&refer=columnist_pesek (accessed 2 July 2009).

40. Louise Armitstead (2008) 'Dubai reveals debt levels to dispel fears over growth',
Daily Telegraph, 24 November, http://www.telegraph.co.uk/news/worldnews/

middleeast/dubai/3510908/Dubai-reveals-debt-levels-to-dispel-fears-over-growth.html (accessed 5 July 2009).

41. Dominic O'Connell and Iain Dey (2008) 'Abu Dhabi wants stake in Emirates for bailout cash', *The Sunday Times*, 30 November, http://business.timesonline.co.uk/tol/business/industry_sectors/transport/article5258243.ece (accessed 29 June 2009).

42. Simeon Kerr and James Drummond (2009) 'Alarm over cost of insuring Dubai debt', *Financial Times*, 15 February, http://www.ft.com/cms/s/0/0ee4f97c-fb8e-11dd-bcad-000077b07658.html (accessed 8 July 2009).

43. Edmund O'Sullivan (2009) 'Dubai looks beyond the debt mountain', *Middle East Economic Digest*, 5 May, http://www.meed.com/commentary/last_word/2009/05/concerns_mount_over_dubais_skyhigh_debt.html (accessed 20 June 2009).

44. 'Brand Dubai will set record straight', *Gulf News*, 14 June 2009, http://archive.gulfnews.com/articles/09/06/14/10322491.html (accessed 29 June 2009).

45. *Associated Press* (2007) 'Dubai shuts down independent Pakistan TV station under pressure', 17 November, http://www.foxnews.com/story/0,2933,312027,00.html (accessed June 1, 2009).

46. Roy Greenslade (2009) 'Why was journalist detained in Dubai?' *Guardian*, 21 April, http://www.guardian.co.uk/media/greenslade/2009/apr/21/press-freedom-wallstreetjournal (accessed 22 May 2009).

47. Ivan Watson (2008) 'Dubai's media censors tackle news, sex and politics', *National Public Radio*, 22 January, http://www.npr.org/templates/story/story.php?storyId=18292869 (accessed 27 February 2008).

48. Tom Gara (2009) 'Regulator orders article critical of Dubai to be unblocked online', *The National*, 21 May, http://www.thenational.ae/article/20090522/NATIONAL/705219840/1010 (accessed 29 June 2009).

49. Secret Dubai, *Secret Dubai diary*, http://secretdubai.blogspot.com (accessed 12 November 2009).

50. The blog was actually written by two women: *Sex and Dubai*, http://www.single-in-dubai.blogspot.com/ (accessed 12 November 2009).

51. Johann Hari (2009a) 'The dark side of Dubai', *Independent*, 7 April, http://www.independent.co.uk/opinion/commentators/johann-hari/the-dark-side-of-dubai-1664368.html (accessed 9 April 2009).

52. Johann Hari (2009b) 'My post about Dubai is now banned in the city', *Huffington Post*, 21 May, http://www.huffingtonpost.com/johann-hari/my-post-about-dubai-is-no_b_206388.html (accessed 30 June 2009).

53. Nour Samaha and Salam Hafez (2009) 'Internet regulator bans violent protest videos', *The National*, 25 June, http://www.thenational.ae/article/20090625/NATIONAL/706249854 (accessed 29 June 2009).

54. Heerkani Chohan (2009) 'Dubai property scandal claim emerges amid media blackout', 28 May, *Independent*, http://www.independent.co.uk/news/world/middle-east/dubai-property-scandal-claim-emerges-amid-media-blackout-1691537.html (accessed 29 June 2009).

55. Human Rights Watch (2009a) 'Just the good news, please: New UAE media law continues to stifle press', 6 April, http://www.hrw.org/node/82150 (accessed 29 June 2009).

56. *Gulf News* (2009) 'Suspension of Arabic daily upheld', 1 July, http://www.gulfnews.com/nation/Media/10327925.html (accessed 3 July 2009); *Agence France-Presse* (2009) 'UAE suspends newspaper over "horse doping"

claims', 2 July, http://www.google.com/hostednews/afp/article/ALeqM5i5VA2 Mcm9Oawldga_X8MGyrh4O5w (accessed 3 July 2009).

57. *Press Gazette* (2006) 'No tax and all year sunshine', 2 June, http://www. pressgazette.co.uk/story.asp?storycode=34382 (accessed 29 June 2009).

58. Dana El-Baltaji (2007) 'Picture perfect: How the story of Dubai's other side can never be told', *Arab Media & Society*, Issue 2, Summer, http://www.arabmediasociety.com/?article=224 (accessed 22 May 2008).

59. Eman Mohammed (2008a) 'Age of glorifying officials over, says UAE media council chief', *Gulf News*, 17 April, http://www.gulfnews.com/Nation/Media /10206222.html (accessed 25 May 2009).

60. Human Rights Watch (2009a).

61. Like many governmental pronouncements, it was still unclear for a period of time whether an NOC was actually required. For example, in a 2007 column in *Gulf News* called 'Ask the Law', an engineer wanted to know if he needed an NOC to change jobs to a 'non-competitor' company (many companies have clauses in their contracts saying employees cannot join competitors). The Emirati lawyer responded, 'The Ministry of Labour currently requires an NOC in case the employee wishes to transfer to another employer. For that reason, the questioner is advised to seek an NOC from his current employer otherwise he will be subject to a six-month ban.' It is telling that a lawyer specializing in labour issues would say this. Either he did not know of the Ministry of Labour's pronouncement or, more likely, officials lower down in the Ministry's hierarchy either did not know of or did not implement the 2006 policy. By 2008, though, the policy must have become much clearer to all concerned. The same Emirati lawyer answering the 'Ask the Law' column responded to a different reader's query about getting an NOC: 'I would like to assure the questioner that he may initiate procedures to transfer sponsorship with his new employer, and there is no need for an NOC from the previous sponsor, after paying the required fees to the Ministry of Labour.' See Diaa Hadid (2006a) 'New UAE job-switch rule 'in place for weeks', *Gulf News*, 8 March, http://archive.gulfnews.com/articles/06/03/08/10023895.html (accessed 29 June 2009); Dina Aboul Hosn (2008) 'Ask the law: No objection certificate', *Gulf News*, 9 May, http://archive.gulfnews.com/articles/08/05/09/10211690.html (accessed 29 June 2009).

62. Zaher Bitar (2008) 'Labour pains: Ban rules are back', *Xpress*, 5 June, http://www.xpress4me.com/news/uae/dubai/20007923.html (accessed 2 June 2009).

63. Martin Morris (2009) 'Ban impacting expat labour under review', *ArabianBusiness.com*, 1 March, http://www.arabianbusiness.com/548323-6-month-labour-ban-in-dubai-under-review (accessed 22 June 2009).

64. Andy Sambidge (2009a) 'Contracting industry chief slams Bahrain sponsor move', *ArabianBusiness.com*, 10 May, http://www.arabianbusiness.com/555083-contracting-industry-chief-slams-bahrain-sponsor-move (accessed 22 June 2009).

65. Andy Sambidge (2009b) 'Police chief calls for end of sponsorship in UAE', *ArabianBusiness.com*, 24 June, http://www.arabianbusiness.com/559899 (accessed 26 June 2009).

66. Ian Parker (2005) 'The mirage: The architectural insanity of Dubai', *The New Yorker*, 17 October, p. 136.

67. A handful of arts venues existed before the latest economic boom, including Majlis Gallery, Green Art Gallery and Dubai International Arts Centre.

68. One woman who is familiar with the arts scene in Dubai pointed out to me that expatriate artists were mostly housewives pursuing art as a hobby, and 'not of high calibre' (personal interview, 7 April 2009).

69. An alternate possibility is freelancing, which until the mid-2000s was illegal, but is now acceptable in some free zones. As a result, in free zones such as Media City a freelancer can now buy a three-year residence visa for AED 7,500, but that is in addition to other costs that are required to get the visa through Media City, which in total add up to AED 45,000, more than USD 12,000. See Scott MacMillan (2008) 'I want to break free!', *Kippreport*, 9 November, http://www.kippreport.com/kipp/2008/11/09/i-want-to-break-free/?bnr=1 (accessed 9 March 2009).

70. Henry Bowles (2008) 'Books in Arabia's boomtown', *Foreign Policy*, January/February, p. 97.

71. One expatriate who grew up in Dubai pointed out to me that musicians, comedians and stage actors did come to Dubai in the 1990s, but much less frequently, and most performers were 'second or third tier'.

72. R. Jay Magill, Jr (2008) 'Cultural pretensions in Dubai: Desert metropolis reinvents itself as art center', *Der Spiegel*, 21 March, http://www.spiegel.de/international/world/0,1518,542874,00.html (accessed 24 March 2009).

73. See Tashkeel's website, http://www.tashkeel.org/aboutus.html (accessed 13 March 2009). See also *Chinar Tree* (2008) ' "We want to cultivate art from Dubai": An interview with Lateefa bint Maktoum at Tashkeel', December, http://chinartree.com/2009/01/08/we-want-to-cultivate-art-from-dubai-an-interview-with-lateefa-bint-maktoum-december-2008/ (accessed 15 March 2009).

74. See, for example, Sharon Waxman (2009) 'An oasis in the desert', *ARTNews*, February, 108, 2, http://www.artnewsonline.com/issues/article.asp?art_id=2627 (accessed 13 March 2009); Susan Moore (2009) 'The rapid emergence of Emirati art', *Financial Times*, 7 March, http://www.ft.com/cms/s/2/74121b62–091d–11de-b8b0–0000779fd2ac.html (accessed 13 March 2009).

75. Saatchi Gallery (2008) 'Ana Finel Honigman on Dubai's Creek Art Fair', 26 March, http://www.saatchi-gallery.co.uk/blogon/2008/03/ana_finel_honigman_on_dubais_c_1.php (accessed 13 March 2009).

76. Vinita Bharadwaj (2009) 'Art of the matter', *Gulf News*, 20 March (accessed 2 April 2009); Diana Eid (2008) 'Taxidermy camel + oversized suitcase = controversial art', *Inventorspot*, 23 April, http://inventorspot.com/articles/oh_so_thats_where_i_put_my_stuffed_camel_12774 (accessed 8 April 2009).

77. The acclaimed Canadian author Margaret Atwood was scheduled as a star attraction but hastily pulled out because of a controversy over censorship. It was reported that a book that was to premiere at the festival was banned because one of the characters was a gay sheikh. It turned out that the book had never been accepted for the festival. Atwood then agreed to appear via videolink. See Claire Armitstead (2009) 'Censorship row echoes through Dubai literary festival', *Guardian*, 2 March, http://www.guardian.co.uk/books/2009/mar/02/censorship-row-dubai-festival (accessed 2 June 2009).

78. John Arlidge (2008) 'Doha: the cultural Dubai', *The Times*, 29 November, http://www.timesonline.co.uk/tol/travel/destinations/middle_east/article5246873.ece (accessed 22 January 2009).

79. *Gulf News* (2008b) 'Culture museum in Dubai will be first in the region', 22 June, http://www.gulfnews.com/Nation/Heritage_and_Culture/10222873.html (accessed 22 January 2009).

80. Isaac John (2006) 'Dubai launches Dh50b culture village project', *Khaleej Times*, 13 May, http://www.khaleejtimes.com/DisplayArticleNew.asp?xfile=data/business/2006/May/business_May333.xml&section=business (accessed 25 February 2008).

81. Two of the earliest universities to open were the University of Wollongong in Dubai in 1993 and the American University in Dubai in 1995, a branch campus of the for-profit American InterContinental University.

82. See the descriptions of the areas of focus on the website of the Mohammed Bin Rashid Al Maktoum Foundation, http://www.mbrfoundation.ae/English/ (accessed 22 March 2009).

83. See Warren Fox (2008) 'The United Arab Emirates and policy priorities for higher education', in Christopher Davidson and Peter Mackenzie Smith (eds) *Higher Education in the Gulf States: Shaping Economies, Politics and Culture*, Saqi, London, pp. 110–26; Andrew Mills (2008) 'Emirates look to the West for prestige', *Chronicle of Higher Education*, 26 September, http://chronicle.com/free/v55/i05/05a00101.htm (accessed 1 April 2009).

84. Zvika Krieger (2008a) 'An academic building boom transforms the Persian Gulf', *Chronicle of Higher Education*, vol. 54, no. 29, 28 March.

85. Fox (2008). For a list of universities and other educational institutions in Dubai, see the official government website of the Dubai Knowledge and Human Development Authority, http://www.khda.gov.ae/en/home/default.aspx (accessed 3 April 2009).

86. Krieger (2008a).

87. John Gill (2008) 'Oiling the learning machine', *Times Higher Education*, 21 August, http://www.timeshighereducation.co.uk/story.asp?sectioncode=26&storycode=403223&c=1 (accessed 1 April 2009).

88. Zvika Krieger (2008b) 'The Emir of NYU', *New York Magazine*, 13 April, http://nymag.com/news/features/46000/ (accessed 1 May 2008).

89. Krieger (2008a).

90. Ethan Bronner (2009) 'Palestinian campus looks to east bank (of Hudson)', *New York Times*, 15 February, http://www.nytimes.com/2009/02/15/world/middleeast/15quds.html (accessed 16 February 2009).

CHAPTER THREE: IRON CHAINS

1. David Keane and Nicholas McGeehan (2008) 'Enforcing migrant workers' rights in the United Arab Emirates', *International Journal on Minority and Group Rights*, vol. 15, no. 1, pp. 81–115. They write: 'In an interview with the Indian consul in Dubai . . . [French] journalists were shown [in 2005] confidential reports that two Asians per day die on the construction sites of Dubai, and that there is a suicide every four days.' Very few deaths on the job are officially reported to the UAE Ministry of Labour for the simple reason that 'Companies are legally obliged to pay two years' salary to the family of any worker who dies in a work-related incident' (p. 93).

2. Wafa Issa (2007a) 'Heat is on to ensure midday break rule', *Gulf News*, 21 June, http://archive.gulfnews.com/indepth/labour/Pay_and_conditions/10134106.html (accessed 28 June 2007).

3. Wafa Issa (2007b) '102 companies fined more than Dh1m for violating break rule', *Gulf News*, 16 July, http://archive.gulfnews.com/indepth/labour/Pay_and_conditions/10139541.html.

4. Tom Arnold (2009) '73 firms fined for violating summer work hours', *ArabianBusiness.com*, 7 July, http://www.arabianbusiness.com/561227–73-firms-fined-for-violating-summer-work-hours (accessed 9 July 2009).
5. Keane and McGeehan (2008) p. 83.
6. Human Rights Watch (2006b) 'Building towers, cheating workers: Exploitation of migrant construction workers in the United Arab Emirates', November, pp. 38–9, http://www.hrw.org/en/reports/2006/11/11/building-towers-cheating-workers (accessed 29 June 2009).
7. Ibid., p. 10.
8. Samir Salama (2006c) 'Retaining passports is "forcible labour" ', *Gulf News*, 13 June, http://archive.gulfnews.com/articles/06/06/13/10046487.html (accessed 22 June 2006).
9. K.C. Zachariah *et al.* (2004) 'Indian workers in UAE: Employment, wages and working conditions,' *Economic and Political Weekly*, 29 May, vol. 39, no. 22, pp. 2227–34.
10. Shadid, Anthony (2006) 'In UAE, tales of paradise lost', *Washington Post*, 12 April, http://www.washingtonpost.com/wp-dyn/content/article/2006/04/11/AR2006041101474.html (accessed 1 May 2006).
11. Human Rights Watch (2006b), p. 29.
12. Human Rights Watch (2009b) 'The island of happiness': Exploitation of migrant workers on Saadiyat Island, Abu Dhabi', 19 May, http://www.hrw.org/en/reports/2009/05/18/island-happiness-0 (accessed 22 May 2009).
13. Anthony (2006); see also Human Rights Watch (2006b), pp. 34–5.
14. Many people in Dubai make the specious argument that, well, this is a lot more money than these workers would make where they come from, which is why they come in the first place. An exchange on Secret Dubai's blog (one of the most widely read blogs from and about Dubai) is indicative of this: 'Sun, sand and slavery', 22 May 2007, http://secretdubai.blogspot.com/2007/05/sun-sand-and-slavery.html (accessed 21 June 2008).
15. Human Rights Watch (2006b), p. 36.
16. Human Rights Watch (2009b).
17. Human Rights Watch (2006b), pp. 26–9.
18. Ash (2007) 'Of greedy appetites and glass houses', *A Most Trying July*, 15 March, http://tryingjuly.blogspot.com/2007/03/judgment-day.html (accessed 22 March 2007).
19. Samir Salama (2006b) 'Unskilled workers can stay for 6 years: Al Ka'abi', *Gulf News*, 8 June, http://gulfnews.com/news/gulf/uae/employment/unskilled-workers-can-stay-for-6-years-al-ka-abi-1.240098 (accessed 12 January 2007).
20. Duraid Al Baik (2007) 'Six-year cap on foreign workers', *Gulf News*, 1 October, http://archive.gulfnews.com/articles/07/10/01/10157293.html. The GCC members are Saudi Arabia, UAE, Kuwait, Bahrain, Qatar and Oman. Throughout the book I refer to the GCC member states as 'the Gulf' or 'Gulf countries.'
21. Wafa Issa (2007c) 'Businesses lash out at residency cap proposal', *Gulf News*, 22 October, http://archive.gulfnews.com/indepth/labour/more_stories/10162184.html
22. Andrew White (2009) 'Expat residency cap as early as 2010 – Minister', 7 July, *ArabianBusiness.com*, http://www.arabianbusiness.com/561192-expat-residency-cap-as-early-as-2010—minister (accessed 7 July 2009).
23. Human Rights Watch (2006c) 'UAE: Workers abused in construction boom: New report highlights the plight of migrant construction workers', 11 November,

http://www.hrw.org/en/news/2006/11/11/uae-workers-abused-construction-boom (accessed 13 November 2006).

24. Elsa Baxter (2009) 'UAE workers report over 300 firms for unpaid wages', *ArabianBusiness.com*, 21 June, http://www.arabianbusiness.com/559453-uae-workers-report-over-300-firms-for-unpaid-wages (accessed 7 July 2009).

25. Human Rights Watch (2009b).

26. Diaa Hadid (2006b) 'Labour protests in 2005', *Gulf News*, 29 April, http://archive.gulfnews.com/indepth/labour/Protests/10036459.html (accessed 12 October 2006).

27. The timeline is taken from Keane and McGeehan (2008) pp. 89–90.

28. Ratha *et al.* (2008) 'Briefing 8: Outlook for remittance flows 2008–2010: Growth expected to moderate significantly, but flows to remain resilient', Migration and Remittances Team Development Prospects Group, World Bank, 11 November, http://siteresources.worldbank.org/INTPROSPECTS/Resources/334934–11103 15015165/MD_Brief8.pdf (accessed 22 January 2009)

29. Subramani Dharmarajan (2007) 'Sonapur: Welcome to the dark side', *Gulf News*, 3 April, http://gulfnews.com/news/gulf/uae/general/sonapur-welcome-to-the-dark-side-1.463591 (accessed 12 October 2009).

30. Sunita Menon (2007) 'Workers live amid pools of sewage', *Gulf News*, 10 March, http://gulfnews.com/news/gulf/uae/employment/workers-live-amid-pools-of-sewage-1.166065 (accessed 15 March 2007).

31. Wafa Issa (2008) '70 per cent of labour accommodations violate safety rules', *Gulf News*, 17 December, http://gulfnews.com/news/gulf/uae/housing-property/70-of-labour-accommodations-violate-safety-rules-1.149524 (accessed 22 January 2009).

32. Lila Allen (2009) 'Dark side of the Dubai dream', *BBC News* (*Panorama*), 6 April, http://news.bbc.co.uk/2/hi/uk_news/magazine/7985361.stm (accessed 29 June 2009).

33. Zaher Bitar and Kamakshi Gupta (2008) 'Four detained over Deira fire', *Xpress*, 28 August, http://www.xpress4me.com/news/uae/dubai/20009363.html (accessed 1 September 2008).

34. Sunita Menon (2006) 'More than 2,000 workers housed in cargo containers', *Gulf News*, 25 November, http://gulfnews.com/news/gulf/uae/employment/more-than-2–000-workers-housed-in-cargo-containers-1.267094 (accessed 2 December 2006).

35. Joy Sengupta (2007) 'Have wheels, will sleep ...', *Khaleej Times*, 9 March, http://www.khaleejtimes.com/DisplayArticleNew.asp?xfile=data/theuae/2007/March/theuae_March269.xml&section=theuae&col= (accessed 12 April 2007).

36. Samir Salama (2007a) 'Hundreds of workers forced to live in attics', *Gulf News*, 19 February, http://gulfnews.com/news/gulf/uae/employment/hundreds-of-workers-forced-to-live-in-attics-1.161866 (accessed 1 October 2009).

37. Bassma Al Jandaly (2006a) 'Workers forced to live in freezing tent by recruiter', *Gulf News*, 2 June, http://gulfnews.com/news/gulf/uae/employment/workers-forced-to-live-in-freezing-tent-by-recruiter-1.83344 (accessed 1 October 2009).

38. Samir Salama (2006a) 'Change in rule for sponsorship transfer of maids hailed', *Gulf News*, 19 January, http://archive.gulfnews.com/articles/06/01/19/10012600.html (accessed 22 March 2008.)

39. Human Rights Watch (2007) 'Exported and exposed: Abuses against Sri Lankan domestic workers in Saudi Arabia, Kuwait, Lebanon, and the United Arab Emirates, 13 November, p. 44, http://www.hrw.org/en/reports/2007/11/13/exported-and-exposed-1 (accessed 21 August 2008).

40. Becky Lucas (2008) 'Filipino Dubai', *TimeOut Dubai*, July.
41. Human Rights Watch (2007), p. 63.
42. Secret Dubai (2005) 'Mute maids of the mall', *Secret Dubai Diary*, 30 November, http://secretdubai.blogspot.com/2005/11/mute-maids-of-malls.html (accessed 12 June 2006). See the comments section for an interesting discussion.
43. This report also stated that 'Women from India, Sri Lanka, Bangladesh, Indonesia, Ethiopia, Eritrea, and the Philippines travel willingly to the UAE to work as domestic servants, but some subsequently face conditions of involuntary servitude such as excessive work hours without pay, unlawful withholding of passports, restrictions on movement, non-payment of wages, and physical or sexual abuse.' See US Department of State (2008b) *Trafficking in Persons Report 2008*, http://www.state.gov/g/tip/rls/tiprpt/2008/index.htm (accessed 2 February 2009). See also the Human Rights Watch (2006a) 'Swept under the rug: Abuses against domestic workers around the world', 27 July, http://www.hrw.org/en/reports/2006/07/27/swept-under-rug (accessed 21 August 2008) and Human Rights Watch (2007).
44. *7days* (2007) 'My torture hell', 28 February, http://www.7days.ae/storydetails.php?id=6619&page=local%20news&title=MY%20TORTURE%20HELL (accessed 22 December 2007).
45. Bassma Al Jandaly (2007a) 'Public warned not to employ runaway housemaids', *Gulf News*, 30 January, http://gulfnews.com/news/gulf/uae/employment/public-warned-not-to-employ-runaway-housemaids-1.131362 (accessed 22 February 2007).
46. *7days* (2005) 'Runaway maids', 1 June, http://www.7days.ae/storydetails.php?id=1702&page=local%20news&title=Runawaymaids (accessed 20 December 2007).
47. Bassma Al Jandaly (2007b) 'Just in case your maid runs away', *Gulf News*, 5 May, http://gulfnews.com/news/gulf/uae/general/just-in-case-your-maid-runs-away-1.177159 (accessed 8 May 2007).
48. Human Rights Watch (2006a), (2007).
49. *7days* (2006) 'We now have a voice', 9 November, http://www.7days.ae/storydetails.php?id=5919%20%20%20%20&page=local%20news&title=We%20now%20have%20a%20voice (accessed 12 December 2007).
50. Bassma Al Jandaly (2006b) 'New contract "will protect rights of maids" ', *Gulf News*, 10 November, http://gulfnews.com/news/gulf/uae/employment/new-contracts-will-protect-rights-of-maids-1.155775 (accessed 12 January 2007).
51. Ashfaq Ahmed (2007) 'Expats want Pakistan ban on housemaids lifted,' *Gulf News*, 30 October, http://gulfnews.com/news/gulf/uae/employment/expats-want-pakistan-ban-on-housemaids-lifted-1.208522 (accessed 12 December 2007).
52. Binsal Abdul Kader (2008) 'Minimum wage means we can no longer afford to hire maids', *Gulf News*, 5 March, http://gulfnews.com/news/gulf/uae/general/minimum-wage-means-we-can-no-longer-afford-to-hire-maids-1.89976 (accessed 12 October 2009).
53. *7days* (2008) 'Shoulder to cry on for victims', 23 June, http://www.7days.ae/storydetails.php?id=41103%20%20%20%20&page=local%20news&title=Shoulder%20to%20cry%20on%20for%20victims (accessed 24 July 2008).
54. US Department of State (2006) *Trafficking in Persons Report 2006*, http://www.state.gov/g/tip/rls/tiprpt/2006/65990.htm (accessed 12 July 2008).
55. E. Benjamin Skinner (2008) *A Crime So Monstrous: Face-to-Face with Modern-Day Slavery*, Free Press, New York, p. 182.
56. Ali Al-Shouk (2007) 'Justice was done', *7days*, 11 July, http://www.7days.ae/storydetails.php?id=30043%20%20%20%20&page=local%20news&title=Dubai%20-%20Justice%20was%20done (accessed 16 August 2008).

57. Alia Al Theeb (2008) 'Man gets jail term of 10 years for human trafficking', *Gulf News*, 14 January, http://gulfnews.com/news/gulf/uae/crime/men-get-jail-term-of-10-years-for-human-trafficking-1.77630 (accessed 22 January 2008).

58. *BBC News* (2007)'Dubai authorities smash vice ring', 5 December, http://news.bbc.co.uk/2/hi/middle_east/7128990.stm (accessed 8 December 2007).

59. US Department of State (2009) *Trafficking in Persons Report 2009*, http://www.state.gov/g/tip/rls/tiprpt/2009/123139.htm (accessed 7 July 2009).

60. Skinner (2008), p. 183.

61. William Finnegan (2008) 'The countertraffickers: Rescuing the victims of the global sex trade', *The New Yorker*, 5 May, http://www.newyorker.com/reporting/2008/05/05/080505fa_fact_finnegan (accessed 12 June 2008).

62. Skinner (2008), pp. 179–80.

63. The film is called *Dubai: Night Secrets*, by Mimi Chakarova. It can be viewed online at http://www.pbs.org/frontlineworld/rough/2007/09/dubai_sex_for_s.html# (accessed 22 November 2008).

64. Sholeh Shahrokhi (2008) 'When tragedy hits: A concise socio-cultural analysis of sex trafficking of young Iranian women', *Wagadu: A Journal of Transnational Women's and Gender Studies*, vol. 5, no. 2, http://web.cortland.edu/wagadu/Volume%205/Articles%20html/wagadu_2008_vol5_chap2_shahrokhi.htm (accessed 20 September 2008).

65. Out and About in Dubai (2008) 'I'm not a prostitute, chump', 5 July, http://www.sdangit.com/2008/07/im-not-a-prostitute-chump.html (accessed 12 December 2008).

66. UNICEF (2006) *Starting Over: Children Return Home from Camel Racing*, The United Nations Children's Fund. See also Sulayman Khalaf (1999) 'Camel racing in the Gulf: Notes on the evolution of a traditional cultural sport', *Anthropos*, vol. 94, nos 1–3, pp. 85–106.

67. Dickey (1990), p. 200.

68. Hassan Fattah (2005a) 'Limits set for boy jockeys in Emirates' camel races', *New York Times*, 3 April, http://www.nytimes.com/2005/04/03/international/middleeast/03camels.html?pagewanted=all (accessed 8 December 2007).

69. Ansar Burney Trust (2007b) 'Trafficking of persons: Our mission against human smuggling and trafficking', http://www.ansarburney.org/human_trafficking-children-jockeys.html (accessed 7 December 2007).

70. UNICEF (2006), p. 5.

71. Dickey (1990), p. 200.

72. US Department of State (1999) *1999 Country Reports on Human Rights Practices: United Arab Emirates*, http://www.state.gov/www/global/human_rights/1999_hrp_report/uae.html (accessed 12 September 2008).

73. Dickey (1990), p. xx.

74. Ansar Burney Trust (2007a) *Child Camel Jockeys in UAE: August 2007*, http://www.ansarburney.org/videolinks/18aug07.html (accessed 25 July 2008).

75. Skinner (2008), p. 181.

76. Ibid., p. 45.

77. Hassan Fattah (2005a).

78. Meena Janardhan (2007) 'Labour-UAE: Worker friendly laws make a difference', *IPS*, 11 January, http://ipsnews.net/news.asp?idnews=36133 (accessed 22 January 2007).

79. Robert Mackey (2005) 'Robot jockeys', *New York Times*, 11 December, http://www.nytimes.com/2005/12/11/magazine/11ideas_section3-11.html (accessed 4 January 2007).

80. US Department of State (2008a) *Trafficking in Persons Report 2008*, http://www.state.gov/g/tip/rls/tiprpt/2008/105389.htm (accessed 25 July 2008).
81. Ansar Burney Trust (2007a).

CHAPTER FOUR: LIVING IN 'FLY-BY' DUBAI

1. Ian Gallagher (2008) 'Revealed: The lonely Bridget Jones world of the British sales manager facing jail in Dubai', *Daily Mail*, 12 July, http://www.dailymail.co.uk/news/article-1034629/Revealed-The-lonely-Bridget-Jones-world-British-sales-manager-facing-jail-Dubai.html (accessed 14 July 2008).
2. The first headline was from 9 July 2008, and the second, 10 July 2008.
3. Roula Khalaf (2006) 'Dubai cultivates oasis of calm where business can flourish', *Financial Times*, 29 September, http://www.ft.com/cms/s/0/abfae89c-4fd9–11db-9d85–0000779e2340.html (accessed 12 January 2009).
4. Hassan Fattah (2005b) 'Young Iranians follow dreams to Dubai', *New York Times*, 4 December, http://www.nytimes.com/2005/12/04/international/middleeast/04dubai.html (accessed 6 January 2009).
5. Praveen Menon (2008) 'A third of Indian workers are white-collar professionals', *The National*, 14 August 2008, http://thenational.ae/article/20080814/NATIONAL/654056929 (accessed 16 August 2008).
6. Michael Slackman (2008) 'Young and Arab in land of mosques and bars', *New York Times*, 21 September, http://www.nytimes.com/2008/09/22/world/middleeast/22dubai.html (accessed 21 January 2009).
7. The theoretical literature on why people migrate is vast and complex. The best overview of various theoretical approaches is contained in Massey *et al.* (1998) *Worlds in Motion: Understanding International Migration at the End of the Millennium*, Oxford University Press, New York. On the culture of migration to Mexico, see Jeffrey Cohen (2004) *The Culture of Migration in Southern Mexico*, University of Texas Press, Austin, TX; also William Kandel and Douglas Massey (2002) 'The culture of Mexican migration: A theoretical and empirical analysis', *Social Forces*, vol. 80, no. 3, pp. 981–1004. On the culture of migration of Indian Muslims to Saudi Arabia and the US, see Syed Ali (2007a) ' "Go west young man": The culture of migration among Muslims in Hyderabad, India,' *Journal of Ethnic and Migration Studies*, vol. 33, no. 1, pp. 37–58.
8. Katherine Zoepf (2006) 'Where the boys are, at least for now, the girls pounce', *New York Times*, 2 November, http://www.nytimes.com/2006/11/02/world/middleeast/02beirut.html (accessed 30 January 2009).
9. Donald Lee (2004) http://www.donaldlee.net/expat/gulf_business_2004_salary_survey.aspx (accessed 10 October 2008).
10. The survey was based on self-reporting by nearly 9,000 respondents: http://www.arabianbusiness.com/salary-survey-report (accessed 6 January 2008). The survey was repeated in early 2009 in the middle of the economic downturn with similar results. See http://www.arabianbusiness.com/research/salary-survey-report-2009 (accessed 2 July 2009).
11. Ghaith Abdul-Ahad (2008) 'We need slaves to build monuments', *Guardian*, 8 October, http://www.guardian.co.uk/world/2008/oct/08/middleeast.construction (accessed 12 November 2008).
12. Gallagher (2008).
13. Katie Walsh (2008) ' "It got very debauched, very Dubai!": Heterosexual intimacy amongst single British expatriates', *Social and Cultural Geography*, vol. 8, no. 4, pp. 507–33.

14. Ibid., p. 516.
15. Ibid., p. 509.
16. Ibid., pp. 515, 517.
17. Ibid., p. 517.
18. David Jones (2008) 'The degenerates of Dubai: How the widespread behaviour of our expats is causing a backlash', *Daily Mail*, 19 July, http://www.dailymail.co.uk/ textbased/news/worldnews/article-1036384/The-degenerates-Dubai-How-wide-spread-behaviour-expats-causing-backlash.html (accessed 20 July 2008). Oddly the link to this article was severed a short while after it was published, and its cached version on Google had also disappeared.
19. Dickey (1990), p. 169.
20. Nadim Audi and Michael Slackman (2008) 'In Dubai, respect, fun and freedom', *New York Times*, 21 September, http://thelede.blogs.nytimes.com/2008/09/21/in-dubai-respect-fun-and-freedom/ (accessed 21 January 2009).
21. Weiner (1982), p. 6.
22. Karen Leonard (2003) 'South Asian workers in the Gulf: Jockeying for places', in Richard Perry and Bill Maurer (eds) *Globalization under Construction: Governmentality, Law, and Identity*, University of Minnesota Press, Minneapolis, MN, pp. 129–70.
23. Diana Milne (2007) 'Can you afford it?', *ArabianBusiness.com*, 8 July, http://www.arabianbusiness.com/property/article/495893-can-you-afford-it (accessed 23 August 2007); Kathryn Lewis (2008) 'School fees force expats to send children home', *The National*, 13 October, http://thenational.ae/article/20081012/ NATIONAL/945890049 (accessed 10 November 2008).
24. Claire Feris-Lay (2009) 'School confirms 90 per cent fee hike despite protests', *ArabianBusiness.com*, 9 February, http://www.arabianbusiness.com/546146-school-confirms-90-fee-hike-despite-protests (accessed 10 February 2009).
25. Milne (2007).
26. Lewis (2008).
27. Walsh (2008).
28. Davis (2006).
29. Gallagher (2008).
30. Milne (2007).
31. Armina Ligaya (2009) 'UAE cities more costly, says survey', *The National*, 7 July, http://www.thenational.ae/article/20090707/BUSINESS/707079946/1133/FOR EIGN (accessed 10 July 2009).
32. Lucas (2008).
33. Mary Nammour (2008) 'Big family + small flat = No residence visa!' *Khaleej Times*, 14 August, http://www.khaleejtimes.com/DisplayArticle08.asp?xfile=data/ theuae/2008/August/theuae_August292.xml&section=theuae (accessed 16 August 2008).
34. Jeremy Lawrence (2008) 'The writing's on the wall', *Time Out Dubai*, May, http://www.timeoutdubai.com/dubai/features/review.php?id=3097 (accessed 22 May 2008).
35. Nina Muslim (2008) 'Filipino population in UAE dwindling amid high costs', *Gulf News*, 13 December, http://gulfnews.com/nation/Society/10266701.html (accessed 2 January 2009).
36. Rob Corder (2009) 'UAE population growth set to stall in 2009', *ArabianBusiness.com*, 15 January, http://www.arabianbusiness.com/543750-uae-population-growth-set-to-stall-in-2009—report (accessed 17 January 2009).

37. Robin Wigglesworth (2009) 'Real estate: Are prices at the bottom?' *Financial Times*, 20 July, http://www.ft.com/cms/s/0/7185479a-7270-11de-ba94-00144feabdc0,dwp_uuid=c23e5f6e-727a-11de-ba94-00144feabdc0.html (accessed 21 July 2009).

CHAPTER FIVE: GUESTS IN THEIR OWN HOMES

1. Kapiszewski (2001), p. 51.
2. Ibid., p. 49.
3. Eman Al Baik (2005) 'Senior expatriates in Dubai can get UAE passport', *Khaleej Times*, 25 July, http://www.khaleejtimes.com/DisplayArticleNew.asp?section=theuae&xfile=data/theuae/2005/july/theuae_july712.xml (accessed 22 August 2007).
4. *Khaleej Times* (2005) 'DNRD clarifies report on UAE passport for expatriates', 26 July, http://www.khaleejtimes.com/DisplayArticleNew.asp?section=theuae&xfile=data/theuae/2005/july/theuae_july749.xml (accessed 22 July 2008).
5. Nada Mussallam (2005) 'Citizenship proposed for skilled expatriates', *Khaleej Times*, 28 August, http://www.khaleejtimes.com/DisplayArticle.asp?xfile=data/theuae/2005/August/theuae_August830.xml&section=theuae&col (accessed 22 July 2008).
6. Joel Bowman (2007) 'UAE flatly rejects citizenship for foreign workers', *ArabianBusiness.com*, 12 December, http://www.arabianbusiness.com/506295-uae-flatly-rejects-citizenship-for-foreign-workers?ln=en (accessed 22 July 2008).
7. Paul Dresch (2005) 'Debates on marriage and nationality in the United Arab Emirates', in Paul Dresch and James Piscatori (eds) *Monarchies and Nations: Globalisation and Identity in the Arab States of the Gulf*, I.B. Tauris: London, p. 140.
8. Kapiszewski (2001), p. 9.
9. Davidson (2008).
10. Classical versions of assimilation theory assumed that migrants would 'melt' into the host society (e.g. Milton Gordon (1964) *Assimilation in American Life*, Oxford University Press, New York). Neo-assimilation theoretical approaches (e.g., Richard Alba and Victor Nee (2003), *Remaking the American Mainstream: Assimilation and Contemporary Immigration*, Harvard University Press, Cambridge, MA) allow for more dynamic interaction, i.e., that migrants can change a host society at the same time they assimilate into it. Segmented assimilation (e.g., Alejandro Portes and Ruben Rumbaut (2006) *Immigrant America: A Portrait*, University of California Press, Berkeley, CA) rejects the notion of melting. This theoretical approach looks at how immigrants may assimilate into different segments of the native population – some may be upwardly mobile while others are downwardly mobile, while still others moderate their pace of cultural assimilation. While these approaches to assimilation have great differences, the notion of host society is an integral concept to all streams of immigration theories.
11. Philip Kasinitz, John Mollenkopf and Mary Waters (2004) 'Worlds of the second generation', in Philip Kasinitz, John Mollenkopf and Mary Waters (eds) *Becoming New Yorkers: Ethnographies of the New Second Generation*, Russell Sage Foundation, New York, pp. 1–19.
12. Rosh (2007) 'Just Talkin', *uaeian*, 26 May, http://blog-uaeian.blogspot.com/2007/05/just-talkin.html (accessed 26 July 2008). Localexpat replied to my question in the comments section of this post at the timestamp 6 June 2007 5:42 AM.

13. This visa category is for professionals for a three-year term that can be renewed only once.
14. This is also the case in Bahrain. See Andrew Gardner (2008) 'Strategic transnationalism: The Indian diasporic elite in Bahrain', *City and Society*, vol. 20, no. 1, pp. 54–78.
15. Though certain types of professionals, like those in the advertising industry, are left out, as Canada has a points system that favours professionals such as doctors, engineers and teachers. This may change, however, as Canada's visa policy may be becoming more restrictive; see Christopher Mason and Julia Preston (2007) 'Canada's policy on immigrants brings backlog', *New York Times*, 27 June, http://www.nytimes.com/2007/06/27/washington/27points.html (accessed 3 August 2007).
16. George Abraham (2007) 'Gulf allure: Canada is losing immigrants', *Khaleej Times*, 19 October, http://www.khaleejtimes.com/DisplayArticleNew.asp?xfile=data/theuae/2007/October/theuae_October494.xml&section=theuae&col= (accessed 25 October 2007).

CHAPTER SIX: STRANGERS IN THEIR OWN LAND

1. United Arab Emirates (2009) *United Arab Emirates Yearbook 2009*, Trident Press, London, pp. 234–5, available at http://www.uaeinteract.com/uaeint_misc/pdf_2009/ (accessed 15 May 2009). This statistic is even more impressive when one takes into account that a great deal of illiteracy before was of adults, and the government is quite proud of its programmes to eradicate illiteracy among adults.
2. Gassan Al-Kibsi *et al.* (2007) 'Getting labor policy to work in the Gulf', *McKinsey Quarterly*, February, pp. 19–29, http://www.mckinseyquarterly.com/Middle_East/Getting_labor_policy_to_work_in_the_Gulf_1930 (accessed 16 March 2008).
3. While official figures show the enrolment rates of men hovering around 25 per cent, the numbers may be slightly deflated as they do not take into consideration men who enrol in university abroad. Even so, their enrolment levels are far less than those of women. See Warren Fox (2008) 'The UAE and policy priorities for higher education', in Christopher Davidson and Peter Mackenzie Smith (eds), *Higher Education in the Gulf States: Shaping Economies, Politics and Culture*, Saqi, London, pp. 110–25.
4. Ashfaq Ahmed (2008) 'Expats make up 99% of private sector staff in UAE,' *Gulf News*, 7 April, http://gulfnews.com/news/gulf/uae/employment/expats-make-up-99-of-private-sector-staff-in-uae-1.96744 (accessed 27 June 2009).
5. Diaa Hadid (2006c) 'Easier work culture lures', *Gulf News*, 5 May, http://gulfnews.com/about-gulf-news/al-nisr-portfolio/tabloid/articles/easier-work-culture-lures-1.235720 (accessed 22 October 2009).
6. Tom Spender (2009) 'Emiratisation process hampered by "lack of reliable data" ', *The National*, 30 March, http://www.thenational.ae/article/20090330/NATIONAL/686322048/1138/YOURVIEW (accessed 25 June 2009).
7. As a direct reaction to the economic meltdown that began in late 2008, the government issued a decree in February 2009 that makes it unlawful to lay off a national employee for any reason other than gross misconduct – i.e. it is now legally almost impossible to fire a national in the private sector. While the intention is to protect the jobs of nationals, a likely outcome is that firms will avoid hiring nationals – especially younger, less-experienced nationals – in the first place, knowing that they will not be able to fire them ever. See Navtej Dhillon

et al. (2009) 'Missed by the boom, hurt by the bust: Making markets work for young people in the Middle East', Brookings Institute, May, p. 23, http://www.brookings.edu/reports/2009/05_middle_east_youth_dhillon.aspx?more=rc   (accessed 19 May 2009).

8. Al-Kibsi *et al.* (2007), p. 25.
9. Spender (2009).
10. Kapiszewski (2001), p. 77.
11. Andy Sambidge (2008) 'Call for new plan to tackle Emirati jobs dilemma', *ArabianBusiness.com*, 25 August, http://www.arabianbusiness.com/528807-call-for-new-plan-to-tackle-emirati-jobs-dilemma (accessed 3 January 2009). See also Kapiszewski (2001), pp. 240–1.
12. *Oxford Analytica* (2007) 'United Arab Emirates: Education trumps Emiratisation', Daily Brief Service, 20 April; Samir Salama (2007b) 'Call for cautious Emiratisation,' *Gulf News*, 20 April, http://gulfnews.com/business/general/call-for-cautious-emiratisation-1.172940 (accessed 22 October 2009); Matthew Brown (2007) 'UAE's drive for Emirati-run economy is thwarted by handouts', *Bloomberg*, 3 October, http://www.bloomberg.com/apps/news?pid=20601085&sid=axmdijbZMi5k&refer=europe (accessed July 25, 2009).
13. Mary Ann Tetreault (2000) 'The economics of national autonomy in the UAE', in Joseph Kechichian (ed) *A Century in Thirty Years: Shaykh Zayed and the United Arab Emirates*. Middle East Policy Council, Washington, DC, pp. 107–48.
14. Davidson (2008), p. 179.
15. Salama (2007b).
16. *ArabianBusiness.com* (2008) 'Gulf Arabs "lazy" and "spoilt", blasts minister,' 28 January, http://www.arabianbusiness.com/509425-gulf-arabs-lazy-and-spoilt-blasts-minister (accessed 2 February 2008).
17. Johann Hari (2009a) 'The dark side of Dubai', *Independent*, 7 April, http://www.independent.co.uk/opinion/commentators/johann-hari/the-dark-side-of-dubai-1664368.html (accessed 9 April 2009).
18. Yasin Kakande (2009) 'Emiratis steer clear of taxi-driving jobs', *The National*, 23 May, http://www.thenational.ae/article/20090524/NATIONAL/705239803/1010/rss (accessed 29 May 2009).
19. Salama (2007b).
20. Abdullah Al Shaiba (2009) 'Let's take Emiratisation campaign to the next level', *Gulf News*, 8 May, http://gulfnews.com/opinions/columnists/let-s-take-Emiratisation-campaign-to-the-next-level-1.67914 (accessed 12 May 2009); Sambidge (2008).
21. Oxford Analytica (2007).
22. Salama (2007b).
23. Brown (2007).
24. *The National* (2009) 'Lack of confidence hampers Emiratisation', 4 May, http://www.thenational.ae/article/20090504/NATIONAL/705049926/1133/BUSINESS (accessed 8 May 2009).
25. Hadid (2006c).
26. See Ingo Forstenlechner (2009) 'Current issues in Emiratisation', paper presented to the Emirates Foundation, Dubai, 5 April, http://www.p-designserver.biz/aboutme.0.html (accessed 30 May 2009).
27. UAE (2009) p. 235.
28. Wafa Issa (2009) 'Fewer Emiratis placed in government jobs', *Gulf News*, 19 May, http://archive.gulfnews.com/nation/Emiratisation/10315241.html (accessed 21 May 2009); Reema Saffarini (2007) 'Companies keen to hit Emiratisation targets',

Gulf News, 12 July, http://archive.gulfnews.com/indepth/labour/Emiritisation/10111442.html (accessed 7 May 2009). The numbers for Tatweer come from discussions with a mid-level expatriate employee in that firm (personal correspondence, 20 January 2009).

29. Spender (2009).
30. Brown (2007). For a more scholarly take on this social contract, see James Onley and Sulayman Khalaf (2006) 'Shaikhly authority in the pre-oil Gulf: An historical–anthropological study', *History and Anthropology*, vol. 17, no. 3, pp. 189–208.
31. Brown (2007); Zaher Bitar (2009) 'Emiratisation: Working partners', 24 February, *Xpress*, http://www.xpress4me.com/articles/09/01/29/20011671.html (accessed 26 February 2009).
32. Brown (2007).
33. Generally, the UAE government gives some of the welfare benefits, while the governments of individual emirates bestow other benefits. Abu Dhabi, as the wealthiest emirate, also has the most extensive benefits. Mohammed Al-Fahim, an Abu Dhabi national and prominent businessman, writes that under Sheikh Zayed, the oil wealth was distributed to nationals in Abu Dhabi as straight cash payments, and each national was give three and sometimes four pieces of land, one for a home in the residential area, the second to build a commercial building on one of the main streets in the centre of town, and the third an industrial site meant for a workshop or industrial project of some kind. The people of Liwa and the outlying villages also received farmland and equipment to cultivate it. Additionally, the government issued a decree that all foreign companies had to be in partnership with a local businessman, ensuring additional income for nationals. See Mohammed Al-Fahim (1995) *From Rags to Riches: A Story of Abu Dhabi*, The London Centre of Arab Studies, London, pp. 140–1.
34. Outside of free zones, for a company to operate it must have a national as a majority-stake owner. Mostly, as I wrote in the last chapter, these nationals do not contribute capital. They own the company on paper, but sign side agreements with the actual owners that gives them an annual 'fee' for which they sign papers for work permits and other governmental actions.
35. Sunita Menon (2008) 'Establishment to build 2,300 low-cost houses for Emiratis in Dubai', *Gulf News*, 9 April, http://www.gulfnews.com/Nation/Government/10204204.html (accessed 2 May 2009).
36. *Gulf News* (2006) 'Residential units for low-income nationals on way', 6 August, http://archive.gulfnews.com/articles/06/08/06/10057856.html (accessed 1 May 2009).
37. Kapiszewski (2001), p. 161.
38. Nada El Sawy (2008b) 'Life on the dole in the UAE', *Financial Times*, 15 September, www.ft.com/cms/s/0/92497e7c-833a-11dd-907e-000077b07658,dwp_uuid=d8cc5c02-3164-11dd-b77c-0000779fd2ac.html (accessed 22 April 2009).
39. Hari (2009a).
40. Though, with so many expatriates leaving Dubai in the midst of the economic contraction in 2009, the percentage of Emiratis in the population will substantially increase.
41. For the maths and a more theoretical explanation, see Peter Blau (1977) *Inequality and Heterogeneity: A Primitive Theory of Social Structure*, Free Press, New York, pp. 19–44.
42. Kapiszewski (2001), pp. 6–7.
43. For example, see an opinion piece by the historian and UAE national Fatima Al Saayegh (2008) 'How can we maintain a national identity?' *Gulf News*,

27 May, http://www.gulfnews.com/nation/Society/10216292.html (accessed 3 May 2009); Eman Mohammed (2008b) 'The debate on UAE national identity', *Gulf News*, 27 May, http://archive.gulfnews.com/indepth/nationalidentity/more_stories /10216190.html (accessed 3 June 2008); *The National* (2008) 'Our national identity must begin at home', 16 April, http://www.thenational.ae/article/20080416/ OPINION/100706505/1006&profile=1006 (accessed 3 June 2008); Nada El Sawy (2008a) 'Foreign influences: Expats force locals to ask who they are', *Financial Times*, 15 May, http://www.ft.com/cms/s/0/e9f2b246-2161-11dd-a0e6-000077b07658,dwp_uuid=571bd9fc-2166-11dd-a0e6-000077b07658.html (accessed 20 May 2009).

44. Davidson (2008), p. 202.
45. *The National* (2008) 'Our national identity must begin at home,' 16 April, http://www.thenational.ae/article/20080416/OPINION/100706505/1006&profil e=1006 (accessed 3 June 2008). The careful reader will note a contradiction between this statistic and one I quoted earlier suggesting basic adult literacy of 93 per cent. It is possible that one or both of these numbers are incorrect, even though both are from government sources. It is also possible that both are correct, and the seeming discrepancy may be due to how each source defines literacy. In neither case is a definition given.
46. Dresch (2005), pp. 136–57.
47. Samir Salama (2006) 'Change in rule for sponsorship transfer of maids hailed', *Gulf News*, 19 January, http://archive.gulfnews.com/articles/06/01/19/10012600.html (accessed 22 March 2008).
48. Abbas Al Lawati (2008) 'Bid to promote national identity', *Gulf News*, 27 May, http://www.gulfnews.com/nation/Society/10216293.html (accessed 2 May 2009).
49. It is generally assumed that parents are critically important for how children behave and what they eventually become when they grow up. Judith Harris, a former writer of textbooks on development psychology, disagrees. In a thorough review of literature in a wide range of fields, she finds that what parents do has almost no effect on how their children turn out. She argues the key factors that influence how children behave are their peers. See Judith Harris (2009) *The Nurture Assumption: Why Children Turn Out the Way They Do*, 2nd ed., Free Press, New York.
50. *Gulf News* (2008a) 'Rapid growth threatens to erode identity', 28 May, http:// archive.gulfnews.com/articles/08/05/28/10216672.html (accessed 2 June 2008).
51. Eman Mohammed (2008) 'The debate on UAE national identity', *Gulf News*, 27 May, http://www.gulfnews.com/Nation/Society/10216190.html (accessed 2 June 2008).
52. Jane Bristol-Rhys (2007) 'Weddings, marriage and money in the United Arab Emirates', *Anthropology of the Middle East*, vol. 2, no. 1, pp. 20–36 (p. 22).
53. Kapiszewski (2001), p. 163.
54. Meriel Beattie (1999) 'Why Emirati weddings are getting less lavish', *BBC News*, 16 December 1999, http://news.bbc.co.uk/2/hi/programmes/crossing_ continents/566491.stm (accessed 15 May 2009); Kathy Evans (1996) 'The price of marriage', *The Middle East*, 1 March; Adel Arafah (2009) 'Marriage fund comes in for flak from FNC', *Khaleej Times*, 15 March, http://www.khaleejtimes.com/ DisplayArticleNew.asp?col=&section=theuae&xfile=data/theuae/2009/March/the uae_March353.xml (accessed 15 May 2009).
55. Amnesty International (2009) *Amnesty International Report 2009: United Arab Emirates*, http://thereport.amnesty.org/en/regions/middle-east-north-africa/uae (accessed 1 June 2009).

56. Karen Thomas (2000) 'Marry a foreigner and you'll pay the price, say Emirates', *Guardian*, 11 April.
57. Zaher Bitar (2007) 'Sad spinsters: Lonely hearts', *Xpress*, 7 June, http://www.xpress4me.com/news/uae/national/20001078.html (accessed 15 May 2009).
58. Mariam Al Serkal (2007) 'Aspirations of young UAE women revealed', *Gulf News*, 7 April, www.gulfnews.com/nation/Society/10116467.html (accessed 15 May 2009).
59. Hari (2009a).

CHAPTER SEVEN: THIS IS THE FUTURE?

1. Wigglesworth (2009).
2. Andy Sambidge (2009e) 'Kuwait begins process to scrap sponsorship', *ArabianBusiness.com*, 9 August, http://www.arabianbusiness.com/564252-kuwait-begins-process-to-scrap-sponsorship (accessed 12 August 2009).
3. Andy Sambidge (2009d), 'Permanent residency for long-term GCC expats – Official', *ArabianBusiness.com*, 13 July, http://www.arabianbusiness.com/561797 (accessed 17 July 2009).

SELECT BIBLIOGRAPHY

Abdul-Ahad, Ghaith (2008) 'We need slaves to build monuments', *Guardian*, 8 October, http://www.guardian.co.uk/world/2008/oct/08/middleeast.construction (accessed 12 November 2008)

Aboul Hosn, Dina (2008) 'Ask the law: No objection certificate', *Gulf News*, 9 May, http://archive.gulfnews.com/articles/08/05/09/10211690.html (accessed 29 June 2009)

Abraham, George (2007) 'Gulf allure: Canada is losing immigrants', *Khaleej Times*, 19 October, http://www.khaleejtimes.com/DisplayArticleNew.asp?xfile=data/theuae/2007/October/theuae_October494.xml&section=theuae&col= (accessed 25 October 2007)

Absal, Rayeesa (2007) '342,000 illegal immigrants took advantage of amnesty', *Gulf News*, 14 November, http://archive.gulfnews.com/indepth/amnesty/main_story/10167345.html (accessed 22 June 2009)

Ahmed, Akbar (1984) ' "Dubai chalo": Problems in the ethnic encounter between Middle Eastern and South Asian Muslim societies', *Asian Affairs*, vol. 15, no. 3, pp. 262–76

Ahmed, Ashfaq (2008) 'Expats make up 99% of private sector staff in UAE', *Gulf News*, 7 April, http://gulfnews.com/news/gulf/uae/employment/expats-make-up-99-of-private-sector-staff-in-uae-1.96744 (accessed 27 June 2009)

Ahmed, Ashfaq (2007) 'Expats want Pakistan ban on housemaids lifted', *Gulf News*, 30 October, http://gulfnews.com/news/gulf/uae/employment/expats-want-pakistan-ban-on-housemaids-lifted-1.208522 (accessed 12 December 2007)

Alba, Richard and Victor Nee (2003) *Remaking the American Mainstream: Assimilation and Contemporary Immigration*, Harvard University Press, Cambridge, MA.

Ali, Syed (2007a) ' "Go west young man": The culture of migration among Muslims in Hyderabad, India', *Journal of Ethnic and Migration Studies*, vol. 33, no. 1, pp. 37–58

Ali, Syed (2007b) 'You must come with us', *Guardian*, 12 November, http://lifeandhealth.guardian.co.uk/family/story/0,,2209519,00.html (accessed 25 July 2009)

SELECT BIBLIOGRAPHY

Ali, Syed (2006) 'Five guys in white come to my door, and I get a new iPod', *Dubai Notes*, 11 November, http://bklyn-in-dubai.livejournal.com/5259.html (accessed 12 November 2009)

Allen, Lila (2009) 'Dark Side of the Dubai Dream', *BBC News (Panorama)*, 6 April, news.bbc.co.uk/2/hi/uk_news/magazine/7985361.stm (accessed 29 June 2009)

Amnesty International (2009) *Amnesty International Report 2009, United Arab Emirates*, http://thereport.amnesty.org/en/regions/middle-east-north-africa/uae (accessed June 1, 2009)

Ansar Burney Trust (2007a) *Trafficking of Persons – Our mission against human smuggling & trafficking*, http://www.ansarburney.org/human_trafficking-children-jockeys.html (accessed 7 December 2007)

Ansar Burney Trust (2007b) *Child Camel Jockeys in UAE – August 2007*, http://www.ansarburney.org/videolinks/18aug07.html (accessed 25 July 2008)

Anthony, John Duke (1975) *Arab States of the Lower Gulf: People, Politics, Petroleum*, Middle East Institute, Washington, DC

Arafah, Adel (2009) 'Marriage fund comes in for flak from FNC', *Khaleej Times*, 15 March, http://www.khaleejtimes.com/DisplayArticleNew.asp?col=&section=theuae &xfile=data/theuae/2009/March/theuae_March353.xml (accessed 15 May 2009)

Arlidge, John (2008) 'Doha: The cultural Dubai', *The Times*, 29 November, http://www.timesonline.co.uk/tol/travel/destinations/middle_east/article5246873.e ce (accessed 22 January 2009)

Armitstead, Claire (2009) 'Censorship row echoes through Dubai literary festival', *Guardian*, 2 March, http://www.guardian.co.uk/books/2009/mar/02/censorship-row-dubai-festival (accessed 2 June 2009)

Armitstead, Louise (2008) 'Dubai reveals debt levels to dispel fears over growth', *Daily Telegraph*, 24 November, http://www.telegraph.co.uk/news/worldnews/middleeast/ dubai/3510908/Dubai-reveals-debt-levels-to-dispel-fears-over-growth.html (accessed 5 July 2009)

Arnold, Tom (2009) '73 firms fined for violating summer work hours', *ArabianBusiness.com*, 7 July, http://www.arabianbusiness.com/561227-73-firms-fined-for-violating-summer-work-hours (accessed 8 July 2009)

Ash (2007) 'Of greedy appetites and glass houses', *A Most Trying July*, 15 March, http://tryingjuly.blogspot.com/2007/03/judgment-day.html (accessed 22 March 2007)

Attwood, Karen and Haneen Dajani (2008) 'Passport holders sell visas illegally', *The National*, 2 July, http://www.thenational.ae/article/20080702/NATIONAL /688537372/1105/ (accessed 22 June 2009)

Audi, Nadim and Michael Slackman (2008) 'In Dubai, respect, fun and freedom', *New York Times*, 21 September, http://thelede.blogs.nytimes.com/2008/09/21/in-dubai-respect-fun-and-freedom/ (accessed 21 January 2009)

Baik, Duraid Al (2007) 'Six-year cap on foreign workers', *Gulf News*, 1 October, http://archive.gulfnews.com/articles/07/10/01/10157293.html (accessed 12 October 2007)

Baik, Eman Al (2005) 'Senior expatriates in Dubai can get UAE passport', *Khaleej Times*, 25 July, http://www.khaleejtimes.com/DisplayArticleNew.asp?section= theuae&xfile=data/theuae/2005/july/theuae_july712.xml (accessed 22 August 2007)

Baltaji, Dana El- (2007) 'Picture perfect: How the story of Dubai's other side can never be told', *Arab Media & Society*, Issue 2, Summer, http://www.arabmediasociety.com/? article=224 (accessed 22 May 2008)

Barrett, Raymond (2009) 'New Jack Emirate: A key to understanding the history of Dubai's seamy underbelly', *Foreign Policy*, April, http://www.foreignpolicy.com/story/cms.php?story_id=4897 (accessed 14 July 2009)

Baxter, Elsa (2009) 'UAE workers report over 300 firms for unpaid wages', *ArabianBusiness.com*, 21 June, http://www.arabianbusiness.com/559453-uae-workers-report-over-300-firms-for-unpaid-wages (accessed 7 July 2009)

Beattie, Meriel (1999) 'Why Emirati weddings are getting less lavish', *BBC News*, 16 December, http://news.bbc.co.uk/2/hi/programmes/crossing_continents/566491.stm (accessed 15 May 2009)

Bernstein, Fred (2008) 'Reaching for the clouds in Dubai', *New York Times*, 8 August, http://www.nytimes.com/2008/08/10/arts/design/10bern.html (accessed 13 March 2009)

Bharadwaj, Vinita (2008) 'Art of the matter', *Gulf News*, 20 March, http://gulfnews.com/news/gulf/uae/heritage-culture/art-of-the-matter-1.92207 (accessed 22 October 2009)

Bitar, Zaher (2009) 'Emiratisation: Working partners', *Xpress*, 24 February, http://www.xpress4me.com/articles/09/01/29/20011671.html (accessed 26 February 2009)

Bitar, Zaher (2008) 'Labour pains: Ban rules are back', *Xpress*, 5 June, http://www.xpress4me.com/news/uae/dubai/20007923.html (accessed 2 June 2009)

Bitar, Zaher (2007) 'Sad spinsters: Lonely hearts', *Xpress*, 7 June, http://www.xpress4me.com/news/uae/national/20001078.html (accessed 15 May 2009)

Bitar, Zaher and Kamakshi Gupta (2008) 'Four detained over Deira fire', *Xpress*, 28 August, http://www.xpress4me.com/news/uae/dubai/20009363.html (accessed 1 September 2008)

Blau, Peter (1977) *Inequality and Heterogeneity: A Primitive Theory of Social Structure*, New York, Free Press

Boer, Kito de, Diana Farrell, Chris Figee, Susan Lund, Fraser Thompson, and John Turner (2008) 'The coming oil windfall in the Gulf', *McKinsey Global Institute*, January

Bowles, Henry (2008) 'Books in Arabia's boomtown', *Foreign Policy*, January/February, p. 97

Bowman, Joel (2007) 'UAE flatly rejects citizenship for foreign workers', *ArabianBusiness.com*, 12 December, http://www.arabianbusiness.com/506295-uae-flatly-rejects-citizenship-for-foreign-workers?ln=en (accessed 15 December 2007)

Bristol-Rhys, Jane (2007) 'Weddings, marriage and money in the United Arab Emirates', *Anthropology of the Middle East*, vol. 2, no. 1, pp. 20–36

Bronner, Ethan (2009) 'Palestinian campus looks to East Bank (of Hudson)', *New York Times*, 15 February, http://www.nytimes.com/2009/02/15/world/middleeast/15quds.html (accessed 16 February 2009)

Brown, Matthew (2007) 'U.A.E.'s drive for Emirati-run economy is thwarted by hand-outs', *Bloomberg*, 3 October, http://www.bloomberg.com/apps/news?pid=20601085&sid=axmdijbZMi5k&refer=europe (accessed 25 July 2009)

Cassara, John (2006) *Hide and Seek: Intelligence, Law Enforcement, and the Stalled War on Terrorist Finance*, Potomac Books, Washington, DC

Chohan, Heerkani (2009) 'Dubai property scandal claim emerges amid media blackout', *Independent*, 28 May, http://www.independent.co.uk/news/world/middle-east/dubai-property-scandal-claim-emerges-amid-media-blackout-1691537.html (accessed 29 June 2009)

Clark, Phil and Anna Winston (2008) 'Mayne warns Dubai set for "ecological disaster" ', *Building Design: The Architect's Website*, 10 October, http://www.bdonline.co.uk/story.asp?storycode=3124669 (accessed 14 November 2008)

Cohen, Jeffrey (2004) *The Culture of Migration in Southern Mexico*, University of Texas Press, Austin, TX

Coll, Steve (2004) *Ghost Wars*, Penguin, New York

Corder, Rob (2009) 'UAE population growth set to stall in 2009', *ArabianBusiness.com*, 15 January, http://www.arabianbusiness.com/543750-uae-population-growth-set-to-stall-in-2009—report (accessed 17 January 2009)

Cowell, Alan (1988) 'A barometer of riches: How now the dhow?' *New York Times*, 27 October

Dallas, Sandra and Drusilla Menaker (1996) 'The mall of the Middle East', *Business Week*, 25 November

Davidson, Christopher (2008) *Dubai: The Vulnerability of Success*, Hurst, London

Davidson, Christopher (2005) *The United Arab Emirates: A Study In Survival*, Lynne Rienner, Boulder, CO

Davis, Mike (2006) 'Fear and money in Dubai', *New Left Review*, September–October, vol. 41, pp. 47–68, http://www.newleftreview.org/?view=2635 (accessed November 15, 2006)

Deulgaonkar, Parag (2009) 'Residence visas to boost property market', *Emirates Business 24/7*, 18 February, http://www.business24-7.ae/articles/2009/2/pages/02182009_fd18091bd07443628a393b46dcdf4544.aspx (accessed 14 April 2009)

Dharmarajan, Subramani (2008) 'Unbearable demands: Broken promise', *Xpress*, 23 October, http://www.xpress4me.com/news/uae/dubai/20010165.html (accessed 4 November 2008)

Dharmarajan, Subramani (2007) 'Sonapur: Welcome to the dark side', *Gulf News*, 3 April, http://gulfnews.com/news/gulf/uae/general/sonapur-welcome-to-the-dark-side-1.463591 (accessed 12 October 2009)

Dhillon, Navtej, Djavad Salehi-Isfahani, Paul Dyer, Tarik Yousef, Amina Fahmy and Mary Kraetsch (2009) 'Missed by the boom, hurt by the bust: Making markets work for young people in the Middle East', *Brookings Institute*, May, p. 23, http://www.brookings.edu/reports/2009/05_middle_east_youth_dhillon.aspx?more=rc (accessed 19 May 2009)

Dickey, Christopher (1990) *Expats: Travels in Arabia from Tripoli to Teheran*, Atlantic Monthly Press, New York

Dinakar, Sethuram (1999) 'The Russian crunch has Dubai crying . . . But the mob is still moving goods', *Business Week*, 8 March

Dresch, Paul (2005) 'Debates on marriage and nationality in the United Arab Emirates', in Paul Dresch and James Piscatori (eds), *Monarchies and Nations: Globalisation and Identity in the Arab States of the Gulf*, I.B. Taurus, London, pp. 136–57

Dubai Department of Tourism and Commerce Marketing, http://dubaitourism.co.ae/EServices/Statistics/HotelStatistics/tabid/167/language/en-US/Default.aspx (accessed 27 February 2009)

Dubai Knowledge and Human Development Authority, http://www.khda.gov.ae/en/home/default.aspx

Dynamic Architecture, http://www.dynamicarchitecture.net/home.html (accessed 5 February 2009)

Eid, Diana (2008) 'Taxidermy Camel + Oversized Suitcase = Controversial Art', *Inventorspot*, 23 April, http://inventorspot.com/articles/oh_so_thats_where_i_put_my_stuffed_camel_12774 (accessed 8 April 2009)

Evans, Kathy (1996) 'The price of marriage', *The Middle East*, 1 March

Evans, Kathy (1994) 'Dubai: State of sin', *Guardian*, 26 November

Evans, Kathy (1992) 'Lazy days on the beach and stunning starlit desert nights', *Guardian*, 2 December

Fahim, Mohammed, Al- (1995) *From Rags to Riches: A Story of Abu Dhabi*, The London Centre of Arab Studies, London

Farrell, Diana and Susan Lind (2008) 'The new role of oil wealth in the world economy', *The McKinsey Quarterly*, January

Fattah, Hassan (2006) 'Emirate wakes up famous. Thank you, America.' *New York Times*, 2 March, http://www.nytimes.com/2006/03/02/international/middleeast/02dubai.html (accessed 3 June 2007)

Fattah, Hassan (2005a) 'Limits Set for Boy Jockeys in Emirates' Camel Races', *New York Times*, 3 April, http://www.nytimes.com/2005/04/03/international/middleeast/03camels.html?pagewanted=all (accessed 8 December 2007)

Fattah, Hassan (2005b) 'Young Iranians follow dreams to Dubai', *New York Times*, 4 December, http://www.nytimes.com/2005/12/04/international/middleeast/04dubai.html (accessed 6 January 2009)

Feris-Lay, Claire (2009) 'School confirms 90% fee hike despite protests', *ArabianBusiness.com*, 9 February, http://www.arabianbusiness.com/546146-school-confirms-90-fee-hike-despite-protests (accessed 10 February 2009)

Field, Michael (1985) *The Merchants: The Big Business Families of Saudi Arabia and the Gulf States*, Overlook Press, Woodstock, NY

Finnegan, William (2008) 'The countertraffickers: Rescuing the victims of the global sex trade', *The New Yorker*, 5 May, http://www.newyorker.com/reporting/2008/05/05/080505fa_fact_finnegan (accessed 12 June 2008)

Forstenlechner, Ingo (2009) 'Current issues in Emiratisation', paper presented to the Emirates Foundation, Dubai, 5 April, http://www.p-designserver.biz/aboutme.0.html (accessed 30 May 2009)

Fox, Warren (2008) 'The UAE and policy priorities for higher education', in Christopher Davidson and Peter Mackenzie Smith (eds), *Higher Education in the Gulf States: Shaping Economies, Politics and Culture*, Saqi, London, pp. 110–25

Gallagher, Ian (2008) 'Revealed: The lonely Bridget Jones world of the British sales manager facing jail in Dubai, *Daily Mail*, 12 July, http://www.dailymail.co.uk/news/article-1034629/Revealed-The-lonely-Bridget-Jones-world-British-sales-manager-facing-jail-Dubai.html (accessed 14 July 2008)

Gara, Tom (2009) 'Regulators orders article critical of Dubai to be unblocked online', *The National*, 21 May, http://www.thenational.ae/article/20090522/NATIONAL/705219840/1010 (accessed 29 June 2009)

Gardner, Andrew (2008) 'Strategic transnationalism: The Indian diasporic elite in Bahrain', *City and Society*, 20, 1, pp. 54–78

Gill, John (2008) 'Oiling the learning machine', *Times Higher Education*, 21 August, http://www.timeshighereducation.co.uk/story.asp?sectioncode=26&storycode=403223&c=1 (accessed 1 April 2009)

Gordon, Milton (1964) *Assimilation in American Life*, Oxford University Press, New York

Graz, Liesl, (1992) *The Turbulent Gulf: People, Politics and Power*, I.B. Tauris, London

Greenslade, Roy (2009) 'Why was journalist detained in Dubai?' *Guardian*, 21 April, http://www.guardian.co.uk/media/greenslade/2009/apr/21/press-freedom-wall-streetjournal (accessed 22 May 2009)

Gulf News (2008a) 'Rapid growth threatens to erode identity', 28 May, http://archive.gulfnews.com/articles/08/05/28/10216672.html (accessed 2 June 2008)

Gulf News (2008b) 'Culture museum in Dubai will be first in the region', 22 June, http://www.gulfnews.com/Nation/Heritage_and_Culture/10222873.html (accessed 22 January 2009)

Hadid, Diaa (2006a) 'New UAE job-switch rule "in place for weeks" ', *Gulf News*, 8 March, http://archive.gulfnews.com/articles/06/03/08/10023895.html (accessed 29 June 2009)

Hadid, Diaa (2006b) 'Labour protests in 2005', *Gulf News*, 29 April, http://archive.gulfnews.com/indepth/labour/Protests/10036459.html (accessed 12 October 2006)

Hadid, Diaa (2006c) 'Easier work culture lures', *Gulf News*, 5 May, http://gulfnews.com/about-gulf-news/al-nisr-portfolio/tabloid/articles/easier-work-culture-lures-1.235720 (accessed 22 October 2009)

Hari, Johann (2009a) 'The dark side of Dubai', *The Independent*, 7 April, http://www.independent.co.uk/opinion/commentators/johann-hari/the-dark-side-of-dubai-1664368.html (accessed 9 April 2009)

Hari, Johann (2009b) 'My post about Dubai is now banned in the city', *Huffington Post*, 21 May, http://www.huffingtonpost.com/johann-hari/my-post-about-dubai-is-no_b_206388.html (accessed 30 June 2009)

Harris, Judith (2009) *The Nurture Assumption: Why Children Turn Out the Way They Do*, Free Press, New York (second edition)

Heard-Bey, Frauke (1982) *From Trucial States to United Arab Emirates*, Longman, London

Henderson, Joan (2006) 'Tourism in Dubai: Overcoming Barriers to Destination Development', *International Journal of Tourism Research*, vol. 8, no. 2, pp. 87–99

Hickman, Leo (2008) 'Chilling developments in Dubai', *Guardian*, 18 December, http://www.guardian.co.uk/environment/2008/dec/18/artificial-beach-dubai-environment (accessed 25 December 2008)

Hodson, Mark (1995) 'Shop of the desert', *The Sunday Times* (London), 3 December

Horner, Susan and John Swarbrooke (2004) *International Cases in Tourism Management*, Butterworth-Heinemann, Oxford

Human Rights Watch (2009a) *Just the Good News, Please: New UAE Media Law Continues to Stifle Press*, 6 April, http://www.hrw.org/node/82150 (accessed 29 June 2009)

Human Rights Watch (2009b) *'The Island of Happiness': Exploitation of Migrant Workers on Saadiyat Island, Abu Dhabi*, 19 May, http://www.hrw.org/en/reports/2009/05/18/island-happiness-0 (accessed 22 May 2009)

Human Rights Watch (2007) *Exported and Exposed: Abuses against Sri Lankan Domestic Workers in Saudi Arabia, Kuwait, Lebanon, and the United Arab Emirates*, 13 November, http://www.hrw.org/en/reports/2007/11/13/exported-and-exposed-1 (accessed 21 August 2008)

Human Rights Watch (2006a) *Swept Under the Rug: Abuses against Domestic Workers Around the World*, 27 July, http://www.hrw.org/en/reports/2006/07/27/swept-under-rug (accessed 21 August 2008)

Human Rights Watch (2006b) *Building Towers, Cheating Workers; Exploitation of Migrant Construction Workers in the United Arab Emirates*, 11 November, http://www.hrw.org/en/reports/2006/11/11/building-towers-cheating-workers (accessed 29 June 2009)

Human Rights Watch (2006c) *UAE: Workers Abused in Construction Boom: New Report Highlights the Plight of Migrant Construction Workers*, 11 November, http://www.hrw.org/en/news/2006/11/11/uae-workers-abused-construction-boom (accessed 13 November 2006)

Issa, Wafa (2009) 'Fewer Emiratis placed in government jobs', *Gulf News*, 19 May, http://archive.gulfnews.com/nation/Emiratisation/10315241.html (accessed 21 May 2009)

Issa, Wafa (2008) '70% of labour accommodations violate safety rules', *Gulf News*, 17 December, http://gulfnews.com/news/gulf/uae/housing-property/70-of-labour-accommodations-violate-safety-rules-1.149524 (accessed 22 January 2009)

Issa, Wafa (2007a) 'Heat is on to ensure midday break rule', *Gulf News*, 21 June, http://archive.gulfnews.com/indepth/labour/Pay_and_conditions/10134106.html (accessed 28 June 2007)

Issa, Wafa (2007b) '102 companies fined more than Dh1m for violating break rule', *Gulf News*, 16 July, http://archive.gulfnews.com/indepth/labour/Pay_and_conditions/10139541.html (accessed 22 July 2007)

Issa, Wafa (2007c) 'Businesses lash out at residency cap proposal', *Gulf News*, 22 October, http://gulfnews.com/news/gulf/uae/employment/businesses-lash-out-at-residency-cap-proposal-1.79038 (accessed 5 October 2008)

Janardhan, Meena (2007) 'Labour-UAE: Worker friendly laws make a difference', *IPS*, 11 January, http://ipsnews.net/news.asp?idnews=36133 (accessed 22 January 2007)

Jandaly, Bassma Al (2008) 'Short-term visas for realty buyers in Dubai', *Gulf News*, 24 June, http://www.gulfnews.com/BUSINESS/Real_Estate_Property/10223343.html (accessed 22 February 2009).

Jandaly, Bassma Al (2007a) 'Public warned not to employ runaway housemaids', *Gulf News*, 30 January, http://gulfnews.com/news/gulf/uae/employment/public-warned-not-to-employ-runaway-housemaids-1.131362 (accessed 22 February 2007)

Jandaly, Bassma Al (2007b) 'Just in case your maid runs away', *Gulf News*, 5 May, http://gulfnews.com/news/gulf/uae/general/just-in-case-your-maid-runs-away-1.177159 (accessed 8 May 2007)

Jandaly, Bassma Al (2006b) 'New contracts "will protect rights of maids" ', *Gulf News*, 10 November, http://gulfnews.com/news/gulf/uae/employment/new-contracts-will-protect-rights-of-maids-1.155775 (accessed 12 January 2007)

Jandaly, Bassma Al (2006a) 'Workers forced to live in freezing tent by recruiter', *Gulf News*, 2 June, http://gulfnews.com/news/gulf/uae/employment/workers-forced-to-live-in-freezing-tent-by-recruiter-1.83344 (accessed 1 October 2009)

John, Isaac (2006) 'Dubai launches Dh50b Culture Village project', *Khaleej Times*, 13 May, http://www.khaleejtimes.com/DisplayArticleNew.asp?xfile=data/business/2006/May/business_May333.xml&section=business (accessed 25 February 2008)

Jones, David (2008) 'The degenerates of Dubai: How the widespread behaviour of our expats is causing a backlash', *Daily Mail*, 19 July, http://www.dailymail.co.uk/textbased/news/worldnews/article-1036384/The-degenerates-Dubai-How-wide-spread-behaviour-expats-causing-backlash.html (accessed 20 July 2008)

Kader, Binsal Abdul (2008) 'Minimum wage means we can no longer afford to hire maids', *Gulf News*, 5 March, http://gulfnews.com/news/gulf/uae/general/minimum-wage-means-we-can-no-longer-afford-to-hire-maids-1.89976 (accessed 12 October 2009)

Kakande, Yasin (2009) 'Emiratis steer clear of taxi-driving jobs', *The National*, 23 May, http://www.thenational.ae/article/20090524/NATIONAL/705239803/1010/rss (accessed 29 May 2009)

Kandel, William and Douglas Massey (2002) 'The culture of Mexican migration: A theoretical and empirical analysis', *Social Forces*, vol. 80, no. 3, pp. 981–1004

Kanna, Ahmed, ed. (2010) *The Superlative City: Dubai and the Urban Condition in the Early Twenty-First Century*, Harvard University Press, Cambridge, MA.

Kantaria, Annabel (2008) 'Expats in Dubai: Shop to stop dropping as Dubai summer hits its height', *Daily Telegraph*, 1 August, http://www.telegraph.co.uk/expat/4205374/Expats-in-Dubai-Shop-to-stop-dropping-as-Dubai-summer-hits-its-height.html (accessed 21 January 2009)

Kapiszewski, Andrzej (2001) *Nationals and Expatriates: Population and Labour Dilemmas of the Gulf Cooperation Council States*, Ithaca Press, Reading, UK

Kasinitz, Philip, John Mollenkopf and Mary Waters (2004) 'Worlds of the second generation', in Philip Kasinitz, John Mollenkopf and Mary Waters (eds) *Becoming New Yorkers: Ethnographies of the New Second Generation*, Russell Sage Foundation, New York, pp. 1–19

Kazmi, Aftab (2006) 'Dubai's water resources "insufficient,"' *Gulf News*, 5 July, http://archive.gulfnews.com/articles/06/07/05/10051564.html (accessed 24 March 2009)

Keane, David and Nicholas McGeehan (2008) 'Enforcing migrant workers' rights in the United Arab Emirates', *International Journal on Minority and Group Rights*, vol. 15, no. 1, pp. 81–115

Kennicott, Phillip (2007) 'Arabian Heights: Oil-rich Dubai raises its international profile with towers meant to be icons – but icons of what?' *Washington Post*, 28 October, http://www.washingtonpost.com/wp-dyn/content/article/2007/10/25/AR2007102501225.html (accessed 12 November 2007)

Kerr, Simeon and James Drummond (2009) 'Alarm over cost of insuring Dubai debt', *Financial Times*, 15 February, http://www.ft.com/cms/s/0/0ee4f97c-fb8e-11dd-bcad-000077b07658.html (accessed 8 July 2009)

Khalaf, Roula (2006) 'Dubai cultivates oasis of calm where business can flourish', *Financial Times*, 29 September, http://www.ft.com/cms/s/0/abfae89c-4fd9-11db-9d85-0000779e2340.html (accessed 12 January 2009)

Khalaf, Sulayman (1999) 'Camel racing in the Gulf: Notes on the evolution of a traditional cultural sport', *Anthropos*, vol. 94, nos 1–3, pp. 85–106

Khan, Shahid Ali (2000) 'Saudis biggest spenders at Dubai Shopping Festival', *Saudi Gazette*, 14 February

Al-Kibsi, Gassan, Claus Benkert, and Jörg Schubert (2007) 'Getting labor policy to work in the Gulf', *McKinsey Quarterly*, February, pp. 19–29

Krane, Jim (2009) *City of Gold: Dubai and the Dream of Capitalism*, St. Martin's Press, New York

Krieger, Zvika (2008a) 'An academic building boom transforms the Persian Gulf', *The Chronicle of Higher Education*, 28 March, http://chronicle.com/article/An-Academic-Building-Boom/20922 (accessed 22 June 2009)

Krieger, Zvika (2008b) 'The Emir of NYU', *New York Magazine*, 13 April, http://nymag.com/news/features/46000/ (accessed 1 May 2008)

Landais, Emmanuelle (2009) 'Experts seek to address water usage, scarcity challenges at special forum', *Gulf News*, 23 March, http://archive.gulfnews.com/nation/Environment/10297759.html (accessed 24 March 2009)

Lawati, Abbas Al (2008) 'Bid to promote national identity', *Gulf News*, 27 May, http://www.gulfnews.com/nation/Society/10216293.html (accessed 2 May 2009)

Lawrence, Jeremy (2008) 'The writing's on the wall', *Time Out Dubai*, May

Leonard, Karen (2003) 'South Asian workers in the Gulf: Jockeying for places', in Richard Perry and Bill Maurer (eds), *Globalization under Construction: Governmentality, Law, and Identity*, University of Minnesota Press, Minneapolis, MN, pp. 129–70

Lewis, Kathryn (2008) 'School fees force expats to send children home', *The National*, 13 October, http://thenational.ae/article/20081012/NATIONAL/945890049 (accessed 10 November 2008)

Lienhardt, Peter (2001), *Shaikhdoms of Eastern Arabia* (ed. Ahmed Al-Shahi), Palgrave, Basingstoke, UK

Ligaya, Armina (2009) 'UAE cities more costly, says survey', *The National*, 7 July, http://www.thenational.ae/article/20090707/BUSINESS/707079946/1133/FOREI GN (accessed 10 July 2009)

Longva, Anh (1997) *Walls Built on Sand: Migration, Exclusion, and Society in Kuwait*, Westview, Boulder, CO

Lotter, Phillip and Tristan Cooper (2008) 'Demystifying Dubai Inc.: A guide to Dubai's corporatist model and Moody's assessment of its rising leverage', *Moody's Investors Service*, October

Lucas, Becky (2008) 'Filipino Dubai', *TimeOut Dubai*, July

Mackey, Robert (2005) 'Robot jockeys', *New York Times*, 11 December, http://www.nytimes.com/2005/12/11/magazine/11ideas_section3-11.html (accessed 4 January 2007)

MacMillan, Scott (2008) 'I want to break free!' *Kippreport*, 9 November, http://www.kippreport.com/kipp/2008/11/09/i-want-to-break-free/?bnr=1 (accessed 9 March 2009)

Magill, R. Jay, Jr (2008) 'Cultural pretensions in Dubai: Desert metropolis reinvents itself as art center', *Der Spiegel*, 21 March, http://www.spiegel.de/international/world/0,1518,542874,00.html (accessed 24 March 2009)

Maier, Matthew (2005) 'Rise of the Emirates empire', *Business 2.0*, October, http://money.cnn.com/magazines/business2/business2_archive/2005/10/01/835925 1/index.htm (accessed 10 February 2009)

Mohammed Bin Rashid Al Maktoum Foundation, http://www.mbrfoundation.ae/English/ (accessed 22 March 2009)

Mason, Christopher and Julia Preston (2007) 'Canada's policy on immigrants brings backlog', *New York Times*, 27 June, http://www.nytimes.com/2007/06/27/washington/27points.html (accessed 3 August 2007)

Massey, Douglas, Joaquin Arango, Graeme Hugo, Ali Kouaouci, Adela Pelligrino and J. Edward Taylor (1998) *Worlds in Motion: Understanding International Migration at the End of the Millennium*, Oxford University Press, New York

Mehta, Suketu (2004) *Maximum City: Bombay Lost and Found*, Penguin, New Delhi

Menon, Praveen (2008) 'A third of Indian workers are white-collar professionals', *The National*, 14 August, http://thenational.ae/article/20080814/NATIONAL/654056929 (accessed 16 August 2008)

Menon, Sunita (2008) 'Establishment to build 2,300 low-cost houses for Emiratis in Dubai', *Gulf News*, 9 April, http://www.gulfnews.com/Nation/Government/10204204.html (accessed 2 May 2009)

Menon, Sunita (2007) 'Workers live amid pools of sewage', *Gulf News*, 10 March, http://gulfnews.com/news/gulf/uae/employment/workers-live-amid-pools-of-sewage-1.166065 (accessed 15 March 2007)

Menon, Sunita (2006) 'More than 2,000 workers housed in cargo containers', *Gulf News*, 25 November, http://gulfnews.com/news/gulf/uae/employment/more-than-2-000-workers-housed-in-cargo-containers-1.267094 (accessed 2 December 2006)

Mills, Andrew (2008) 'Emirates look to the West for prestige', *Chronicle of Higher Education*, 26 September, http://chronicle.com/article/Emirates-Look-to-the-West-for/8165 (accessed 1 April 2009)

Milne, Diana (2007) 'Can you afford it?', *ArabianBusiness.com*, 8 July, http://www.arabianbusiness.com/property/article/495893-can-you-afford-it (accessed 23 August 2007)

Mimi Chakarova (2007) *Dubai: Night Secrets* (director), http://www.pbs.org/frontlineworld/rough/2007/09/dubai_sex_for_s.html# (accessed 22 November 2008)

Mohammed, Eman (2008a) 'Age of glorifying officials over, says UAE media council chief', *Gulf News*, 17 April, http://www.gulfnews.com/Nation/Media/10206222.html (accessed 25 May 2009)

Mohammed, Eman (2008b) 'The debate on UAE national identity', *Gulf News*, 27 May, http://www.gulfnews.com/Nation/Society/10216190.html (accessed 2 June 2008)

Moore, Susan (2009) 'The rapid emergence of Emirati art', *Financial Times*, 7 March, http://www.ft.com/cms/s/2/74121b62-091d-11de-b8b0-0000779fd2ac.html (accessed 13 March 2009)

Morris, Martin (2009) 'Ban impacting expat labour under review', *ArabianBusiness.com*, 1 March, http://www.arabianbusiness.com/548323-6-month-labour-ban-in-dubai-under-review (accessed 22 June 2009)

Mortimer, Joseph (2006) 'From Russia with love', *Arabian Travel News*, 3 December, http://www.itp.net/news/494288 (accessed 3 March 2009)

Muslim, Nina (2008) 'Filipino population in UAE dwindling amid high costs', *Gulf News*, 13 December, http://gulfnews.com/nation/Society/10266701.html (accessed 2 January 2009)

Mussallam, Nada (2005) 'Citizenship proposed for skilled expatriates', *Khaleej Times*, 28 August, http://www.khaleejtimes.com/DisplayArticle.asp?xfile=data/theuae/2005/August/theuae_August830.xml&section=theuae&col (accessed 22 August 2007)

Nammour, Mary (2008) 'Big family+small flat=No residence visa!' *Khaleej Times*, 14 August, http://www.khaleejtimes.com/DisplayArticle08.asp?xfile=data/theuae/2008/August/theuae_August292.xml&section=theuae (accessed 16 August 2008)

Norton, Charlie (2007) 'Dubai: if you're not loaded and decadent, you can't come in', *The Sunday Times*, 10 June, http://www.timesonline.co.uk/tol/travel/article 1878608.ece (accessed 8 January 2008)

O'Connell, Dominic, and Iain Dey (2008) 'Abu Dhabi wants stake in Emirates for bailout cash', *The Sunday Times*, 30 November, http://business.timesonline.co.uk /tol/business/industry_sectors/transport/article5258243.ece (accessed 29 June 2009)

O'Sullivan, Edmund (2008) 'Dubai looks beyond the debt mountain', *Middle East Economic Digest*, 5 May, http://www.meed.com/commentary/last_word/2009/05/concerns_mount_over_dubais_skyhigh_debt.html (accessed 20 June 2009)

Onley, James (2009) 'The Raj reconsidered: British India's informal empire and spheres of influence in Asia and Africa', *Asian Affairs*, vol. 40, no. 1, pp. 44–62

Onley, James (2007) *The Arabian Frontier of the British Raj: Merchants, Rulers, and the British in the Nineteenth Century Gulf*, Oxford University Press, Oxford

Onley, James and Sulayman Khalaf (2006) 'Shaikhly authority in the pre-oil Gulf: An historical-anthropological study', *History and Anthropology*, 17, 3, pp. 189–208

Out and About in Dubai (2008) 'I'm not a prostitute, chump', 5 July, http://www.sdangit.com/2008/07/im-not-a-prostitute-chump.html (accessed 12 December 2008)

Oxford Analytica Daily Brief Service (2007) 'United Arab Emirates: Education trumps Emiratisation', 20 April

Parker, Ian (2005) 'The mirage: The architectural insanity of Dubai', *The New Yorker*, 17 October, pp. 128–43

Pesek, Willia (2009), 'Dubai's edifice complex is falling on hard times', *Bloomberg*, 6 February, http://www.bloomberg.com/apps/news?pid=20601039&sid=aYDcH7_GEdkc&refer=columnist_pesek (accessed 2 July 2009)

Portes, Alejandro and Ruben Rumbaut (2006) *Immigrant America: A Portrait*, University of California Press, Berkeley, CA

Rai, Lekha (1996) 'Dubai Shopping Festival', *Advertising Age*, 9 December

Ratha, Dilip, Sanket Mohapatra and Zhimei Xu (2008) 'Briefing 8: Outlook for remittance flows 2008–2010: Growth expected to moderate significantly, but flows to remain resilient', *Migration and Remittances Team Development Prospects Group, The World Bank*, 11 November, http://siteresources.worldbank.org/INTPROSPECTS/Resources/334934-1110315015165/MD_Brief8.pdf (accessed 22 January 2009)

Real Nick, The (2009) 'The Real Nick's really visionary strategic plan to property investment', *Some Like It Not*, 7 April, http://some-like-it-not.blogspot.com/2009/04/real-nicks-really-visionary-strategic.html (accessed 15 April 2009)

Rehman, Aamir (2008) *Dubai & Co.: Global Strategies for Doing Business in the Gulf States*, Mc-Graw Hill, New York

Richey, Warren (1982) 'Tiny Dubai, an Emirate trade hub, beset by area rivalry', *Christian Science Monitor*, 9 December.

Ridgeway, William (2005) 'Dubai – The scandal and the vice', *The Social Affairs Unit*, 5 April, http://www.socialaffairsunit.org.uk/blog/archives/000345.php (accessed 18 September 2008)

Rose, Steve (2005) 'Sand and freedom' *The Guardian*, 28 November, http://www.guardian.co.uk/artanddesign/2005/nov/28/architecture (accessed 22 June 2008)

Rosh (2007) 'Just talkin', *uaeian*, 26 May, http://blog-uaeian.blogspot.com/2007/05/just-talkin.html (accessed 26 July 2008)

Roy, Shubhajit (2007) 'Are you an American scholar? You aren't welcome in India', *Indian Express*, 11 February, http://www.indianexpress.com/news/are-you-an-american-scholar-you-arent-welcome-in-india/23071/ (accessed 22 February 2007)

Runnette, Charles (2007) 'Confessions on a Dubai dance floor', *New York Times*, 25 March, http://travel.nytimes.com/2007/03/25/travel/tmagazine/03talk.dubai.t.html (accessed 20 January 2009)

Russell, Henry (1995) 'Jousting for jobs: You want to work in Dubai? So does everyone else', *Resident Abroad*, April, pp. 26, 28

Saatchi Gallery (2008) 'Ana Finel Honigman on Dubai's Creek Art Fair', 26 March, http://www.saatchi-gallery.co.uk/blogon/2008/03/ana_finel_honigman_on_dubais_c_1.php (accessed 13 March 2009)

Saayegh, Fatima Al (2008) 'How can we maintain a national identity?', *Gulf News*, 27 May, http://www.gulfnews.com/nation/Society/10216292.html (accessed May 3, 2009)

Saffarini, Reema (2007) 'Companies keen to hit emiratisation targets', *Gulf News*, 12 July, http://archive.gulfnews.com/indepth/labour/Emiritisation/10111442.html (accessed 7 May 2009)

Salama, Samir (2007a) 'Hundreds of workers forced to live in attics', *Gulf News*, 19 February, http://gulfnews.com/news/gulf/uae/employment/hundreds-of-workers-forced-to-live-in-attics-1.161866 (accessed 1 October 2009)

Salama, Samir (2007b) 'Call for cautious Emiratisation', *Gulf News*, 20 April, http://gulfnews.com/business/general/call-for-cautious-emiratisation-1.172940 (accessed 22 October 2009)

Salama, Samir (2006a) 'Change in rule for sponsorship transfer of maids hailed', *Gulf News*, 19 January, http://archive.gulfnews.com/articles/06/01/19/10012600.html (accessed 22 March 2008)

Salama, Samir (2006b) 'Unskilled workers can stay for 6 years: Al Ka'abi', *Gulf News*, 8 June, http://gulfnews.com/news/gulf/uae/employment/unskilled-workers-can-stay-for-6-years-al-ka-abi-1.240098 (accessed 12 January 2007)

Salama, Samir (2006c) 'Retaining passports is "forcible labour" ', *Gulf News*, 13 June, http://archive.gulfnews.com/articles/06/06/13/10046487.html (accessed 22 June 2006)

Samaha, Nour and Salam Hafez (2009) 'Internet regulator bans violent protest videos', *The National*, 25 June, http://www.thenational.ae/article/20090625/NATIONAL/706249854 (accessed 29 June 2009)

Sambidge, Andy (2009a) 'Contracting industry chief slams Bahrain sponsor move', *ArabianBusiness.com*, 10 May, http://www.arabianbusiness.com/555083-contracting-industry-chief-slams-bahrain-sponsor-move (accessed 22 June 2009)

Sambidge, Andy (2009b) 'Police chief calls for end of sponsorship in UAE', *ArabianBusiness.com*, 24 June, http://www.arabianbusiness.com/559899 (accessed 26 June 2009)

Sambidge, Andy (2009c) 'UAE raises minimum salary limit for expats with family', *ArabianBusiness.com*, 2 July, http://www.arabianbusiness.com/560719-uae-to-raise-minimum-salary-limit-for-expats-with-family (accessed 3 July 2009)

Sambidge, Andy (2009d) 'Permanent residency for long-term GCC expats – Official', *ArabianBusiness.com*, 13 July, http://www.arabianbusiness.com/561797 (accessed 17 July 2009)

Sambidge, Andy (2009e) 'Kuwait begins process to scrap sponsorship', *ArabianBusiness.com*, 9 August, http://www.arabianbusiness.com/564252-kuwait-begins-process-to-scrap-sponsorship (accessed 12 August 2009)

Sambidge, Andy (2008) 'Call for new plan to tackle Emirati jobs dilemma', *ArabianBusiness.com*, 25 August, http://www.arabianbusiness.com/528807-call-for-new-plan-to-tackle-emirati-jobs-dilemma (accessed 3 January 2009)

Sassen, Saskia (2007) *A Sociology of Globalization*, W. W. Norton, New York

Sawy, Nada El (2008a) 'Foreign influences: Expats force locals to ask who they are', *Financial Times*, 15 May, http://www.ft.com/cms/s/0/e9f2b246-2161-11dd-a0e6-000077b07658,dwp_uuid=571bd9fc-2166-11dd-a0e6-000077b07658.html (accessed 20 May 2009)

Sawy, Nada El (2008b) 'Life on the dole in the UAE', *Financial Times*, 15 September, www.ft.com/cms/s/0/92497e7c-833a-11dd-907e-000077b07658,dwp_uuid=d8cc5c02-3164-11dd-b77c-0000779fd2ac.html (accessed 22 April 2009)

Sayegh, Fatma Al- (1998) 'Merchants' role in a changing society: The case of Dubai, 1900-90', *Middle Eastern Studies*, vol. 34, no. 1, pp. 87–102

Secret Dubai, *Secret Dubai Diary*, http://secretdubai.blogspot.com

Sengupta, Joy (2007) 'Have wheels, will sleep …', *Khaleej Times*, 9 March, http://www.khaleejtimes.com/DisplayArticleNew.asp?xfile=data/theuae/2007/March/theuae_March269.xml&section=theuae&col= (accessed 12 April 2007)

Sengupta, Kim and Daniel Howden (2009) 'Pirates: The $80m Gulf connection', *Independent*, 21 April, http://www.independent.co.uk/news/world/africa/pirates-the-80m-gulf-connection-1671657.html (accessed 22 April 2009)

Serkal, Mariam Al (2007) 'Aspirations of young UAE women revealed', *Gulf News*, 7 April, www.gulfnews.com/nation/Society/10116467.html (accessed 15 May 2009)

Setser, Brad and Rachel Ziemba (2009) 'GCC Sovereign Funds: Reversal of Fortune', working paper, *Council on Foreign Relations*, New York, January, http://www.cfr.org/content/publications/attachments/CGS_WorkingPaper_5.pdf (accessed 22 February 2009)

Sex and Dubai, *Sex and Dubai*, http://www.single-in-dubai.blogspot.com

Shadid, Anthony (2006) 'In UAE, tales of paradise lost', *Washington Post*, 12 April, http://www.washingtonpost.com/wp-dyn/content/article/2006/04/11/AR2006041101474.html (accessed 1 May 2006)

Shahrokhi, Sholeh (2008) 'When tragedy hits: A concise socio-cultural analysis of sex trafficking of young Iranian women', *Wagadu: A Journal of Transnational Women's and Gender Studies*, 5, 2, http://web.cortland.edu/wagadu/Volume%205/Articles%20html/wagadu_2008_vol5_chap2_shahrokhi.htm (accessed 20 September 2008)

Shaiba, Abdullah Al (2009) 'Let's take emiratisation campaign to the next level', *Gulf News*, 8 May, http://gulfnews.com/opinions/columnists/let-s-take-emiratisation-campaign-to-the-next-level-1.67914 (accessed 12 May 2009)

Sharif, Arif (2008) 'Dubai can't find the taxis to make its skyscrapers commodious', *Bloomberg*, 14 July, http://www.bloomberg.com/apps/news?pid=20601109&sid=aUYy8mpe6e6o&refer=home (accessed 17 July 2009)

Shouk, Ali Al- (2007) 'Justice was done', *7days*, 11 July, http://www.7days.ae/storydetails.php?id=30043%20%20%20%20&page=local%20news&title=Dubai%20-%20Justice%20was%20done (accessed 16 August 2008)

Skinner, E. Benjamin (2008) *A Crime So Monstrous: Face-to-Face with Modern-Day Slavery*, Free Press, New York

Slackman, Michael (2008) 'Young and Arab in Land of Mosques and Bars', *New York Times*, 21 September, http://www.nytimes.com/2008/09/22/world/middleeast/22dubai.html (accessed 21 January 2009)

Soros, George (1998) 'Towards a global open society', *The Atlantic Monthly*, January, http://www.theatlantic.com/issues/98jan/opensoc.htm (accessed 29 June 2008)

Spender, Tom (2009) 'Emiratisation process hampered by "lack of reliable data" ', *The National*, 30 March, http://www.thenational.ae/article/20090330/NATIONAL/686322048/1138/YOURVIEW (accessed 25 June 2009)

Stewart, Christopher (2008) 'The axis of commerce', *Portfolio.Com*, September, http://www.portfolio.com/news-markets/international-news/portfolio/2008/08/13/US-Trades-With-Iran-Via-Dubai (accessed 12 May 2009)

Surk, Barbara (2007) 'Jail time is cost for not paying debts in Dubai', *Seattle Times*, 12 June, http://seattletimes.nwsource.com/html/nationworld/2003744014_debtors12.html (accessed 14 April 2009)

Taryam, Abdullah (1987) *The Establishment of the United Arab Emirates, 1950–85*, Croom Helm, London

Tashkeel, http://www.tashkeel.org/aboutus.html

Tetreault, Mary Ann (2000) 'The economics of national autonomy in the UAE', in Joseph Kechichian (ed.), *A Century in Thirty Years: Shaykh Zayed and the United Arab Emirates*, Middle East Policy Council, Washington, DC, pp. 107–48

Theeb, Alia Al (2008) 'Man gets jail term of 10 years for human trafficking', *Gulf News*, 14 January, http://gulfnews.com/news/gulf/uae/crime/men-get-jail-term-of-10-years-for-human-trafficking-1.77630 (accessed 22 January 2008)

Thomas, Karen (2000) 'Marry a foreigner and you'll pay the price, say Emirates', *Guardian*, 11 April

Thornton, Emily and Stanley Reed (2008) 'Who's afraid of Mideast money?' *Business Week*, 10 January, http://www.businessweek.com/magazine/content/08_03/b4067042272294.htm (accessed 3 July 2009)

Trofimov, Yaroslav (1995) 'United Arab Emirates Inc.', *Jerusalem Post*, 15 June

United Arab Emirates (2009) *United Arab Emirates Yearbook 2009*, Trident Press, London, http://www.uaeinteract.com/uaeint_misc/pdf_2009/ (accessed 15 May 2009)

United Nations Children's Fund (UNICEF) (2006) *Starting Over: Children Return Home from Camel Racing*

United States Department of State (2009) *Trafficking in Persons Report 2009*, http://www.state.gov/g/tip/rls/tiprpt/2009/123139.htm (accessed 7 July 2009)

United States Department of State (2008) *Trafficking in Persons Report 2008*, http://www.state.gov/g/tip/rls/tiprpt/2008/105389.htm (accessed 25 July 2008)

United States Department of State (2006) *Trafficking in Persons Report, United Arab Emirates*, 5 June, http://www.state.gov/g/tip/rls/tiprpt/2006/65990.htm (accessed 12 July 2008)

United States Department of State (1999) *1999 Country Reports on Human Rights Practices: United Arab Emirates*, http://www.state.gov/www/global/human_rights/1999_hrp_report/uae.html (accessed 12 September 2008)

Verma, Sonia (2009) 'Sun, sea and sewage in the playground of the rich in Dubai', *The Times*, 29 January, http://www.timesonline.co.uk/tol/travel/news/article 5607619.ece (accessed 22 February 2009)

Walsh, Katie (2008) 'Travelling together? Work, intimacy, and home amongst British expatriate couples in Dubai', in Anne Coles and Anne-Meike Fechter (eds), *Gender and Family among Transnational Professionals*, Routledge, New York, pp. 63–84

Walsh, Katie (2007) ' "It got very debauched, very Dubai!" Heterosexual intimacy amongst single British expatriates', *Social and Cultural Geography*, vol. 8, no. 4, pp. 507–33

Watson, Ivan (2007) 'Iran's Neighbor Dubai a Place of Intrigue', *National Public Radio (US) Morning Edition*, 9 May, http://www.npr.org/templates/story/story.php?storyId=10089956 (accessed 13 March 2009)

Waxman, Sharon (2009) 'An oasis in the desert', *ARTNews*, February, vol. 108, no. 2, http://www.artnewsonline.com/issues/article.asp?art_id=2627 (accessed 13 March 2009)

Weiner, Myron (1982) 'International Migration and Development: Indians in the Persian Gulf', *Population and Development Review*, vol. 8, no. 1, pp. 1–36

White, Andrew (2009) 'Expat residency cap as early as 2010 – Minister', *ArabianBusiness.com*, 7 July, http://www.arabianbusiness.com/561192-expat-residency-cap-as-early-as-2010—minister (accessed 7 July 2009)

Wigglesworth, Robin (2009) 'Real estate: Are prices at the bottom?' *Financial Times*, 20 July, http://www.ft.com/cms/s/0/7185479a-7270-11de-ba94-00144feabdc0,dwp_uuid=c23e5f6e-727a-11de-ba94-00144feabdc0.html (accessed 21 July 2009)

Wilson, Graeme (1999) *Father of Dubai: Sheikh Rashid bin Saeed Al Maktoum*, Media Prima, Dubai

Worth, Robert (2009) 'Laid-off foreigners flee as Dubai spirals down', *New York Times*, 11 February, http://www.nytimes.com/2009/02/12/world/middleeast/12dubai.html (accessed 13 February 2009)

Zachariah, K.C., B.A. Prakash, S. Irudaya Rajan (2004) 'Indian workers in UAE: Employment, wages and working conditions', *Economic and Political Weekly*, 29 May, vol. 39, no. 22, pp. 2227–34

Zoepf, Katherine (2006) 'Where the boys are, at least for now, the girls pounce', *New York Times*, 2 November, http://www.nytimes.com/2006/11/02/world/middleeast/02beirut.html (accessed 30 January 2009)

INDEX